Collaborating on Enterprise Projects

Using Microsoft Project Server 2010

Gary L. Chefetz
Dale A. Howard
Treb Gatte
Tony Zink

Collaborating on Enterprise Projects
Using Microsoft Project Server 2010

Copyright © 2011 Chefetz LLC dba MSProjectExperts

Publisher: Chefetz LLC
Authors: Gary L. Chefetz, Dale A. Howard, Treb Gatte, Tony Zink
Editor: Rodney L. Walker
Cover Design: Emily Baker
Cover Photo: Peter Hurley

ISBN: 978-1-934240-15-1

LCCN: 2010942278

Published and distributed by Chefetz LLC dba MSProjectExperts, 90 John Street, Suite 404, New York, NY 10038. (646) 736-1688 http://www.msprojectexperts.com

We provide the information contained in this book on an "as is" basis, without warranty. Although we make every effort to ensure the accuracy of information provided herein, neither the authors nor the publisher shall have any liability to any person or entity with respect to any loss or damage caused or allegedly caused directly or indirectly by the information contained in this work.

MSProjectExperts publishes a complete series of role-based training/reference manuals for Microsoft's Enterprise Project Management software including Microsoft Project and Microsoft Project Server. Use our books for self-study or for classroom learning delivered by professional trainers and corporate training programs. To learn more about our books and courseware series for Administrators, Implementers, Project Managers, Portfolio Managers, Resource Managers, Executives, Team Members, and Developers, or to obtain instructor companion products and materials, contact MSProjectExperts by phone (646) 736-1688 or by email info@msprojectexperts.com.

Contents

Contents

Contents

Contents

About the Authors

Gary Chefetz is the founder and President of MSProjectExperts, which exists to support businesses and organizations that choose the Microsoft enterprise project management platform. Gary has worked with Microsoft Project since 1995 and has supported Microsoft Project users since the introduction of Project Central in early 2000. Gary continues to receive the prestigious Microsoft Project Most Valuable Professional (MVP) award for his contributions to the Project community and possesses the Microsoft Certified IT Professional (MCITP) and the Microsoft Certified Trainer (MCT) certifications. As a long-time MVP, he works closely with the Microsoft Project product team and support organizations. Gary is dedicated to supporting Microsoft Project Server implementations through his business efforts with clients and through his contributions in TechNet forums. Contact Gary Chefetz online in one of the Microsoft Project forums on TechNet or e-mail him at:

gary.chefetz@msprojectexperts.com

Dale Howard is an enterprise project management trainer/consultant and is Vice President of Educational Services of MSProjectExperts. Dale possesses the Certified Technical Trainer (CTT) and Microsoft Certified Technology Specialist (MCTS) certification for Microsoft EPM, and has more than 15 years of experience training and consulting in productivity software. He has worked with Microsoft Project since 1997 and volunteers many hours each week answering user questions in the various Microsoft Project communities. Dale continues to receive the prestigious Most Valuable Professional (MVP) yearly award for Microsoft Project since 2004 for his expertise with the software and for his contributions to the user communities. Dale is married to Mickey and lives in Dunedin Florida. Contact Dale online in one of the Microsoft Project forums on TechNet or e-mail him at:

dale.howard@msprojectexperts.com

Treb Gatte is a seasoned business expert with significant experience with the Project Server tool as well as with process and project management. Treb has over 20 years of experience in project management, business process development, and software development management. Treb was the Microsoft Program Manager responsible for Setup, Upgrade and Business Intelligence features for the Microsoft Project Server 2010 release. He also has experience as the former Project Manager for a large national bank's Project Server implementation. Treb holds a BS in Management from Louisiana State University and an MBA from Wake Forest University. Contact Treb at:

treb.gatte@msprojectexperts.com

About the Exercises in this book

The exercises in this book are based on the download and setup available for *Managing Enterprise Projects using Microsoft Project Server 2010*, ISBN 978-1-934240-11-3. To obtain these files, you must own a copy of this book.

Introduction

Thank you for choosing *Collaborating on Enterprise Projects Using Microsoft Project Server 2010*. Herein find a complete learning guide and reference to working as a project team member on projects using the Microsoft EPM platform. Our goal in writing this book is to help you effectively use Project Web Access as an enterprise project collaboration tool.

This book takes a systematic approach for manager and team members to learn to use Project Server. The first module provides you with an overview of Project Server. In the second module, you learn how to use the Project Web App user interface. The next module teaches you how to use the project proposal workflow in Project Server. Next you learn how to enter time and task progress in Project Web App and in Microsoft Outlook. The following four modules show you how to set up important personal settings options, how to use the SharePoint Project Site features, how to request and submit Status Reports, how to work in the Project Center, and work with project views and editing projects in Project Web App. The book concludes with an in-depth exploration of the SharePoint Business Intelligence tools connected to Project Server.

Throughout each module, you get a generous amount of Notes, Warnings, and Best Practices. Notes call your attention to important additional information about a subject. Warnings help you avoid the most common problems experienced by others and Best Practices provide tips for using the tool based on our field experience.

Because you have read this book, we believe that you will be much more effective using Project Web App as an enterprise project collaboration tool. If you have questions about the book or are interested in our professional services, please contact us at our office. If you have questions about Microsoft Project or Project Server, contact us through the TechNet forums for Project Server.

Gary L. Chefetz

Dale A. Howard

Treb Gatte

Module 01

Introducing Microsoft Project Server

Learning Objectives

After completing this module, you will be able to:

- Understand the PMI definition of a project

- Understand Project Server's enterprise project management terminology

- Describe the project communications life cycle used in Project Server

- Be familiar with Project Server team collaboration tools

- Understand how Microsoft SharePoint Server (MSS) provides functionality in Project Server

- Acquire an overview understanding of OLAP and Business Intelligence (BI) tools

- Understand how tracking methods impact progress reporting

Inside Module 01

What Is Microsoft Project Server?

Microsoft Project Server 2010 is an enterprise project management (EPM) automation system. Microsoft designed Project Server to support business and industry-specific project management and tracking requirements. Project Server 2010 is an out-of-the-box project and assignment tracking system, as well as a platform for business-specific configuration and customization. Using Project Server 2010, your organization can manage dozens, hundreds, or thousands of projects, along with dozens, hundreds, or thousands of resources.

Project Server 2010 is Microsoft's fifth-generation, server-based project management solution. The previous generations of Microsoft's EPM tool included Project Central, along with Project Server 2002, 2003, and 2007. The combination of Microsoft Project Professional 2010 and Project Server 2010 provides a powerful enterprise portfolio management system that is rich in features but fraught with complexity and challenges. Our goal is to help you maximize the feature benefits and minimize the frustrations.

Understanding Project Management Theory

According to *A Guide to the Project Management Body of Knowledge* (PMBOK Guide, 4th Edition) from the Project Management Institute (PMI), a project is "a temporary endeavor undertaken to create a unique produce, service, or result." According to this definition, a project is:

- **Temporary** – Every project has a definite beginning and end.

- **Unique** – Every project is something your organization has not done before, or has not done in this manner.

Because Microsoft Project 2010 is a project management tool, you use the software most effectively in the context of the normal project management process. Therefore, it is important to become acquainted with each of the phases of the project management process and with the activities that take place during each phase. According to the Project Management Institute, the project management process consists of five phases including Definition, Planning, Execution, Control, and Closure.

Understanding Enterprise Project Management Terminology

In the world of enterprise project management, you hear the terms program and portfolio. For the purposes of this book, a **program** is "a collection of related projects" and a **portfolio** is "a collection of programs and/or projects within a business unit or across an entire enterprise". Many companies have their own interpretation of these terms, reflecting their approach to project management. Sometimes the sheer size of the organization drives these definitions.

The concept of a portfolio is flexible, depending on the size of the deployment. A smaller organization may have a single portfolio of projects, whereas a larger business may conceive of an enterprise portfolio made up of numerous departmental or line-of-business portfolios, each containing its own set of programs and projects. However your organization conceives programs and portfolios, you can model them in Project Server 2010.

Understanding Project Server Terminology

Two terms that you must understand in the context of the Project Server 2010 environment are **enterprise project** and **enterprise resource**. Very specific criteria determine whether a project is an enterprise or non-enterprise project, and whether a resource is an enterprise or local resource. In addition, you must also understand how to **check in** and **check out** a project. Finally, it is helpful to understand two other terms, **portfolio analysis** and **portfolio analyses**.

Enterprise Project

An **enterprise project** is any project stored in the Project Server database using one of the following methods:

- You create the project using the Project Professional 2010 client while connected to Project Server 2010 and save the project in the Project Server database.

- You import the project to the enterprise using the *Import Project Wizard* in Project Professional 2010.

- You create a proposed project using the demand management process from the *Project Center* page in Project Web App.

The system stores all enterprise projects in the Project Server database. Any project not stored in the Project Server database, such as a project saved as an .MPP file, is termed a **non-enterprise project** or a **local project**.

Enterprise Resource

An **enterprise resource** is any resource stored in the Enterprise Resource Pool in the Project Server database using one of the following methods:

- The Project Server administrator creates the resource in the Enterprise Resource Pool using the Project Professional 2010 client while connected to Project Server 2010.

- The Project Server administrator imports the resource into the Enterprise Resource Pool using the Import Resources Wizard in Project Professional 2010.

- The Project Server administrator creates the resource using Project Web App.

If a resource exists in an enterprise project but does not exist in the Enterprise Resource Pool, then this resource is termed a **non-enterprise resource** or **local resource**. This means that the resource is local to the project only.

Check In and Check Out

The terms **check in** and **check out** apply to enterprise objects such as projects, resources, calendars, fields, lookup tables, and even to the Enterprise Global file. As a project manager, when you open an enterprise project for editing, the system checks out the project to you exclusively. While you have the project open, no other user can edit your project. When you close the enterprise project, the system checks in the project so that other users can edit the project, if they have the permission to do so.

Portfolio Analysis

The term **portfolio analysis** refers to an analysis of a group of projects for the purposes of selecting projects for execution by best matching the strategic objectives of the organization and fitting resource and cost constraints within the parameters set by management consensus. This term differs dramatically from Microsoft's previous definition in Project Server 2007.

Portfolio Analyses

When you encounter the term **portfolio analyses** in Project Server 2010, it refers to the collection of individual analysis studies performed by various users in the system to determine the viability of proposed project investments in the system.

Using Enterprise Resource Management Tools

A centralized **Enterprise Resource Pool** is vital to the advanced resource management functionality in Project Server 2010. The Enterprise Resource Pool contains resources and resource attributes that drive functionality, such as matching people to tasks using skills or based on department or location. The system models these resource attributes using custom enterprise fields that contain a lookup table. These custom fields might describe practice groups, location, department, or other company-specific information that project and resource managers use to intelligently assign resources to task assignments, and that management can use to drive reporting and analysis. After defining custom fields for your organization, your Project Server administrator assigns values for these fields to each resource in the Enterprise Resource Pool.

Understanding the Communications Life Cycle

A key piece of the core functionality in Project Server 2010 provides a cyclical assignment and update process between project managers and team members. This cycle is the heart of Project Server's work and resource management system. Work assignments flow from the plan to resources performing the work, and resources report progress data back to the plan. This project communication cycle flows through the following steps:

1. The project manager saves the project plan in the Project Server database, as shown in Figure 1 - 1. This action saves the project in the **Draft** database only. At this point, neither team members nor executives can see the project anywhere in Project Web App.

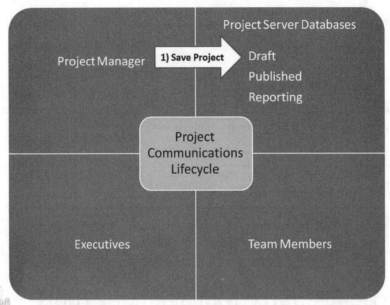

Figure 1 - 1: Save the project in Project Server Draft database

2. When the project manager publishes a project, as shown in Figure 1 - 2, the system writes the project data to the *Published* and *Reporting* databases. If enabled by the Project Server administrator, the system sends an e-mail message to each project team member to notify them of their new task assignments. Using an embedded link in the e-mail message, they can quickly click to view their task assignments in the project through Project Web App or through Outlook. Publishing makes project data visible in the *Project Center* and *Project Detail* views, and the system includes the project data in the next cube build.

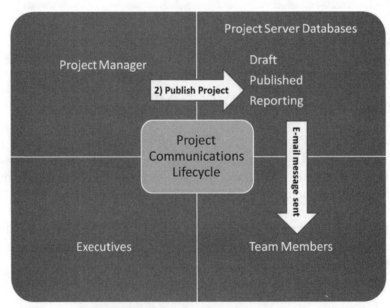

Figure 1 - 2: Publish the project with e-mail sent to team members

3. At the end of each reporting period, team members enter their actual progress on the project and send the task updates to the project manager via the Project Web App interface, as shown in Figure 1 - 3. Actual progress includes completion percentages and/or hours worked on each task, based on the organization's reporting method. The updates are visible to the project manager, but the system does not apply the updates to the plan until the project manager accepts the updates in the next step, or unless the project manager uses automation rules.

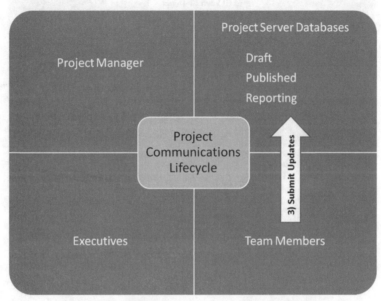

Figure 1 - 3: Team members submit actual progress

4. The project manager receives and reviews each set of task updates from project team members as shown in Figure 1 - 4. The project manager can individually accept or reject each task update, or process them in batches using automation rules.

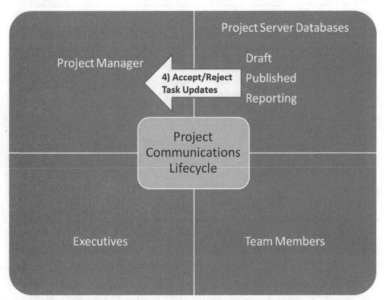

Figure 1 - 4: Project manager reviews and processes updates

5. After accepting or rejecting each task update, the project manager saves the latest schedule changes in the *Draft* database, as shown in Figure 1 - 5.

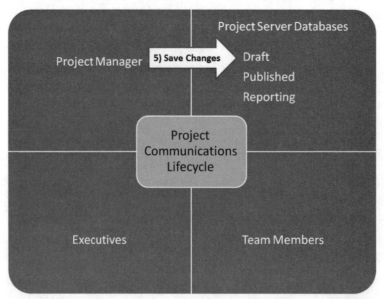

Figure 1 - 5: Project manager saves the latest schedule changes

6. After saving the project, the project manager publishes the latest project schedule changes to the *Published* and *Reporting* databases, as shown in Figure 1 - 6. This makes the schedule changes visible in the *Project Center* page, the *Timesheet* and *Tasks* pages for team members, along with the *Reporting* database and the OLAP cubes.

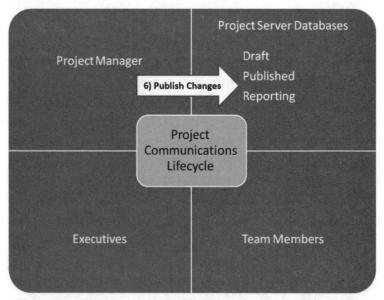

Figure 1 - 6: Project manager publishes the latest schedule changes

At any time throughout the life of the project, executives within the organization can view the organization's entire portfolio of projects, as shown in Figure 1 - 7. Project Server 2010 provides numerous view entry points, including the *Project Center* and *Resource Center* pages in Project Web App, which are gateways to detailed project and resource information.

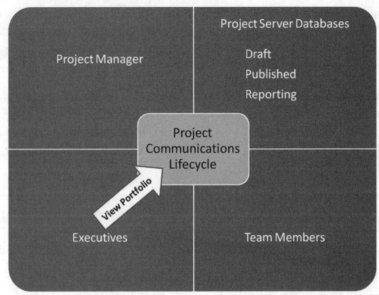

Figure 1 - 7: Executives view the organization's project portfolio

Understanding SharePoint Collaboration Tools

Beyond the core communication between project managers and project team members, Project Server 2010 provides additional features for project team collaboration. Some of these features are native to Project Server, whereas others leverage integration with Microsoft SharePoint Server 2010 (MSS) and Microsoft Windows SharePoint Foundation. These features include:

- **Status Reports** – Status Reports allow project managers, resource managers, and executives to establish single or periodic status reports to which team members must respond. Team members may also create their own unrequested reports and submit them at any time. The status report feature can save a manager time, as it automatically compiles a team report from individual responses.

- **Automated Alerts and Reminders** – Project Server 2010 features an automated reminder system that generates e-mail notices for a variety of situations, including reminding team members of upcoming and overdue task work, and of status reports that are due. In addition to reminders, alerts provide instant notification when certain events occur, such as a new task assignment. All users have the ability to set their own alerts and reminders, and managers have the added ability to set reminders for their resources.

- **Exchange Integration** – This feature allows users to display Project Web App tasks on the Outlook task list and status the tasks using the percent complete method.

- **Task Reassignment** – The system supports a team lead structure where functional leaders participate in the work distribution and management process. If the project manager enables task reassignment for team members in a project, team members can transfer work to each other, subject to the project manager's approval.

- **Ad hoc Reporting** – You can quickly print information from data grids in Project Web App, selecting and ordering fields and formatting the results. You can also export grid data and analysis cube data to Microsoft Excel for additional manipulation and reporting.

- **Risks** – Team members can identify, prioritize, and track project risks using the Project Server list feature created as part of each project's Project Site in SharePoint. You can link risks to tasks, or to issues, documents, and other risks. The links create indicators that appear in the *Project Center* views, where the system flags a project with an icon indicating it contains risks. Similarly, the system flags tasks in *Project* views when they have risks linked to them.

- **Issues** – Team members log and track project issues from creation to resolution using the Project Server list feature created as part of each project's Project Site in SharePoint. As with risks, you can link issues to tasks, or to risks, documents, and other issues. The links create indicators that appear in the *Project Center* views, where the system flags a project with an icon indicating it contains issues. Similarly, the system flags tasks in *Project* views when they have issues linked to them.

- **Documents** – Project Web App provides a general public document library available to all system users. The public document library is an excellent place to make common process documentation available as part of a standardized environment. Each project has its own document library within the Project Site in SharePoint, into which users can load documents and link them to tasks, issues, risks and other documents in the system.

- **Deliverables** – Project managers can define deliverables linked to tasks that other project managers can consume in their projects, thereby creating a new way of cross-linking projects. With the addition of Microsoft SharePoint Server (MSS) to the server farm, managers can apply SharePoint workflows to the deliverables. Workflows are new in the 2010 version of MSS.

- **Project Proposals** – System users can create and submit project proposals for consideration and approval. This feature enables the enterprise to build a demand-management system for new projects in the enterprise. You can tailor the approval process to meet your organization's workflow.

- **Resource Plans** – Used in conjunction with project proposals and enterprise projects, resource plans provide a means to estimate and measure future resource loads.

- **Timesheets** – Timesheets provide enterprise users with fully functional time reporting capabilities that can collect time at any reporting level. Most importantly, the timesheet feature includes the ability to create a full audit trail, allowing system implementers to create regulatory-compliant solutions. You can use timesheet data to drive task progress or maintain this data without using it to drive task updates. You can also use the *Tasks* page to collect task progress as in previous versions of Project Server.

Understanding Tracking Methods

The default method of tracking progress chosen by your organization has a significant impact on both project team members and project managers, and how they interact with Project Web App. Specifically, the tracking method selected determines the appearance of the *Tasks* page and the *Detailed Assignments* page in Project Web App, and determines what type of data team members must report on either of these two pages. Beyond this, the tracking method selected also affects each project manager as it affects the type of data the project manager must approve in the *Approval Center* page in Project Web App.

After selecting the default tracking method for your organization, the Project Server administrator must also choose whether to "lock down" the selected method. With the tracking method locked down, project managers and team members **must** use this method for tracking progress in every enterprise project. Project Server 2010 offers four methods for tracking task progress:

- **Percent of Work Complete** allows team members to enter % Work Complete and a Remaining Work estimate on each task assignment.

- **Actual Work Done and Work Remaining** allows team members to enter the cumulative amount of Actual Work value and to adjust the Remaining Work estimate on each task assignment.

- **Hours of Work Done per Period** allows resources to enter the hours of Actual Work completed for the current period and to adjust the Remaining Work estimate on each task assignment.

- **Free Form** tracking allows the user to enter progress using any of the three previous methods.

Percent of Work Complete is the system default method for tracking progress unless your organization selects another method.

In addition to selecting the default method of tracking progress in Project Server 2010, the Project Server administrator must also define what constitutes a "current task" in the system. This definition determines which tasks team members see by default on their *Tasks* page in Project Web App. By default, the system defines a "current task" as any task that meets one of the following criteria:

- An unstarted task scheduled in the past.

- A task that is in-progress but is not yet completed.

- A rejected task that the team member has not resubmitted.

- A task completed in the last two reporting periods (10 days) prior to the current week.

- A task scheduled to start in the next two reporting periods (10 days) after the current week.

The Project Server administrator has the option to leave the default setting for "current tasks" at 2 reporting periods (10 days), or to increase or decrease the number of reporting periods as needed by your organization.

Understanding Business Intelligence

Business Intelligence (BI) is a set of processes, tools, and techniques for gathering, organizing, and analyzing large volumes of complex data in an effort to develop an accurate understanding of business dynamics, and you use it to improve strategic and tactical business decision-making. In other words, the purpose of BI is to capture large amounts of data, make some sense out of it, and use it to make sound business decisions. The ultimate goal is to develop the ability to spot problems and trends, and to make informed decisions to mitigate risks, improve efficiencies, and identify opportunities.

Organizations spend time and money implementing Project Server 2010 to capture work data, make sense out of it, and use it to make decisions such as:

- Spotting problems and trends - Is the project running late or over budget?

- Mitigating risks - What can we do to avoid missing our launch deadline?

- Improving efficiencies - Who is the best-qualified person to perform the work?

- Identifying opportunities - What if we design the database and the user interface at the same time?

A well-designed BI system should do the following:

- Extract large amounts of complex data from one or more sources, such as CRM, supply chain management, ERP, and EPM systems

- Centralize, organize, and standardize information in repositories such as data warehouses or data marts

- Provide analytical tools through multiple delivery methods that allow business and technical specialists to run queries against the data and to perform analyses to uncover patterns and diagnose problems

- Present the right information, at the right time, in the right format in order to make the right decisions and take the right actions to achieve the right performance

Project Server helps to do these things already. It aggregates different types of complex work data from different locations into a central set of databases and OLAP cubes, or BI Data Store, such as those shown in Figure 1 - 8.

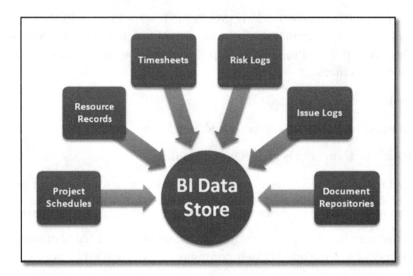

Figure 1 - 8: Aggregating Project Server Data into the BI Data Store

Project Server 2010, when used in conjunction with Microsoft SharePoint Server 2010, also provides a set of rich analytical tools to build reports and visuals for analysis of that data, such as the following:

- Project Center Reports

- Project Detail Reports

- Project Professional Reports

- Microsoft Visio Diagrams

- Microsoft Excel Tabular and Pivot-Style Reports

- Key Performance Indicators

- Balanced Scorecards

- Interactive Dashboards

As a manager, you may have access to all of these types of *Business Intelligence* reports. In addition, you may have access to the *Business Intelligence Center* page in Project Web App. Using the *Business Intelligence Center* page, you can not only view all types of reports, you also have permission to create your own reports. For example, Figure 1 - 9 shows a custom Excel report containing an Excel PivotTable and PivotChart, opened in the *Business Intelligence Center* page. This custom Excel report shows the total amount of work for all IT projects, broken down by project type and by year. Every time a manager or executive opens this report, the system refreshes the data to show the latest information about all IT projects.

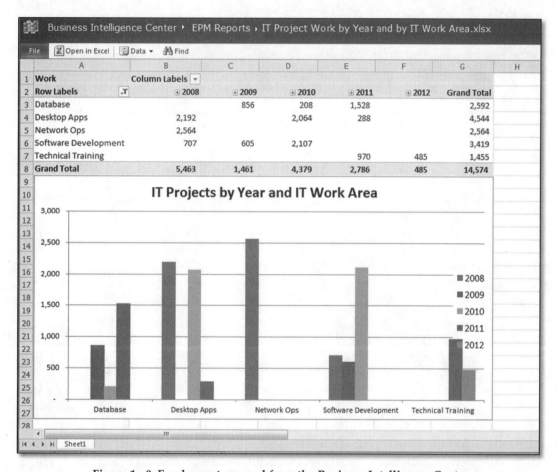

Figure 1 - 9: Excel report, opened from the Business Intelligence Center

 In Module 09, *Working with Business Intelligence*, I provide an in-depth presentation of all the features available in the *Business Intelligence Center* page in Project Web App.

Module 02

Preparing to Use Project Server

Learning Objectives

After completing this module, you will be able to:

- Understand and use the Project Web App user interface

- Log in to Project Web App from the workstation of another user

- Become familiar with Project Server ribbon navigation

- Use the new grid objects in Project Web App pages

Inside Module 02

Using the Project Web App User Interface

When you log in to Project Web App with a valid user account, the system presents the *Home* page. Figure 2 - 1 shows the *Home* page for a user named George Stewart who has Project Manager permissions in the system. Notice that the *Home* page of Project Web App consists of two parts: a *Quick Launch* menu on the left and a main content area in the middle.

 All of the screenshots included in this book show Project Web App for a user who is a member of only the Project Managers group. If you are a member of any group with higher permissions, such as the Portfolio Managers or Administrators groups, the system displays more features in Project Web App.

If you are already familiar with SharePoint websites, you probably recognize the Project Web App user interface as a standard SharePoint site layout. Project Server 2010 fully embeds the entire Project Web App interface into Share-Point. All of the Project Web App pages function just like any other SharePoint site.

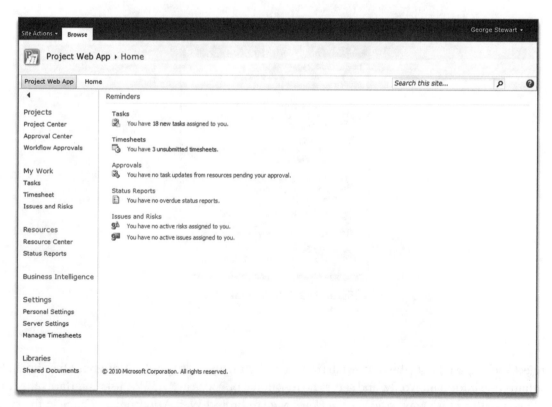

Figure 2 - 1: Project Web App Home page for a project manager

The *Quick Launch* menu contains links to all areas of Project Web App that you can reach based on your security permissions. The main content area contains *Reminders* about your action items including tasks, timesheets, approvals, status reports, and issues and risks. Across the top of the page, Project Server 2010 offers you a number of additional options and selections as well. Starting at the upper left of the screen and working across, you first see the *Site Actions* menu, a SharePoint artifact that provides standard SharePoint options as shown in Figure 2 - 2. These include:

1. The *Edit Page* selection allows you to put the page into edit mode to introduce additional web parts or change the page layout. Editing the page from this menu selection affects all users by the changes.

2. The *New Document Library* selection allows you to create a new document library to attach to the PWA site.

3. You can access the full range of available content types that you can create by selecting the *More Options* menu item, which includes new sites and document libraries.

4. The *View All Site Content* selection allows you to see the entire site's content in one page.

5. The *Edit in SharePoint Designer* selection allows you to edit the site using SharePoint Designer. Note that you cannot edit the PWA site using SharePoint Designer; however you can edit subordinate sites and Project sites using SharePoint Designer.

6. Finally, the *Site Settings* selection takes you to the *Site Settings* page for Project Web App. As a project manager, this page allows you only a small amount of administration capabilities for your Project Server 2010 instance.

Figure 2 - 2: Site Actions Menu

7. Project Web App inherits the *Browse* tab from SharePoint, and it is visible throughout the site. In PWA, this contains title information only, and serves no functional purpose in the PWA user interface other than to provide you with a quick way to access the *Home* page in Project Web App from any page in the system.

To return to the *Home* page from any other page in Project Web App, click the *Browse* tab and then click the *Home* tab or the *Project Web App* tab.

In the far upper-right corner of the page shown in Figure 2 - 3, notice that your name appears with a *Personal Menu* shown in Figure 2 - 4. This menu contains selections that allow you to change your personal settings, personalize the page, sign out, or sign in as a different user.

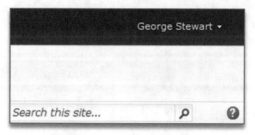

Figure 2 - 3: Personal Menu

Figure 2 - 4: Personal Menu
with personal settings options

Immediately below the personal menu is a search tool you can use to search for specific information in the Project Web App site. To use this tool, enter your search terms in the *Search* field and then click the *Search* button (it looks like a magnifying glass).

To the right of the search tool, click the *Help* icon
 to see context-sensitive help displayed in a floating window.

Logging into Project Web App from another Workstation

Project Server 2010 allows you to log in to Project Web App from another user's workstation while the user is logged on to your corporate network with his/her own network user ID. To log in to Project Web App from another user's workstation, click the *Personal Menu* and then click the *Sign in as Different User* item on the menu, as shown previously in Figure 2 - 4.

The system displays the standard Windows network logon dialog shown in Figure 2 - 5. In the *Windows Security* dialog, begin by clicking *Use another account* option. Enter your domain and user ID in the *User name* field, enter your network password in the *Password* field, and then click the *OK* button. The system automatically logs you in to Project Web App using your network user credentials, and displays your name in the upper right hand corner of the screen.

Figure 2 - 5: Connect dialog

Using the Quick Launch Menu

The Project Web App user interface offers a *Quick Launch* menu on the left side of every primary page. This menu lists your viewable selections based on your role in the project management environment. In Figure 2 - 6 shown to the left, the *Quick Launch* menu contains menu options for a user with Project Manager permissions. Notice that the options available on the *Quick Launch* menu include:

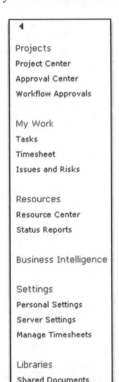

Figure 2 - 6: Quick Launch Menu

- The *Projects* section contains three links. Click the *Project Center* link to navigate to the *Project Center* page where you can view your project portfolio. Click the *Approval Center* link to view and navigate to the *Approval Center* page, where you approve task updates (task progress) from your team members. Click the *Workflow Approvals* link to navigate to the *Project Server Workflow Tasks* page where you approve or reject steps in the workflow for new proposed projects. If you click the *Projects* section header, the system navigates to the *Project Center* page.

- The *My Work* section contains three links. Click the *Tasks* link to navigate to the *Tasks* page to view and update tasks assigned to you. Click the *Timesheet* link to navigate to the *Timesheet* page where you can view and update your timesheet for the current reporting period. Click the *Issues and Risks* link to navigate to the *Issues and Risks* page where you can view issues and risks assigned to you in all of your projects. If you click the *My Work* section header, the system navigates to the *Tasks* page.

- The *Resources* section contains two links. Click the *Resource Center* link to navigate to the *Resource Center* page where you can view resource availability and assignment information. Click the *Status Reports* link to navigate to the *Status Reports* page where you can create or respond to a *Status Report* request. If you click the *Resources* section header, the system navigates to the *Resource Center* page.

- Click the *Business Intelligence* link to access the *Business Intelligence Center* page where you can view all types of *Business Intelligence* reports and perform project data analysis.

- The *Settings* section contains three links. Click the *Personal Settings* link to navigate to the *Personal Settings* page where you can set up e-mail subscriptions for alerts and reminders, set up alerts and reminders for your resources, manage your own queued jobs, manage your delegates, or act as a delegate. Click the *Server Settings* link to navigate to the *Server Settings* page and configure the options available to you as a project manager. Click the *Manage Timesheets* link to view a list of all of your past, current, and future timesheets. If you click the *Settings* section header, the system navigates to the *Personal Settings* page.

> **Warning:** The default permissions for the Project Managers group **do not** allow project managers to manage delegates or to serve as a delegate. If this functionality is beneficial for the project managers in your organiztion, your Project Server adminstrator must enable all of the *Delegate* permissions in the Project Managers group. For the purposes of writing this book, I have enabled every *Delegate* permission for project managers so that you can see this powerful functionality.

- The *Libraries* section contains only one link. Click the *Shared Documents* link to navigate to the *Shared Documents* page where you can view or share public documents with everyone using the Project Server system. Click the *Libraries* section heading to navigate to the *All Site Content* page where you can see all available public content.

A new feature in the *Quick Launch* menu for Project Server 2010 allows you to collapse the menu to give you more room to display the rest of the page. This feature is particularly handy when you view pages that contain a data grid object, such as the *Tasks* or *Timesheet* pages. Click the *Collapse* icon, the small left-pointing triangle image shown in Figure 2 - 7, to collapse the *Quick Launch* menu completely. When you collapse the *Quick Launch* menu, the system displays the *Expand* icon, which reverses the direction of the triangle image. Click the *Expand* icon to expand the *Quick Launch* menu.

**Figure 2 - 7: Collapse
the Quick Launch menu**

Using the Ribbon Menus

Every Project Web App page that contains a data grid includes a *Ribbon* with one or more ribbon tabs at the top of the page. When you click a *Ribbon* tab, Project Server 2010 displays one or more buttons on the *Ribbon*, depending on your Project Server permissions. For example, Figure 2 - 8 shows the *Project Center* page for a user with project manager permissions. Notice the *Projects* ribbon at the top of the page, along with the *Projects* tab at the top of the *Projects* ribbon.

Figure 2 - 8: Project Center page

Notice that the *Project Center* ribbon has one context-sensitive tab, the *Projects* tab. Some pages contain only the *Browse* tab when the software handles their functionality within the page itself. The *Projects* ribbon contains menu selections in seven sections: *Project, Navigate, Zoom, Data, Share, Show/Hide* and *Project Type*. If you used prior versions of Project Server, you can see right away that Project Web App has a much richer set of available functionality than ever before. For example, Project Web App now supports project editing in the browser, a new feature in Project Server 2010. Notice that the *Project* section contains an *Update List* button. This button allows you to synchronize data between projects and SharePoint lists, which is another new feature for 2010. Notice also that the *Navigate* section includes a *Project Site* button, which allows you to navigate to the Project Site for a selected project. **Project Site** is the new terminology for what Microsoft called a **Project Workspace** in Project Server 2007.

Some pages contain more than one context-sensitive tab, such as the *Project Details* page. This page contains three such tabs, including the *Project, Task,* and *Options* tabs, grouped together under the *Schedule Tools* section, as shown in Figure 2 - 9. You navigate to the *Project Detail* page by clicking on the name of a project in the *Project Center* page. The *Project Detail* page contains both a *Project* and a *Task* tab because you must access both project-level and task-level functions to leverage the features on this page. Notice the convenient *Status* bar notification just below the *Task* ribbon.

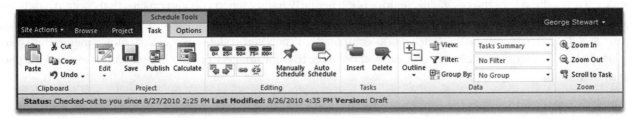

Figure 2 - 9: Project Details page with the Task ribbon selected

In the *Task* ribbon shown in Figure 2 - 9, notice the *Clipboard* section on the far left and the *Editing* and *Tasks* sections in the center. These three sections contain the new web-based project editing tools available in Project Server 2010 using familiar functionality similar to what you find in Project Professional 2010. This exciting new capability supports much stronger project management collaboration, allowing numerous users to participate in project schedule development, or even to manage simple projects from end-to-end, including project tracking, without using Project Professional 2010.

The project editing tools in Project Web App are a small subset of the editing tools you find in Project Professional 2010, and are limited in their functionality. For example, you cannot specify a *Units* value when assigning resources to tasks; the system uses the 100% units value automatically. When setting dependencies between tasks, the system limits you to only the Finish-To-Start (FS) dependency, and you cannot add Lag time or Lead time. Despite these limitations, this new capability represents a giant advance in Project Web App usability.

If you click the *Project* tab, the system displays the *Project* ribbon shown in Figure 2 - 10. This ribbon provides redundant *Edit* and *Save* buttons and provides the only way to close and check in a project after editing on the web via the *Close* button in the *Project* section. The *Navigate* section includes the new *Project Permissions* button that allows you to set project-level permissions specific to your selected project. Note in Figure 2 - 10 that the system grays out the *Edit* button because I have the project open for editing.

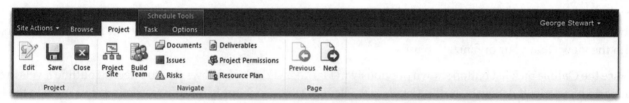

Figure 2 - 10: Project Details page with the Project ribbon selected

Note that the *Project* tab in the *Project Details* page differs significantly from the *Project* tab you see in the *Project Center* page. This is because the operations available on the *Project* tab in the *Project Center* page apply to all projects in the data grid, while the operations available on the *Project* tab in the *Project Details* page apply to only the project open for editing.

Click the *Options* tab and the system displays the *Options* ribbon shown in Figure 2 - 11. Notice that the *Link To* section contains buttons that allow you to create links from tasks to documents, issues and risks contained in the *Project Site* for the selected project. You can even create any one of these objects and link them all in one operation. The *Options* ribbon also provides quick access to the *Close Tasks to Updates* feature, a feature also available from the *Project Center* page as well.

Figure 2 - 11: Project Details page with the Options ribbon selected

Applying and Working with Views

Project Web App pages that contain data grids include a *Data* section in their default ribbon. You use the tools in the *Data* section of the ribbon to apply various views and to control those views by restricting data outline levels, applying filter conditions and grouping the data in the view. Figure 2 - 12 shows the *Data* section of the *Resource* ribbon on the *Resource Center* page.

**Figure 2 - 12: Data Section
of the Resource Ribbon**

The *View* selector allows you to select any view that you can access on the page that you are viewing. Although Project Server ships with a number of out-of-the-box views, for the most part you work with customized versions of the views or an entirely different set of views created specifically for your organization. You should familiarize yourself with the views that your organization uses.

Notice the *Outline* pick list button shown previously in Figure 2 - 12, which allows you to select all outline levels in the data grid or restrict the view by outline level up to 9 levels. When you apply outline restrictions to a view in the Resource Center, it acts upon the grouping structure in the view. When you apply outline restrictions to a *Project Detail* view, it acts upon the project structure itself. Selecting *Outline Level 1* from the pick list, for example, restricts the view to display only the most top-level data lines. Similarly, if you select *Outline Level 3* from the pick list, the system displays only the first three levels of data and collapses the rest of the data below it.

The *Filter* selector provides two options: *No Filter* and *Custom Filter*. You use the *No Filter* option to clear a custom filter once you have applied it. To filter a view, from the *Data* section of the ribbon, select the *Custom Filter* item from the *Filter* pick list. The system displays the *Custom Filter* dialog shown in Figure 2 - 13.

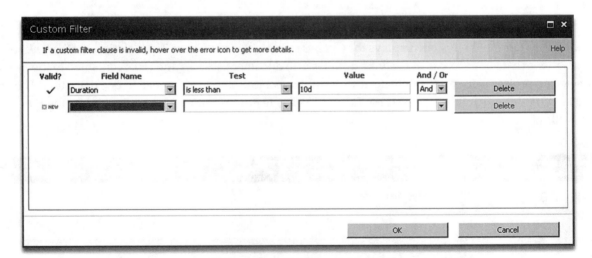

Figure 2 - 13: Custom Filter Dialog

The *Custom Filter* dialog allows you to build a filter by creating test conditions for the fields available in the view. In order to filter on a field in Project Web App, it must be included in the view. You use the *Field Name* selector to choose the field for your first filter condition. Use the *Test* selector to apply an available test condition from the list as shown in Figure 2 - 14.

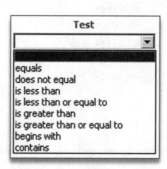

Figure 2 - 14: Test Conditions

In the *Value* field, you must then enter a valid value for your test. When you test against a *Text* field, you enter a *Text* value, when you test against a *Date* field, you must enter a valid *Date* format and you must enter numeric data for fields containing numeric values.

The *Group By* selector is the last tool in the *Data* section of the ribbon shown previously in Figure 2 - 12. Like the *Field* selector in the *Custom Filter* dialog, the *Group By* selector displays only fields that are available in the view. You cannot group your fields using data fields not included in the view. When you apply a group by value, the system redisplays the view grouped by the unique values it finds in the field. Logically, not all data fields are good candidates for grouping. For instance, grouping by *Resource Name* in a *Resource Center* view would not make sense as most resource names are unique unto themselves. On the rare occasions that names are repeated in the resource pool, the most you can gain from this grouping is to understand how many times the repetition occurs in your resource pool. Grouping by *Resource Type*, however, is a very useful exercise because it organizes your resources in a logical presentation.

Manipulating the Data Grid

Some Project Web App pages contain a data grid that displays task, resource, or assignment data. Some data grids, such as the *Project Center* page, have a vertical split bar separating the grid into two sections, while other pages contain a single grid only. For example, notice that the *Project Center* page, shown previously in Figure 2 - 8, consists of two sections: the project list on the left side of the split bar, and the Gantt chart on the right side. To work with the data in the grid most effectively, it is important to know how to take the following actions:

- **Moving the Split Bar** - You move the split bar in the grid by floating your mouse pointer anywhere over the split bar itself. When the mouse pointer changes from a single arrow to a double-headed arrow, as shown in Figure 2 - 15, click and hold the mouse button to "grab" the split bar and then drag it to the new position on the screen.

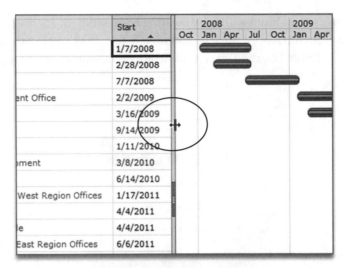

Figure 2 - 15: Move the Split Bar

- **Changing Column Widths** - To change the width of any column in the grid, float the mouse pointer any-where on the right edge of the column in the header row. The mouse pointer changes from a single arrow to a double-headed arrow, as shown in Figure 2 - 16. Click and hold to "grab" the right edge of the column, and drag the edge of the column to the desired width.

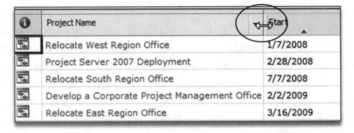

Figure 2 - 16: Widen the Project Name Column

To widen any column to "best fit" the data in the column, you can use the Microsoft Excel trick by double-clicking the gridline on the right edge of the column header.

- **Moving Columns** - To move any column in the grid, click and hold the column header of the column you want to move. Drag the column into its new position in the grid and then drop it. Notice in Figure 2 - 17 that I am dragging the *% Complete* column to a new position to the left of the *Start* column. Notice how the column floats over the other columns in a transparent format as I move it across the other columns.

Project Name	% Complete Start	Finish	% Complete
Relocate West Region Office	1/7/2008	7/28/2008	100%
Project Server 2007 Deployment	2/28/2008	7/28/2008	100%
Relocate South Region Office	7/7/2008	2/9/2009	100%
Develop a Corporate Project Management Office	2/2/2009	12/14/2009	100%
Relocate East Region Office	3/16/2009	12/17/2009	100%
Develop Corporate Assets Database	9/14/2009	1/21/2010	100%
Relocate North Region Office	1/11/2010	7/2/2010	100%

Figure 2 - 17: Drag the % Complete column to the left of the Start column

- **Sorting Columns** - To sort the data in the grid, float your mouse pointer over the column header of the column upon which you want to sort, and then click the pick list button. The system displays the pick list shown in Figure 2 - 18 for the *Start* column. Click either the *Sort Ascending* or *Sort Descending* item on the pick list to apply the type of sorting you want. Remember that you can apply sorting to only one column in a data grid.

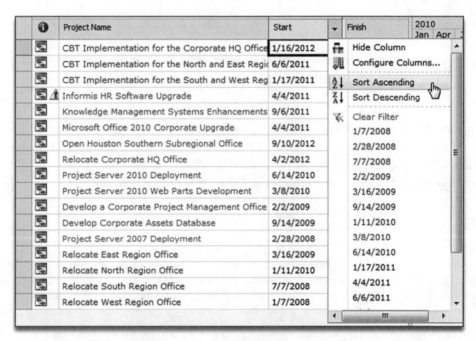

Figure 2 - 18: Apply Ascending sorting on the data in the Start column

- **AutoFilter** - To auto filter the data in any column, float your mouse pointer over the column header of the column whose data you want to filter, and then click the pick list button. Select any value on the list of column values, such as the list of dates in the *Start* column shown previously in Figure 2 - 18. To remove the auto filter, click the pick list again and select the *Clear Filter* item on the pick list.

- **Hiding and Unhiding a Column**: To hide any column, float your mouse pointer over the column header of the column you want to hide, and then click the pick list button. Click the *Hide Column* item in the pick list to hide the selected column. To unhide a column, float your mouse pointer over any column header, click the pick list button, and click the *Configure Columns* item on the pick list. The system displays the *Configure Col-*

umns dialog shown in Figure 2 - 19. In the *Configure Columns* dialog, select the option checkbox of the column(s) you want to unhide and then click the *OK* button.

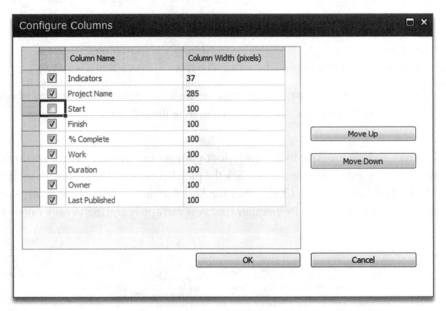

Figure 2 - 19: Unhide column in the Configure Columns dialog

Notice in the *Configure Column* dialog shown previously in Figure 2 - 19 that Project Server 2010 also allows you to set column widths and the column display order, as well as hiding and unhiding column. To change the width of any column, enter the width in pixels in the *Column Width* field. To change the display order of columns, select any column and use the *Move Up* and *Move Down* buttons. Click the *OK* button when finished.

 Project Server 2010 automatically saves any changes you make to the layout of a grid (such as column order, column width, etc.) in your user profile. The layout of the grid reappears the next time you return to the page. These changes affect the current user only and do not affect other users.

Printing the Data Grid

Project Server 2010 allows you to print a report from a data grid or export the data grid information to Microsoft Excel. To print a data grid, click the *Print* option in the *Share* section of the ribbon on a page containing a data grid, such as on the *Project Center* page. The system opens the *Print Grid* window in its own Internet Explorer window, and then displays the *Print* dialog in front of the window, and with the default printer selected, as shown in Figure 2 - 20.

The *Print Grid* window is a duplicate of the grid in the parent window. Notice in Figure 2 - 20 that the *Print Grid* window shows the *Project Center* page, for example. In this window, you can rearrange and resize the columns, but you cannot hide or unhide columns. Before you can change the data in the *Print Grid* window, however, you must close the *Print* dialog. After you change the arrangement of the data in the data grid, use the **Ctrl + P** keyboard shortcut to display the *Print* dialog again.

Click the *Print* button in the *Print* dialog to print the data grid. If you print the data grid that includes a Gantt chart, such as the *Project Center* page, the system prints both the data grid and the Gantt chart. The ability to print the Gantt chart in Project Web App is a new feature in Project Server 2010. In prior versions of Project Server, you could apply additional formatting to the grid prior to printing; this feature is no longer available in the 2010 version.

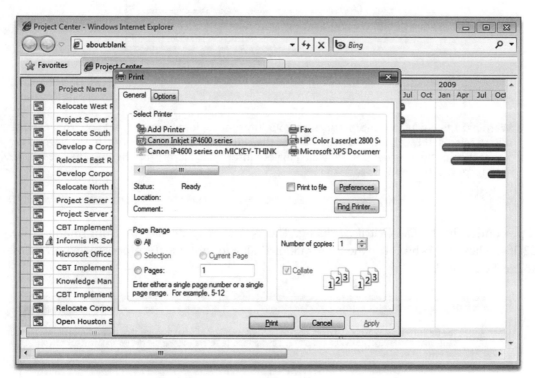

Figure 2 - 20: Print Grid window with the Print dialog displayed

 Warning: If you attempt to print a data grid that exceeds 100 lines of information in the grid, Project Server 2010 does not allow you to print the data grid. Instead, the system forces you to export the data grid to Microsoft Excel. From Excel, you can then print the data grid.

Exporting the Data Grid to Excel

In addition to printing the data grid, you can also export the data grid to a Microsoft Excel workbook by clicking the *Export to Excel* button from the *Share* section of the ribbon on a page containing a data grid. When you select this option, the system displays the *File Download* dialog shown in Figure 2 - 21.

Figure 2 - 21: File Download dialog

 Warning: The default security settings for your Internet Explorer may prevent you from exporting a data grid to Microsoft Excel. If this is the case, add the URL of the Project Web App home page to the *Trusted Site* section of the *Internet Options* dialog in your Internet Explorer, and then set the *Security Level* setting for the *Trusted Sites* zone to *Low*.

Click the *Open* button in the *File Download* dialog. The system may display the confirmation dialog shown in Figure 2 - 22. If so, click the *Yes* button in the confirmation dialog to continue the process of exporting the data grid to a Microsoft Excel workbook.

Figure 2 - 22: Confirmation dialog when exporting data to Excel

The system opens Microsoft Excel and exports the grid into a blank workbook, as shown in Figure 2 - 23.

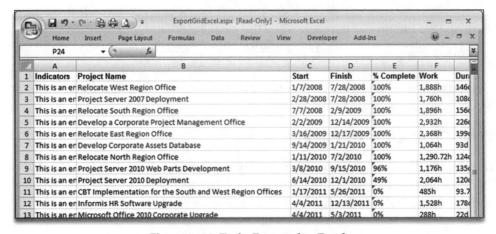

Figure 2 - 23: Tasks Exported to Excel

Warning: When you export grid data to Microsoft Excel, the exporting process exports the data in **every column**, including hidden columns. Keep in mind that in Microsoft Excel, it is very simple to delete a column or to hide a column.

Hands On Exercise

Exercise 2-1

Explore the features of the Project Web App user interface.

1. Log into Project Web App instance for your training.

If you do not intend to use the Project Server 2010 instance included with the sample files for this book, enter a URL for one of your own orgaization's Project Server instances in the *Account Properties* dialog.

2. Click the *Resource Center* link in *Resources* section of the *Quick Launch* menu.

3. Click the *Browse* tab in the upper left corner of the *Resource Center* page.

4. Click the *Home* link at the top of the *Quick Launch* menu to return to the *Home* page of Project Web App.

5. Click the *Project Center* link in the *Projects* section of the *Quick Launch* menu.

6. Collapse the *Quick Launch* menu by clicking the *Collapse* icon at the top of the menu. The *Collapse* icon is the small left-pointing triangle in the upper left corner of the *Quick Launch* menu.

7. Examine the buttons in each section of the *Projects* ribbon.

8. Drag the split bar to the right side of the *Duration* column.

9. Widen the *Indicators* column to a width that shows the indicators for every project.

10. Drag the *Duration* column and drop it in between the *Start* and *Finish* columns.

11. Float your mouse pointer over the *Project Name* column header, click the pick list button, and then select the *Sort Ascending* item on the menu.

12. Float your mouse pointer over the *Start* column header, click the pick list button, and then select the *Sort Ascending* item on the menu.

13. Float your mouse pointer over the *% Complete* column, click the pick list button, and then select the *Hide Column* item on the menu.

14. Float your mouse pointer over the Project Name column header, click the pick list button, and then select the *Configure Columns* item on the menu.

15. In the *Configure Columns* dialog, select the checkbox to the left of the *% Complete* row, and then click the *OK* button. Notice how the system unhides the *% Complete* column.

16. Click the *Export to Excel* button from the *Share* section of the *Projects* ribbon.

17. If the system displays a *File Download* dialog, click the *Open* button in the dialog.

18. If you see a *Microsoft Office Excel* warning dialog concerning file formats, click the *Yes* button in the warning dialog.

19. Examine the data in the Excel workbook, and then close Microsoft Excel without saving the file.

20. Expand the *Quick Launch* menu by clicking the *Expand* icon in the upper left corner of the *Project Center* page. The *Expand* icon is the small right-pointing triangle.

Module 03

Creating New Proposed Projects

Learning Objectives

After completing this module, you will be able to:

- Understand lifecycle management
- Understand phases and stages in a workflow
- Create a new project proposal
- Add a resource plan to a proposal
- Build a team for a resource plan

Inside Module 03

Understanding Lifecycle Management

One of the most exciting new capabilities Project Server 2010 provides is a sophisticated demand, decision-making and lifecycle management system. This system allows your organization to capture project requests and work through a manual or automated procedure to collect information about proposed projects and ultimately use Project Server 2010's new Portfolio decision-making tools to select the organization's portfolio of projects and then manage each project through an appropriate governance lifecycle.

Project Server 2010 provides a complete cradle-to-grave lifecycle management capability by combining a built-in proposal creation process with the decision-making tools that were formerly included with Microsoft Office Portfolio Server 2007, and the ability to govern the end-to-end process using a workflow that moves projects through a series of user-defined *Stages*. You can define lifecycles (workflows) to control all types of governance or process lifecycles.

The sample workflow that ships with Project Server 2010 uses the predefined enterprise custom fields with the names that start with the word *sample.* The system also contains pre-defined *Phases, Stages,* and *Project Detail Pages (PDPs)* used to construct an example of an end-to-end lifecycle. Microsoft provides this sample to help you understand how lifecycle management works, so I use this as my example for this module as well.

The highest form of automated governance you can achieve using Project Server 2010 is to apply workflows to your project types specifically customized for each type of project you allow into the system. With a workflow, you can automate business logic, interact with external data systems, and create multiple branching decision trees–all of this limited only by your development capabilities. Even when you use only simple linear workflows, you can establish powerful governance control of your organization's project lifecycle(s). To get up and running quickly with workflows in Project Server 2010, you can customize the sample workflow to some extent, you can explore third-party solutions that provide graphical interfaces for building sophisticated workflows, or you can use Microsoft's Dynamic Workflow starter solution.

Understanding Demand Management

Project Server 2010 provides you with the tools for very basic demand management without using workflows by providing the ability to display multiple *Project Detail Pages* in the project drilldown window in Project Web App. Those of you who have worked with earlier versions of Project Server will be astounded with the changes Microsoft made to this window, which now has the ability to display multiple project information pages as well as provide an interface to edit the project itself. The most basic form of demand management you can perform uses this window to display *Project Detail Pages* that expose required fields for a specific *Project Type.* When a user creates an instance of that *Project Type,* the system compels the user to fill in the required fields before completing the initial save. When you add workflows to this equation, your company can build extremely complex demand and lifecycle management scenarios.

Understanding Decision Management

Project Server provides decision support tools integrated from previous versions of Portfolio Server. To force projects through a selection process that includes a portfolio analysis step, you must govern your projects using a workflow. Of course, you can use the portfolio analysis capabilities without a workflow, without limiting your analysis ability, which is largely a function of the metadata you capture and create for use in your analyses. Some organizations choose to implement Project Server strictly for portfolio analysis and not for project management.

Introducing Project Types

Project Types are an important innovation in the Project Server 2010 metadata architecture. They give you the ability to establish, as the feature name suggests, project types. The important thing to know about *Project Types* is that you use them to connect workflows with *Enterprise Project Templates* and *Project Site Templates.* This is a very big advance in Project Server's capabilities. Previous versions of Project Server were limited to using only one template for all *Project Workspaces* (Project Server 2007). The system now supports multiple *Project Site* (Project Server 2010) templates connected through *Project Types,* which also gives you the ability to specify a unique base project template for each project type.

A *Project Type* consists of a *Project Template,* a set of *Project Detail Pages,* an optional *Workflow* and a *Project Site* template. You can associate a *Project Type* with one or more departments in Project Server. Figure 3 - 1 shows an illustration of the collection of objects contained in the definition of a *Project Type.*

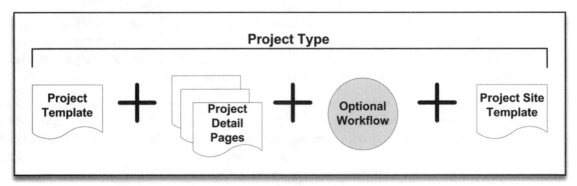

Figure 3 - 1: Project Type Representation

When an *Enterprise Project Type* does not have an associated workflow, an Administrator must specifiy the PDPs that display for the EPT. When an *Enterprise Project Type* does have a workflow, the display of PDPs is controlled by the workflow.

- A **Project Template** is a pre-built schedule model that ideally contains a well-structured schedule with generic resources assigned to tasks as well as duration and effort information that the author estimated in the template. To the degree that the template can eliminate manual schedule building, the more valuable it is to the managers who use them. When your Project Server administrator does not specify a specific project template for a *Project Type,* the system uses a blank project template.

- **Project Detail Pages** are web-part based web pages that your Project Server administrator creates to display and collect project related information. *Project Detail Pages* appear in the Project drilldown window in Project Server Web App. Sometimes a workflow controls the display of PDPs while *Project Types* that are not associated with a workflow allow users to select through the pages manually without the system governing the order of their access. *Project Detail Pages* can contain Project Server 2010 enterprise custom fields and other web parts that display information, or interact with data such as an Excel Services workbook. These can also contain InfoPath forms integrated programmatically.

- **Workflows** are code-based solutions that can control the entire lifecycle flow of projects in Project Server 2010, from proposal through project closure. Workflows can contain very sophisticated business logic such as processing a project request through an automated criteria-based selection or rejection process. Complex workflows can contain multi-branching process logic and can interact with external data sources. Microsoft Project Server 2010 contains one sample workflow that you can use with the *Sample Proposal* that ships with the system. The sample workflow interacts with the portfolio analysis and selection tool in Project Server 2010, forcing project approval through that process. The system requires a workflow to accomplish this.

- **Project Site Templates** are what Project Server uses to create project sites for new projects (formerly named *Project Workspaces* in previous editions). Your Project Server administrator can build new project site templates to meet the specific requirements of your project types, rather than living with the one-size-fits-all model used in previous Project Server versions. If your Project Server administrator does not specify a *Project Site* template for a *Project Type*, the system uses the default *Project Site* template.

Understanding Phases and Stages

To support lifecycle management through workflow, Microsoft Project Server 2010 provides standard lifecycle elements *Phases* and *Stages*. *Phases* are a collection containing at least one *Stage* that contains at least one *Project Detail Page*. While *Phases* primarily serve as containers or groupings, *Stages* contain a number of properties and constituents that support a governance flow.

Figure 3 - 2 shows the *Workflow Stages* page which displays the *Phases* and *Stages* Microsoft ships to support the sample workflow. You cannot access this page unless you have administrator rights in the system.

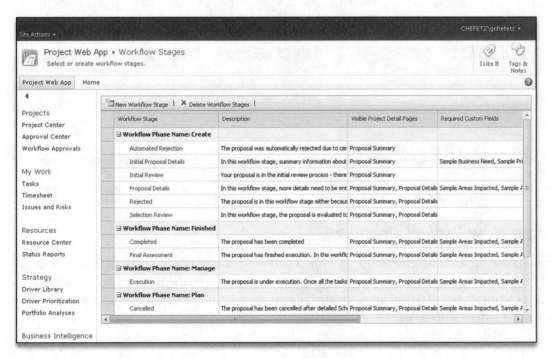

Figure 3 - 2: Workflow Stages page

Notice in the figure that the sample *Stages* are grouped by their respective *Phase*. Notice also that the *Create* workflow phase contains six stages: Automated Rejection, Initial Proposal Details, Initial Review, Proposal Details, Rejected and Selection Review. Each of these *Stages* represents a step in the sample workflow and contains at least one PDP. Your Project Server administrator can define *Project Detail Pages* in a variety of ways to include required fields as well as to apply automated progress control in and out of stages using workflow.

Understanding Project Detail Pages

The base element of the Phase/Stage construct is the *Project Detail Page* or PDP. A PDP is a special kind of web part page that displays in the project drilldown window. While *Stages* can contain more than one PDP, they must contain at least one PDP and often contain multiple PDPs that may show up in multiple stages. In fact, it is common that the system always displays a page that shows the current state of the workflow in every stage, it is also common for the schedule page to display within numerous stages.

From the Project Web App *Quick Launch* menu, select the *Project Center* link from the *Project* section. The system displays the *Project Center* shown in Figure 3 - 3.

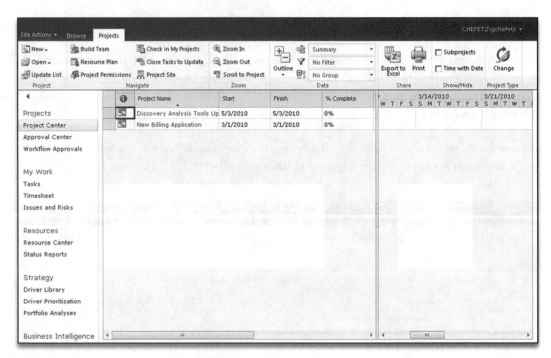

Figure 3 - 3: Project Center

Creating a New Project Proposal

The proposal construct and implementation in Project Server 2010 is radically different than Project Server 2007, as you might imagine with the all the new functionality and supporting elements that I just described. For 2007, proposals were a distinct entity and contained functionality unique to the proposal feature. In 2010, this separate construct is gone in favor of workflow.

Definition of a Proposal in Project Server 2010

Simply put, a proposal is a normal Project Server project record defined as a proposal by its state in a workflow. Unlike its predecessor, Project Server 2010 makes this a soft construct rather than a hard construct. In the 2007 model, you converted a proposal into a full-fledged project, in the 2010 model; you release it into production using a select or reject process.

Initiating a Proposal

For this example, I use the *Sample Proposal* project type that installs with Project Server 2010. To invoke the sample workflow you click on the *New* menu in the upper left corner of the *Projects* ribbon and select the *Sample Proposal* item from the pick list shown in Figure 3 - 4.

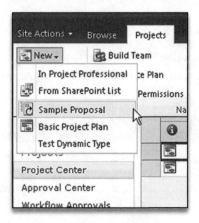

Figure 3 - 4: New menu

When you click on the selection, the system starts a new instance of the *Sample Proposal* workflow and displays the first *Project Detail Page* shown in Figure 3 - 5.

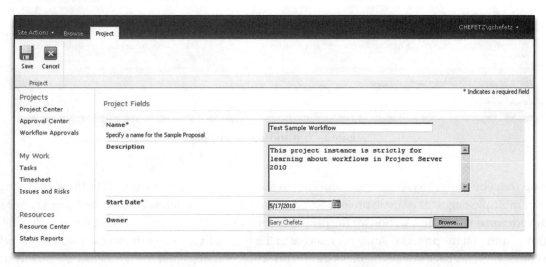

Figure 3 - 5: Sample Proposal Initiation page

Notice that this page contains only three fields accepting user entry, *Name, Description* and *Start Date*. Notice also, the asterisks at the end of the *Name* field and *Start Date* field, which indicate that these are required fields. You cannot save your entries on this page until you provide information in these fields. After you complete your entries, click the *Save* button in the *Project* section of the *Project* ribbon. Note that after clicking the button, the system displays a series of messages in upper right hand corner of the screen to indicate that it is working on your request. The first message you see is *Processing* followed by *Creating Sample Proposal* as shown in Figure 3 - 6.

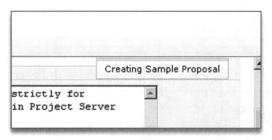

Figure 3 - 6: Processing messages

When the processing completes, the system displays the *Workflow Status* page shown in Figure 3 - 7. This is the second *Project Detail Page* that the system displays in the sample workflow process.

Figure 3 - 7: Workflow Status page

Keep in mind that you are still looking at and working in the project drilldown window in Project Web App, which now displays multiple pages for a single project. Notice that above the top left section of the *Quick Launch* menu you now see an additional navigation section for the project that you are in the process of creating, in my case "Test Sample Workflow," and that the project displays as selected in the menu. Every stage in a workflow has a *Workflow Status* page. The *Workflow Status* page always displays by default when you first enter a stage. Below the project name selection is another link, *Proposal Summary*. This link corresponds with the one shown in the table in the middle of the page in the *Available Pages in this Workflow Stage* section. All *Project Detail Pages* that are available for the current stage are accessible from either the left hand navigation or the *Workflow Status* page. When you click the link in one of the sections, the system displays the selected *Project Detail Page*. Figure 3 - 8 shows the *Proposal Summary*.

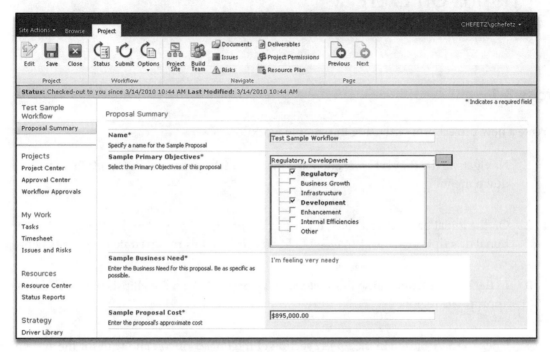

Figure 3 - 8: Proposal Summary page

Enter your own clever choices and remarks in these fields, including a value in the *Sample Proposal Cost* field that is below one million dollars. It is very important that you **do not enter a value over a million dollars** if you wish to completely work through the sample workflow, as crossing this cost threshold will cause your project to be automatically rejected. I selected the *Regulatory* item from the *Sample Primary Objective* area. Notice the options available in the *Project* and *Workflow* sections of the *Project* ribbon. At this point, you can save your information and submit it later, or you can save and then click the *Submit* button. To proceed to the next workflow stage, click the *Submit* button. The system displays the *Message from webpage* dialog shown in Figure 3 - 9.

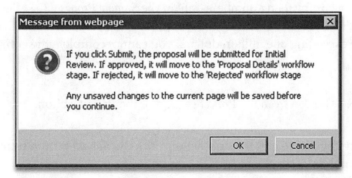

Figure 3 - 9: Message from Webpage dialog

Click the *OK* button to continue. The system accepts your input and moves the workflow to an approval checkpoint where an authorized approver must approve the initial request before it moves to the next stage in the workflow.

Hands On Exercise

Exercise 3-1

Create a new project proposal using the sample workflow.

1. Navigate to the *Project Center* and click the *New* pick list and select *Sample Proposal* from the drop down menu.

2. On the initial page enter a name for your new proposed project in the *Name* field, enter an optional description in the *Description* field and select a future start date for your new project.

3. In the *Region* section of the *Proposal Summary* page, click on the ellipsis button ![...] and choose the appropriate region.

4. Click the *Save* button in the *Project* section of the *Project* ribbon and wait for the system to create your new proposal. Notice that the system reports progress in the upper right hand corner of the display area in a yellow rectangle. Progress indicators include *Processing, Creating Sample Proposal,* and *Save completed successfully.* Depending on the speed of your system, not all of these may have time to display on the screen.

5. When the system displays the *Workflow Status* page, select the *Proposal Summary* item from either the *Quick Launch* menu or the data grid in the center of the page.

6. On the *Proposal Summary* page, click on the ellipsis button ![...] in the *Sample Primary Objectives* section and select values accordingly, then enter a sentence or two in the *Sample Business Need* field. Enter a cost by using numbers only in the *Sample Proposal Cost* field, but do not enter a value that exceeds $1,000,000.00 unless you want to test the automatic rejection feature. Note: If you enter a value exceeding one million dollars, you cannot complete the entire series of exercises in this module.

7. Click the *Save* button from the *Project* section of the *Project* ribbon.

8. After the system completes the save action, click the *Submit* button from the *Workflow* section of the *Project* ribbon.

9. When the system prompts, click the *OK* button in the *Message from webpage* dialog. Wait until the system completes processing and redisplays the *Workflow Status* page.

Approving a New Project Proposal

To both view and approve the request, select the *Workflow Approvals* link from the *Project* section of the *Quick Launch* menu. The system displays the *Project Server Workflow Tasks My Tasks* page, which contains the *Workflow Approvals* page, shown in Figure 3 - 10.

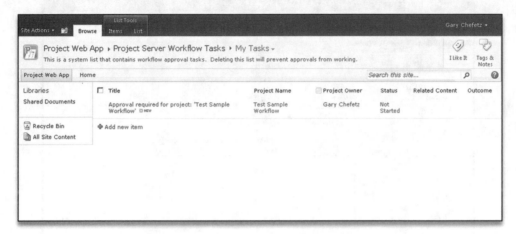

Figure 3 - 10: Workflow Approvals page

Notice the *Approval required for project: 'Test Sample Workflow'* item that appears on the list. Note also that this is a standard SharePoint task list. Float your mouse pointer over the item to reveal the checkbox next to the item and select the checkbox. The page display changes to reveal the *Workflow Approvals* page shown in Figure 3 - 11.

 The approval step in this case does not authorize the project for execution, it simply authorizes the project to move to the next stage in the workflow.

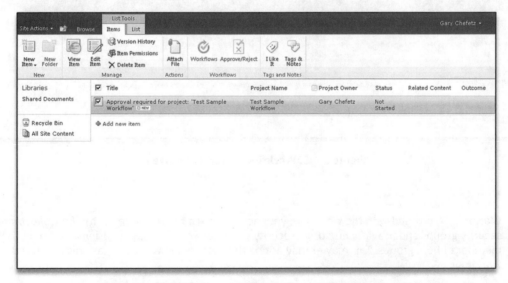

Figure 3 - 11: Workflow Approvals page with item selected

After you select the item, the *List Tools* ribbon appears. Select the *Edit Item* button from the *Manage* section of the ribbon. The system opens the item for editing in the dialog shown in Figure 3 - 12.

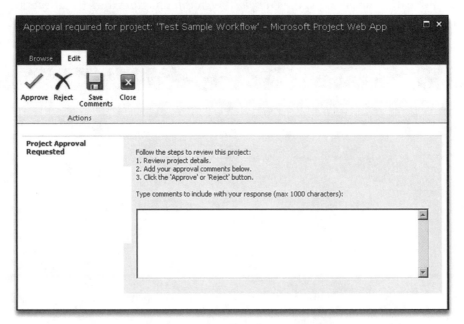

Figure 3 - 12: Edit Approval Item

The *Sample Workflow* requires that one person with approval rights approve the request. The system also supports *Majority* and *Consensus* approval types. Notice that you can approve, reject, or simply add and save comments before closing the item. In this case, you want to select the *Approve* button from the *Actions* section of the ribbon to approve the request and move it forward in the workflow. The system redisplays the *Workflow Approvals* page, which now shows that you have approved the request and can move to the next workflow stage after the *Initial Request* stage as shown in Figure 3 - 13.

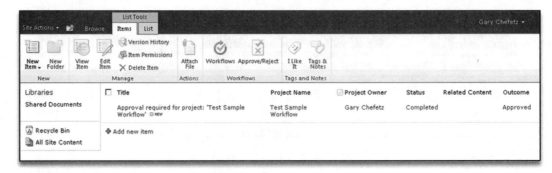

Figure 3 - 13: Workflow request approved

Warning: To proceed with the workflow, your account must be a member of the *Portfolio Managers* security group, and the *Administrators* security group, or you must log on using an account that is a member of both groups. This may or may not be the case for all workflows, as this is determined in the workflow.

Hands On Exercise

Exercise 3-2

Approve your new proposal for further development. Note that your account must be a member of the *Portfolio Managers* security group in order to perform this exercise. If your current account is not a member of the *Portfolio Managers* security group, log on to Project Web App with an account in this group.

1. Select the *Workflow Approvals* link from the *Projects* section of the *Quick Launch* menu

2. Locate the approval record for the proposal you created, float your mouse pointer over the time to reveal the checkbox next to the item and select it.

3. In the *Manage* section of the *List Tools* ribbon, click the *Edit Item* button.

4. In the resulting dialog window, enter comments in the *Comments* field and click the *Approve* button from the *Actions* section of the *Edit* ribbon. The system returns to the *Workflow Approvals* page.

Completing the Sample Workflow Proposal Details Stage

Once approved, the project proposal advances to the *Proposal Details* stage, which displays five *Project Detail Pages* in addition to the *Workflow Status* page as shown in Figure 3 - 14. Notice the series of pages listed in the left-hand navigation as well as the grid in the *Available Pages in this Workflow Stage* section of the page. Notice the status of each page in the grid display. Before you can advance to the next workflow stage, you must complete the pages marked as incomplete. After completing the required information for all of the PDPs shown in the *Proposal Details* stage, the workflow moves the project into the *Select* phase, where the workflow waits for selection using the portfolio analysis tools where your new project must be committed to the portfolio before you can move on to the *Planning* phase.

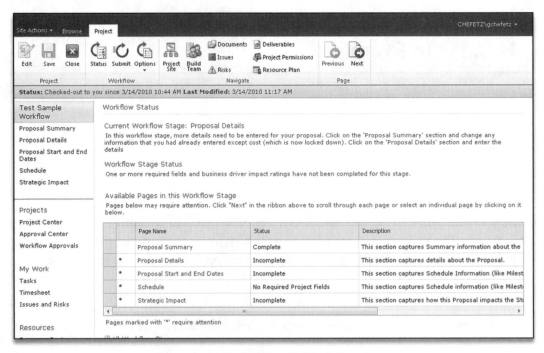

Figure 3 - 14: Project Details Workflow Stage

Behind the scenes, the workflow has already processed some custom business logic included in the automated rejection stage. The stages of the workflow that you advanced through are as shown in Figure 3 - 15.

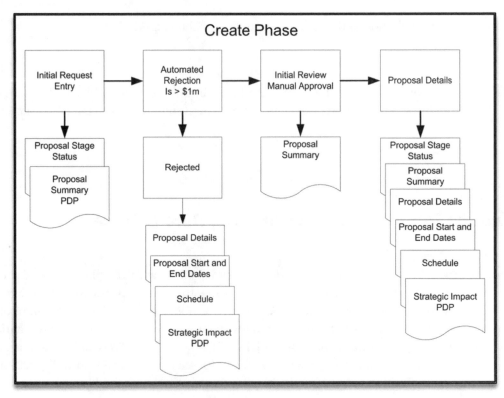

Figure 3 - 15: Workflow Stages for Sample Proposal Create Phase

Behind the scenes, the system created a project file, in this case the default blank project file because the sample does not specify an enterprise project template. It also created a *Project Site* using the custom enterprise template specified for the workflow; in this case, it used the default *Project Site* template because the sample does not specify a custom *Project Site* template.

Your sample workflow is now in the *Proposal Details* stage, a point at which numerous PDPs are exposed, many of which require your attention. You must provide required information before the system will allow you to submit your proposal to the next stage of the workflow unless either the automated or manual initial selection process already rejected your proposal or someone manually rejected it. When you select your started proposal from the *Project Center*, your started proposal should open to the *Workflow Status Page*. Notice that there are three pages marked as incomplete and one that has no required fields. Select the *Proposal Details* link from either the left hand navigation or the grid in the middle of the page. The system displays the *Sample Proposal Details* page shown in Figure 3 - 16.

You can save your information at any time during a workflow and return to the proposal later to complete it. Depending on the design of the workflow, your project may be governed by it from initiation through project closure.

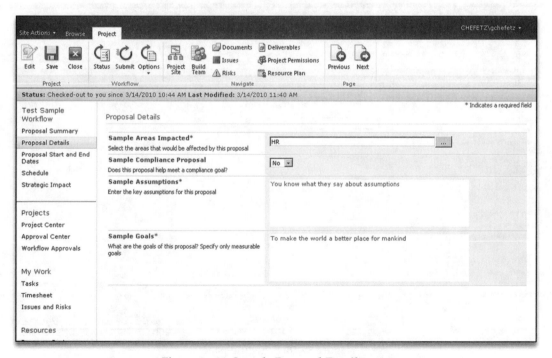

Figure 3 - 16: Sample Proposal Details page

To continue your tour of the sample workflow, add entries to the page and use the *Save* button on the *Project* ribbon to save your entries on each page. The next page that requires attention is the *Proposal Start and Finish Dates* page shown in Figure 3 - 17.

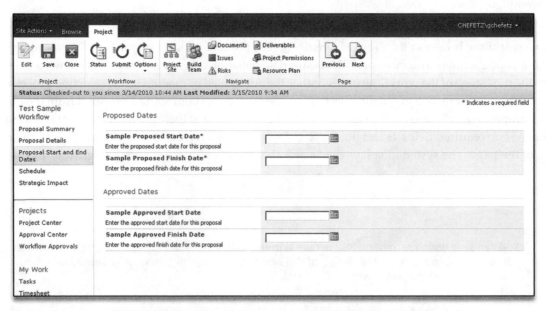

Figure 3 - 17: Proposal Start and Finish Dates page

Provide information in the required fields marked with an asterisk and click the *Save* button to save your entries. Click on the *Schedule* page link and the system displays the *Schedule* page shown in Figure 3 - 18.

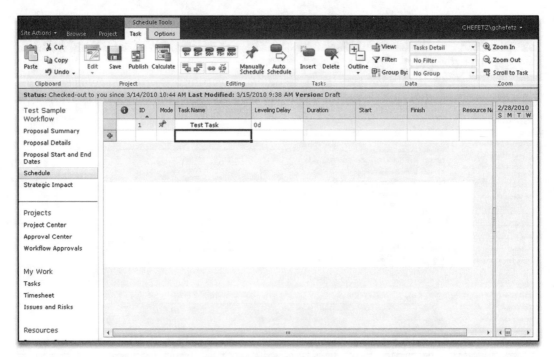

Figure 3 - 18: Schedule page

The *Schedule* page exposes the project schedule for editing. Notice in Figure 3 - 18 that I entered a "Test Task" name to create a single task in the new schedule. At this point in the workflow, there is no requirement for the project to have a developed schedule and there are no required entries for this page. If the sample workflow had an enterprise project template attached, the template schedule would display now. When you click on the *Strategic Impact* link on the left hand menu, the system opens the *Strategic Impact* page shown in Figure 3 - 19.

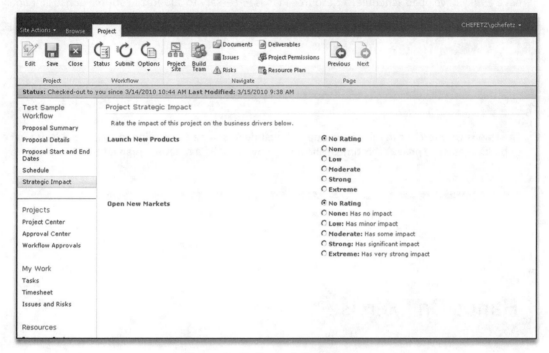

Figure 3 - 19: Strategic Impact page

The *Project Strategic Impact* web part displays the appropriate business drivers based on the department to which the *Project Type* and Business Drivers belong. You must provide information in the page to analyze your portfolio using strategic alignment analysis. The sample workflow includes this page because its creator designed it to use the portfolio analysis capability to select projects for execution.

 Warning: Because the system does not include any predefined business drivers, your Project Server administrator must create business drivers before you can submit your new proposal into the selection process.

At this point, your first sample workflow should be completely through the *Proposal Details* stage and *Create* phase as shown previously in Figure 3 - 15. If you have not completed all the *Project Detail Pages* in the *Proposal Details* stage, do so at this time.

MSProjectExperts recommends that before you submit your proposal, that you build a resource plan for the project in order to use Resource Constraint analysis during Portfolio Anaysis. Portfolio Managers can use resource loading from a Resource Plan or from the project plan. Because this project does not have a fully developed schedule, a Resource Plan is necessary to support Resource Constraint analysis.

The Hands On Exercises in this section do not include Resource Constraint analysis, so it is not necessary to build a resource plan at this time. I show you how to build a resource plan later in this module.

Hands On Exercise

Exercise 3-3

Complete the Sample Workflow Proposal Details Stage.

1. Return to the proposal you started in Exercise 3-1 by navigating to the *Project Center* page. Apply the *Summary* view, if necessary, and locate and select your new proposal in the grid. The system displays the *Workflow Status* page for your proposal.

2. Select the *Proposal Details* item from the *Quick Launch* menu or from the *Available Pages in this Workflow Stage* data grid in the center of the page to open the *Proposal Details* page.

3. Make any selection you like in both the *Sample Areas Impacted* and *Sample Compliance Proposal* fields by using the selection tools.

4. Enter some text in both the *Sample Assumptions* and *Sample Goals* text fields and click the *Save* button in the *Project* section of the *Project* ribbon. Wait for the save action to complete.

5. Select the *Proposal Start and End Dates* item from the *Quick Launch* menu to open the *Proposal Start and End Dates* page.

6. Select future start and end dates in both the *Sample Proposed Start Date* and *Sample Proposed Finish Date* fields using the date pickers. Leave the *Approved Dates* section blank and click the *Save* button in the *Project* section of the *Project* ribbon. Wait for the save action to complete.

7. You can ignore the *Schedule* link for now; this page displays the project schedule, which you have not built yet. If the workflow were associated with a schedule template, you would see it on this page.

8. Select the *Strategic Impact* item from the *Quick Launch* menu and rate your proposal against the available business drivers. When you complete your selections, click the *Save* button in the *Project* section of the *Project* ribbon. Wait for the save action to complete.

9. Click the *Submit* button in the *Workflow* section of the *Project* ribbon and click the *OK* button in the subsequent *Message from webpage* dialog to move your proposal to the *Selection Review* stage.

Editing an Existing Proposal

As you can see, you use the project drilldown pages to edit your project at every stage of the workflow. Both the workflow and specific settings in the *Project Detail Pages* determine what fields you can edit in the various stages of the workflow. Because these vary with each workflow, the experience you will have with workflows in your environment are not predictable. Rather, you must learn each workflow individually. To edit your project simply select it from the *Project Center* and select *Edit* from the *Project* section of the *Project ribbon*.

Because the sample workflow contains code that hooks into portfolio analysis, you cannot move to the next stage of the workflow until a manager approves your project through the portfolio analysis commit process. Assuming that portfolio manager has approved your project, you can return to the *Project Center* and select your new proposal project in the grid. You should now see that the project has advanced to the *Resource Planning* stage, as shown for my new project proposal in Figure 3 - 20. At this point in the process, the project manager actually assigns resources to the tasks in the project moving away from using a *Resource Plan*.

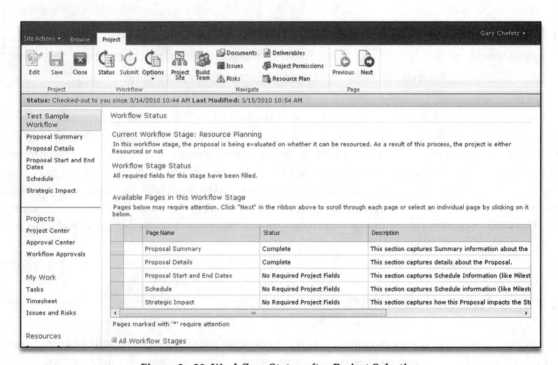

Figure 3 - 20: Workflow Status after Project Selection

The *Resource Planning* stage requires a portfolio manager to perform a resource analysis using the portfolio analysis tools as well, and the manager must commit the project through this process to move it into the *Scheduling* stage. The rest of the workflow progresses through execution and project closure following the diagram shown in Figure 3 - 21.

In the previous example, I did not perform a *Resource Constraint* analysis because the system would have to contain a significant number of projects to exercise the tool in a meaningful way. Normally, you build a resource plan to prepare the project for resource constraint analysis. If you are a resource manager or portfolio manager, you may need to know how to do this. I show you how in the balance of this module.

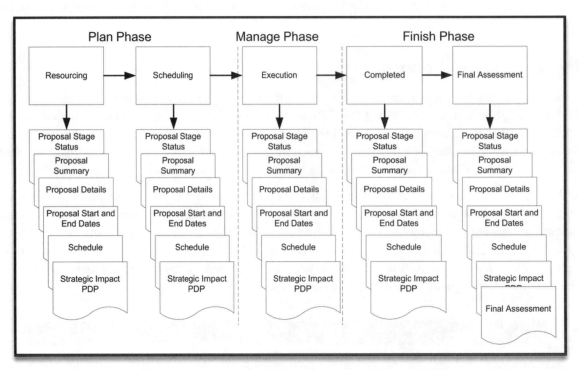

Figure 3 - 21: Workflow Stages for Sample Proposal continued

As you can see in the diagram, the *Project Detail Pages* that the workflow uses remain constant until the final stage, which introduces a *Final Assessment* page, which captures some lessons learned information. Before the plan can move from the *Scheduling* stage to the *Execution* stage, the system requires a manual approval after the project manager submits the project from the *Scheduling* stage. The project manager cannot submit the project from the *Execution* stage to the *Completed* stage until all of the tasks in the project are marked 100% complete. The workflow logic immediately rejects any attempt that the project manager makes to submit the project to this stage while there are incomplete tasks in the plan. Once the project manager marks all tasks complete, the project is eligible for submission to the *Finish* phase.

Creating a Resource Plan

In many if not most Project Server configurations used for Portfolio Analysis, early resource planning relies on *Resource Plans*. A *Resource Plan* is a way to "reserve" a resource for specific periods without assigning the resource to tasks. In the *Sample Workflow* example, building a project team and assigning individual resources to tasks happens during the *Resource Planning* stage that occurs after portfolio selection.

In a typical workflow, after you create a new proposal, and before portfolio selection, you need to commit resources to the proposal to show demand. To create a Resource Plan for a proposal, navigate to the Project Center page in Project Web App. Select your proposal by clicking the row header to the left of its name and then click the Resource Plan button from the Navigate section of the Project ribbon. Project Server 2010 displays the Resource Plan page for the selected proposal shown in Figure 3 - 22.

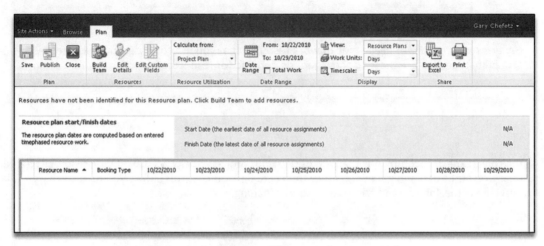

Figure 3 - 22: Resource Plan page for a proposal

Building a Team on a Resource Plan

Notice that the message immediately below the ribbon in Figure 3 - 22, states "Resources have not been identified for this Resource Plan. Click Build Team to add resources." The first step in creating a *Resource Plan* is to add resources to the *Resource Plan*. Click the *Build Team* button from the *Resources* section of the *Plan* ribbon. The system displays the *Build Resource Plan Team* page shown in Figure 3 - 23.

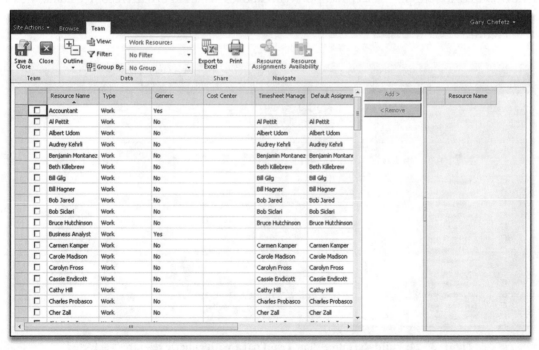

Figure 3 - 23: Build Resource Plan Team page

From the list of resources shown on the *Build Resource Plan Team* page, you must select the resources to serve on your project team. Begin by selecting the option checkbox to the left of each resource who may be a potential team member. You can select any type of resource using this page. Use the *View* pick list in the *Data* section of the *Team* ribbon to change views and select from various subsets of your resource pool. Most organizations are likely to use *Generic* resources to represent resource loading.

Generic resources are a special type of work resource that you use to represent resources by role or capability type. You use these to show generic demand for resources.

MSProjectExperts recommends that you design your process to always use generic resources for early-phase resource demand modeling rather than actual resources. This allows you to easily differentiate between actual loading and proposed resource loading.

If you elect to use actual resources from your resource pool, Project Server 2010 offers you two ways to determine whether each resource is available to serve on your proposed team by using the *Resource Assignments* and *Resource Availability* buttons in the *Navigate* section of the *Team* ribbon. You can use these after selecting one or more resources. Because the expectation is that you are using *Generic* resources exclusively at this point in the process, I do not cover these in this module.

Adding Resources to the Team on a Resource Plan

To add generic resources to your plan, select the option checkboxes to the left of each resource name and then click the *Add* button. The system shows the list of selected resources in the upper right corner of the *Build Resource Plan Team* page shown in Figure 3 - 24.

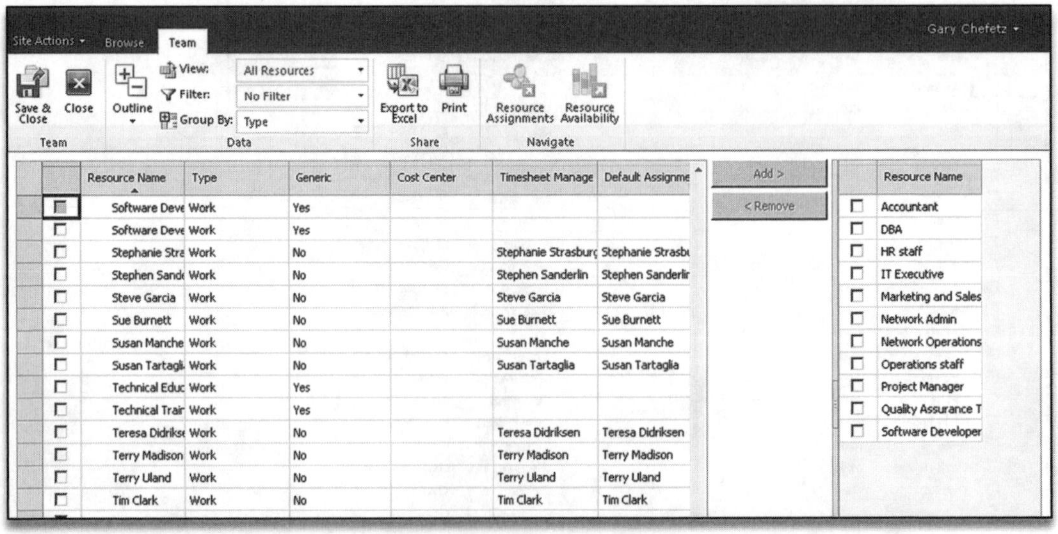

Figure 3 - 24: Build Resource Plan Team page with generic resources selected

Click the *Save and Close* button from the *Team* section of the *Team* ribbon to add the selected resources to the team for the proposal. Project Server 2010 redisplays the *Resource Plan* page with the new team members, as shown in Figure 3 - 25.

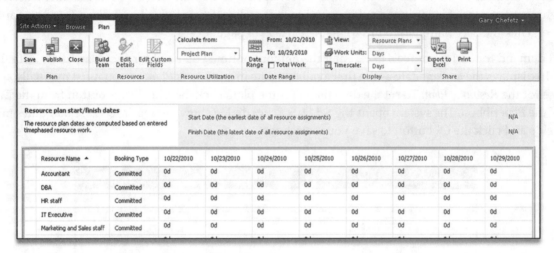

Figure 3 - 25: Resource Plan page with generic team members

Modeling Resource Demand in a Resource Plan

After you add resources to the proposal, you must designate the *Booking Type* for each resource and then "reserve" each resource for the periods for which you need them. Project Server 2010 offers two potential *Booking Type* values for a resource in a *Resource Plan*. Use the **Proposed** booking type to indicate a tentative resource booking when you are not certain that you will use the resource in the *Resource Plan*. Leave the default **Committed** booking type selected to indicate a firm resource commitment to the *Resource Plan*.

To set the *Booking Type* for a resource, select the name of a resource and then click the *Edit Custom Fields* button. Project Server 2010 displays the *Edit Custom Fields* page shown in Figure 3 - 26.

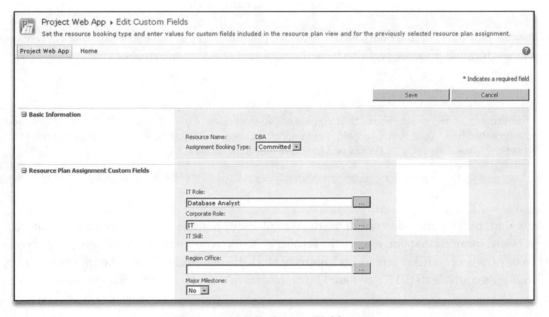

Figure 3 - 26: Edit Custom Fields page

To change the *Booking Type* field value from *committed* to *proposed*, click the *Booking Type* pick list and select the *Proposed* value. In addition to changing the *Booking Type* field value, the system also allows you to set custom resource field values at the assignment level for the selected resource's assignments in the proposal. Notice in Figure 3 - 26 that I can specify assignment-level values for the *IT Role, Corporate Role, IT Skill,* and *Region Office* custom fields. Notice also that assignment-level task field values display on the page as well. After you specify a *Booking Type* value and custom field values, click the *Save* button to return to the *Resource Plan* page.

To model demand for each resource's time, enter the amount of time you need for each period. By default, Project Server 2010 displays the current date as the first available date in a *Resource Plan*, so you must manually specify the date range for the *Resource Plan*. To set the date range for the plan, click the *Date Range* button from the *Date Range* section of the *Plan* ribbon. The system opens the *Set Date Range* dialog shown in Figure 3 - 27. Enter dates in the *From* and *To* fields and click the *Ok* button to save your selections.

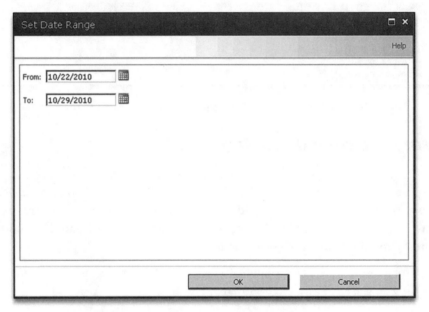

Figure 3 - 27: Set Date Range dialog

Click the *Timescale* pick list to set the timescale for resource planning. Typically, you want to select weeks or months, but for very long- duration projects, you also have the option of selecting quarters or years.

MsProjectExperts recommends that you enter the start date of your proposal in the *From* field and the estimated finish date in the *To* field. For simplicity's sake, MsProjectExperts also recommends that you set the *Timescale* value to *Weeks* or *Months* rather than *Days*.

Click the *Work Units* pick list and select one of the three available options: *Hours, Days,* or *Full-time equivalent.* The default value is *Hours,* meaning that you reserve the resource's work in hours. Select the *Days* option if you wish to reserve work in days, where each day represents 8 hours of work. If you select the *Full-time equivalent* option, you enter the work in full-time equivalents (FTE's), where 1.00 represents full-time work and .50 represents half-time work, for example.

Using the *Full-time equivalent* option is an easy way to reserve full or part-time work for the resources in your resource plan and then to allow the system to calculate the necessary number of hours.

When you select the *Full-time equivalent* option, Project Server 2010 determines the number of hours of work in each time period based on how your Project Server administrator configured your system. The system allows the Project Server administrator to define an FTE as either a specific number of hours per day (such as 8 hours/day), or according to the number of hours each day shown on each resource's calendar in the *Enterprise Resource Pool*.

If you enter work values or FTEs you can display the total work reserved for each resource by selecting the *Show total work* option from the *Date Range* section of the *Plan* ribbon. When you finish selecting your resource plan options, click the *Save* button in the *Plan* section of the *Plan* ribbon.

Because my Proposal runs from early October 2010 through late March 2011, I entered 10/22/2010 in the *From* field, entered 3/25/2011 in the *To* field, and selected *Months* from the *Timescale* pick list. The system redisplays the *Resource Plan* page as shown in Figure 3 - 28.

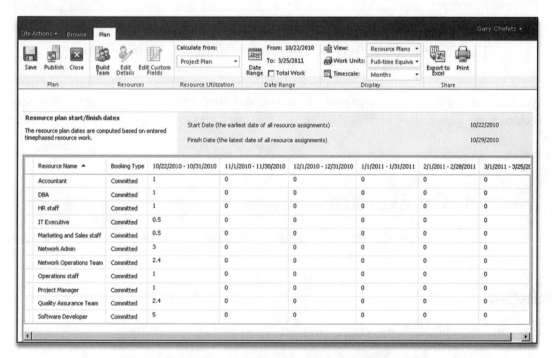

Figure 3 - 28: Resource Plan page shows monthly periods

Figure 3 - 29 shows the same information, but with the *Show total work* option selected. For each resource on the team, enter time in one or more periods to "reserve" the resource during each period. The information you enter shows your "forecast" of anticipated resource utilization over the life of the proposed project, even though you did not assign the resources to tasks.

Figure 3 - 28 shown previously shows the FTE totals that I started entering into the monthly grid. Notice that my anticipated utilization of each resource varies by resource and that these can vary by period as well, even though I did not add values beyond the first month, my intention is to create contoured resource demand across many months.

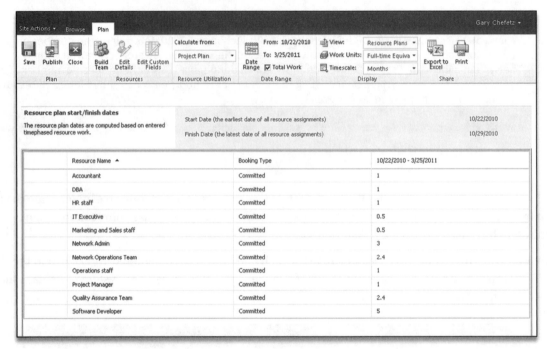

Figure 3 - 29: Resource Plan page shows total resource utilization in one column

When you finish your resource plan for your proposal, click the *Save* button from the *Plan* section of the *Plan* ribbon. Notice that you can also publish the resource plan without publishing the project plan. After the system finishes saving the project, click the *Close* button to close the *Resource Plan* page and return to the *Project Center* page.

Hands On Exercise

Exercise 3-4

Create a Resource Plan on a Proposal in Project Web App.

1. Navigate to the *Project Center* page in Project Web App and select the row header for the proposal you created earlier in this module.

2. In the *Navigate* section of the *Projects* ribbon, click the *Resource Plan* button. Project Web App displays the *Resource Plan* page for the selected proposal.

3. In the *Resources* section of the *Plan* ribbon, click the *Build Team* button. The system displays the *Build Resource Plan Team* page.

4. Add some generic resources to your plan by selecting the option checkboxes to the left of each generic resource name and then click the *Add* button. The system shows the list of selected generic resources in the upper right corner of the *Build Resource Plan Team* page.

5. In the *Team* section of the *Team* ribbon, click the *Save & Close* button to add the selected resources to the team for the proposal. Project Web App redisplays the *Resource Plan* page with the new team members.

6. Select a resource on the *Resource Plan* page. In the *Resources* section of the *Plan* ribbon, click the *Edit Custom Fields* button. Project Web App displays the *Edit Custom Fields* page. Notice that you can set the Assignment Booking Type for a resource in the *Basic Information* section of the page. You can also add other custom field values in the *Resource Plan Assignment Custom Fields* section of the page. Click the *Cancel* button to exit without making changes.

7. In the *Date Range* section of the *Plan* ribbon, click the *Date Range* button. The system opens the *Set Date Range* dialog. Enter dates in the *From* and *To* fields that span several months and click the *OK* button to save your selections.

8. In the *Display* section of the *Plan* ribbon, click the *Work Units* pick list and select the *Full-time Equivalent* item from the pick list.

9. Enter FTE values for at least one column in the monthly grid.

10. In the *Date Range* section of the *Plan* ribbon, select the *Total Work* option to display the FTE totals for your new resource plan.

11. In the *Plan* section of the *Plan* ribbon, click the *Save* button, then click the *Close* button to close your new resource plan

Importing Resources from a Resource Plan

Typically, you apply a resource plan in order to enable the resource constraint analysis in a portfolio analysis. Now that you have moved your proposal through the selection process and built a resource plan, it is time to get your plan detailed with task assignments. Resources in a resource plan are not eligible for assignments in Project unless you copy them from your resource plan into your project. To do this I must open my project from the *Project Center* and then use the *Build Team* tool to accomplish this. Select the row header for your project and click the *Build Team* button from the *Navigate* section of the *Projects* ribbon. The system displays the *Build Team* page shown in Figure 3 - 30.

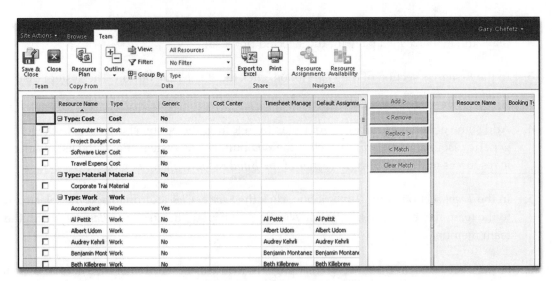

Figure 3 - 30: Build Team for a Project

This is essentially the same tool that you used to build your team for your *Resource Plan*. Notice that the *Team* ribbon now contains a *Copy From* section with a button labeled *Resource Plan* that allows you to copy the resources in your resource plan into your project. To copy the resource into your project, click the *Resource Plan* button and the system redisplays with the resources selected in the *Selected Resources* section on the right as shown in Figure 3 - 31.

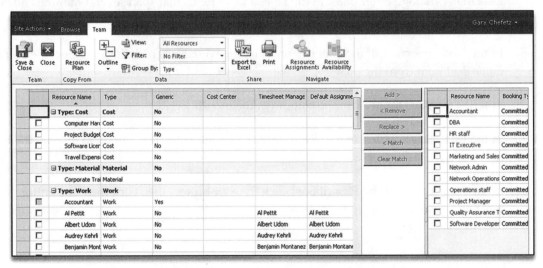

Figure 3 - 31: Build Team tool with Resources Copied from Plan

Now that you copied your resources from the *Resource Plan* you use the *Build Team* tool the same way you did in the previous example. You can add or remove resources at this point and use the *Match* tool to replace your generic resources with human workers. Click the *Save and Close* button when you complete your resource selections. The system returns to your resource plan page.

From the *Build Team* page, you can also determine the availability for one or more selected resources by clicking the *Resource Assignments* button or the *Resource Availability* button.

Using a Resource Plan during Project Execution

As you can see, resource plans are very powerful for modeling resource demand during the proposal process allowing you to create a rich resource model at a high level with very little effort, and a more complex and contoured model with a moderate amount of effort. Resource plans are also very useful during project execution, particularly for projects with long durations or projects where detailed planning is possible for only a near-term horizon. On the *Resource Plan* page shown previously in Figure 3 - 29, notice in the *Resource Utilization* section of the *Plan* ribbon the *Calculate From* pick list shown in focus in Figure 3 - 32.

**Figure 3 - 32: Calculate
From pick list**

As you execute a project that you cannot fully detail, you can use a combination of resources assigned to specific tasks in your project plan and resource loading represented in your resource plan. You do this by selecting the *Project Plan until* item on the pick list and the system displays the *Set Date* dialog shown in Figure 3 - 33.

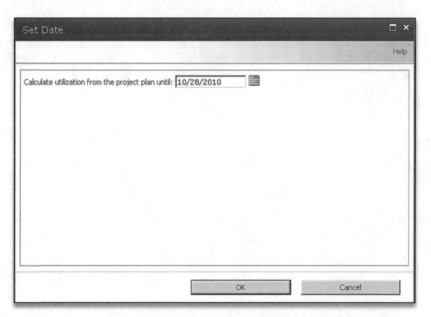

Figure 3 - 33: Set Date dialog

Selecting a date in the dialog tells the system to use the resources assigned to tasks in the project plan to determine utilization until the specified date; and thereafter, use the values in the resource plan allowing you to combine detailed bottom-up planning with high-level top-down planning to support this scenario.

The web-based resource tools you learned about in this module are also useful for organizations where project managers by policy may not select resources for their own teams. In this case, resource managers or other designated staff members use the same tools to apply resources to resource plans and directly to projects.

Proposals Summary

Supported by workflows and project type objects, the proposal feature in Project Sever 2010 is very rich and flexible. So flexible, in fact, that I cannot predict what you have in your environment. As long as you keep in mind that working through a workflow in Project Server is a matter of moving from stage to stage, you should find using the tool with your own configuration an easy experience.

Module 04

Tracking Time and Task Progress

Learning Objectives

After completing this module, you will be able to:

- Create a new timesheet

- Report time on the My Timesheet page

- Plan and submit Administrative Time

- Create a Timesheet for another resource

- Report progress on the Tasks page

- Use the Task Center

- Submit task updates from Outlook

Inside Module 04

Tracking Time in Project Web App

Project Server 2010 allows you to track both time and task progress using the Project Web App interface. Your organization can use a daily timesheet to track hours on all types of work, including both project and non-project work. Using the timesheet system, you can also track non-working time such as vacation or sick leave. Using the Timesheet system in Project Server 2010 allows your organization to account for every hour of work every day for all of your resources.

Your organization can also track task progress in enterprise projects using the default method of tracking progress defined by your Project Server administrator. Table 4 - 1 outlines the potential uses of Timesheets and Tasks Status tracking.

The first major topical section of the module reviews how to track time using the *Timesheets* page in Project Web App. The second major topical section of this module discusses how to track task progress using the *Tasks* page in Project Web App.

Function	Single Entry Mode	Double Entry Mode	Timesheet Stand Alone Mode	Tasks Stand Alone Mode
Timesheets	Timesheets track: • Billable hours • Non-billable hours • Administrative time • Project task progress Automatic data exchange with tasks	Timesheets track • Billable hours • Non-billable hours • Administrative time • Project task progress User initiated data exchange with tasks	Timesheets track • Administrative time No data exchange with tasks	Not used
Tasks	Work routing using Team tasks, Reassign task Management of Material resources	Tasks track of project task progress. User initiated data exchange with timesheets	Not used	Tasks track project task progress No data exchange with timesheets

Table 4 - 1: The Different Uses of Timesheets and Task Status Tracking

Single Entry Mode

Single Entry Mode enables you to enter your time once and have it feed both timesheets and task updates. Environments where tracking of project tasks and administrative time is important will typically use this mode as shown in Figure 4 - 1.

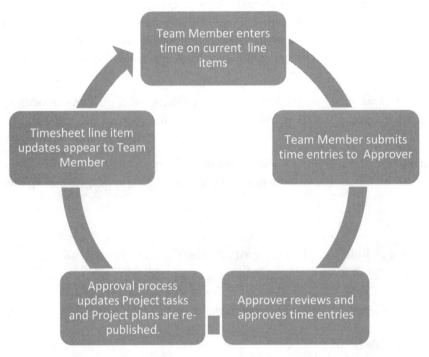

Figure 4 - 1: Single Entry Mode Time Tracking Process Steps

Double Entry Mode

Double Entry Mode enables you to separate task updates from timesheet entries. This capability is desirable in situations where customer billing uses timesheet data and task updates to keep the project plan up to date. For example, if you have a fixed bid contract, your billing must match a given number regardless of the actual number of hours invested in the project.

Standalone Modes

Standalone Modes indicate that you are using either timesheets or tasks but not using them together. Environments that have no billing need will likely not need timesheet capabilities. Environments that are only tracking time will not need task status capabilities.

The time tracking process is typically a repeated process that happens on a regular schedule. Many organizations have weekly time tracking reporting periods. The needs of your organization determine your time tracking reporting period length.

Timesheet Items Tracked

Timesheets help organizations determine where it is investing its efforts and whether there is sufficient capacity to maintain those efforts. Timesheets capture three types of data to fulfill this information need.

Project Tasks

This timesheet item represents your planned activities for a given time period to support the outcomes of the associated project.

Administrative Time Categories

This timesheet item represents a capture mechanism to reflect the number of hours you spend on non-project work. The default Project Server configuration has categories for *Administrative time, Sick Leave* and *Vacation*. Your Project Server administrator can add additional categories to meet your organization's specific needs.

Personal Tasks

Sometimes, your work does not fit in your project tasks or your administrative time categories. In this case, Project Server provides the ability to add personal tasks to your timesheet to capture this time.

Accessing Your Timesheet

To navigate to your timesheet, use any of the following methods as shown in Figure 4 - 2.

- To go to your current period timesheet, do the following:

- Click the *Timesheet* link in the *My Work* section of the *Quick Launch* menu.

- To go to the *Manage Timesheets* page, do one of the following:

- Click the *Manage Timesheet* link in the *Settings* section of the *Quick Launch* menu

- Click the *Timesheets* link in the *Reminders* section of the page.

- Click the ___ *unsubmitted timesheet* link in the *Reminders* section of the page (if available).

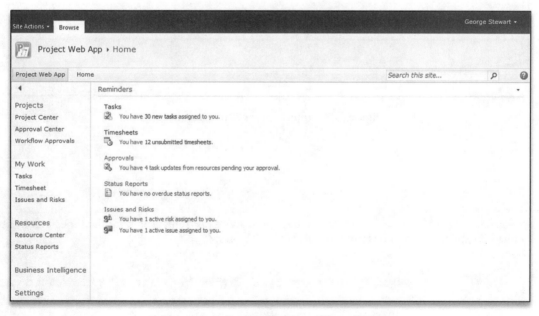

Figure 4 - 2: Project Web App Home Page

Understanding the Timesheet Page

The *Timesheet* page enables you to capture your time spent on all planned and administrative activities for the current time reporting period. New in Project Server 2010, when you first access the *Timesheet* link, Project Server automatically creates your timesheet for the current time reporting period.

To access your timesheet, click the *Timesheet* link in the *My Work* section of the Project Web App *Quick Launch* menu. When selected, you see the page similar to that appearing in Figure 4 - 3 . If you need more room horizontally to see your timesheet, click the *Triangle* button at the top of the *Quick Launch* menu, as highlighted in Figure 4 - 3.

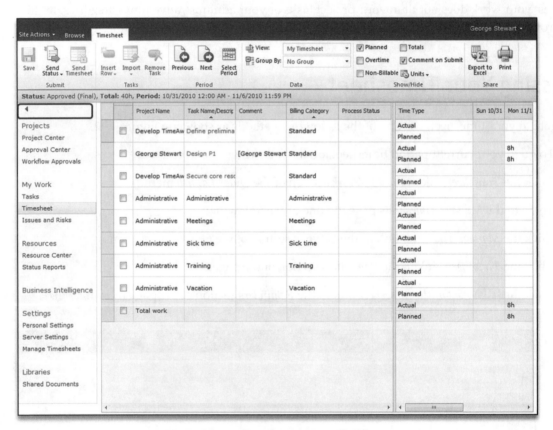

Figure 4 - 3: Project Server 2010 Timesheet

You can collapse the *Quick Launch* menu to provide more horizontal room for the timesheet by selecting the *Triangle* button at the top of the *Quick Launch* menu.

Timesheet Ribbon

The *Timesheet* ribbon is new in Project Server 2010. This module covers all aspects of the *Timesheet* ribbon functionality. The initial items covered are the display control options. The default display of the *Timesheet* page includes these columns.

- Project Name

- For administrative time categories, this column contains the term *Administrative*.

- Task Name/Administrative Time Description

- Descriptive name of the timesheet line item

- Comment

- Data field for you to add a comment related to this timesheet line item entry

- Billing Category

- This optional field enables you to designate a billing category for a particular timesheet line item. For example, if the administrator set up a *Merger* billing category, you can set this value to designate a line item as a *Merger* effort.

- Process Status

- Data field that informs you of the current state of the timesheet line item in regards to the approval cycle.

- To the right of the *Approval Status* column, you also see a timesheet grid containing one week of daily cells for reporting your work.

> The default settings in Project Server 2010 configure the *My Timesheet* page to allow the daily entry of work. Your Project Server administrator can change the configuration to allow users to enter an entire week of work for a seven-day period in a single cell.

Time Types

Each task in the timesheet includes two *Time* types by default, which is *Actual* and *Planned*. You use the first line to enter actual work hours. The second line displays the planned or scheduled work hours for the task. When you enter actual work hours for a task, Project Server 2010 assumes all hours are billable regular (non-overtime) work and it calculates the task cost using the *Standard Rate* value from the Enterprise Resource Pool. Some organizations, however, need to track overtime work in addition to regular work, and to differentiate between billable and non-billable work.

To add an additional *Time* type to track overtime work for each project task, click the *Overtime* checkbox in the *Show/Hide* section of the *Timesheet* ribbon as shown in Figure 4 - 4. For *Non-Billable* time, click the *Non-Billable* checkbox. These time types appear in the time phased entry grid on the right. Notice that *Overtime* and *Non-Billable Time* types only apply to project tasks.

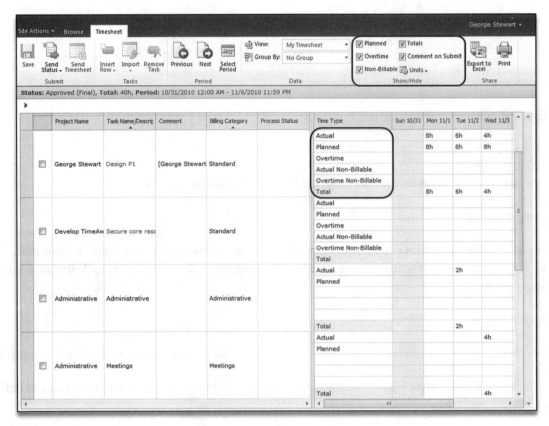

Figure 4 - 4: Show/Hide Line Options

To remove the lines for overtime work and non-billable work, click the appropriate checkboxes on the *TImesheet* ribbon.

Other Show/Hide Options

The *Show/Hide* section of the *Timesheet* ribbon also contains two other options. The *Comment on Submit* option determines whether a pop-up box into which you can enter timesheet level comments appears when you submit your timesheet. While the system enables this option by default, you can change it by unchecking the checkbox. The *Units* pick list enables you to decide the display formats of *Work, Duration* and *Date* fields on the page. For example, if you want to enter your updates as number of days, change the *Units* value for *Work* to *Days*.

The default unit used (minutes, hours, days, weeks) for time entered in the time phased grid is controlled by the *Units* pick list in the *Timesheet* ribbon.

Information Bar

The *Information* bar beneath the ribbon shows you information about the current timesheet period, the total number of hours entered and the current status of the timesheet. It turns *Yellow* when you make changes to the timesheet. This visual indicator helps remind you to save or submit your entries.

Period Selectors

By default, the timesheet opens in the current time reporting period. However, you may have cause to navigate to another time reporting period. As shown in Figure 4 - 5, you can either use the *Previous* and *Next* buttons to change periods or you can choose a specific period from the *Select Period* pick list.

Figure 4 - 5: Period Navigation Ribbon Buttons

Changing Views and Grouping

The *View* pick list shown in Figure 4 - 6 enables you to select which *Timesheet* view to use. Your Project Server administrator determines the views that appear in this list.

The *Group By* pick list enables you to group your timesheet lines by process status or by project. Use *Process Status* grouping when you have a number of entries that are in progress or rejected so that you can see all of a given status together. Use *Group By Project* grouping when you are entering time for a number of project-related tasks.

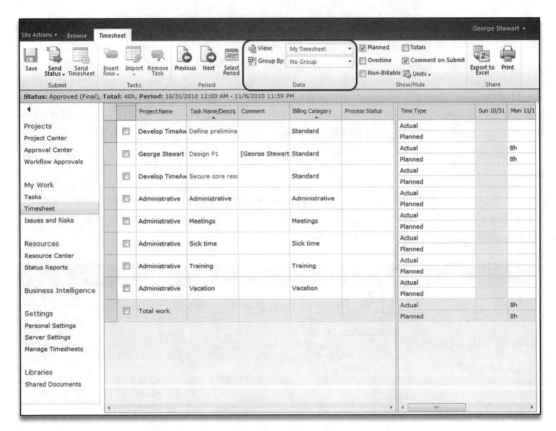

Figure 4 - 6: Ribbon View/Grouping Options

Hands On Exercise

Exercise 4-1

1. Log in to Project Web App and click the *Timesheet* link in the *My Work* section of the *Quick Launch* menu. If you do not see any tasks in the timesheet, from the *Period* section of the *Timesheet* ribbon, click the *Next* button to advance to the next period.

2. Examine the *Planned* work and *Actual* work (if any) for both *Project* tasks and *Administrative* tasks during the reporting period.

3. Deselect the *Overtime* and *Non-Billable* items in the ribbon to hide the *Overtime Work* and *Non-Billable Work* lines from your timesheet.

4. Navigate to the *Manage Timesheets* page from the link in the *Settings* section of the *Quick Launch* menu and examine the time periods for existing timesheets, if any.

5. Click the *View* pick list in the ribbon and apply each of the available views.

Entering Time in the Timesheet

On the *Timesheet* page, you enter actual time spent on project and non-project work. There are a number of ways to enter time, including each of the following:

- Enter actual work manually in the daily timesheet grid for each of the items listed.

- Add a new line to the timesheet to enter time on an item not listed.

- Import the planned work as the actual work.

- If you are in Double Entry mode, you can import task progress from the *Tasks* page.

Entering actual work manually in the daily timesheet grid is simple. At the end of each day, enter the amount of time you spent that day on any task listed in the timesheet. In addition, you may want to add a comment in the *Comment* field for any task requiring additional information. After you enter your time each day, click the *Save* button to save the latest changes to your timesheet.

Figure 4 - 7 shows George Stewart's timesheet for the week of October 31. Notice that George entered a combination of task work and administrative time for the week. The *Information* bar shows that George has entered a total of 40 hours for the week.

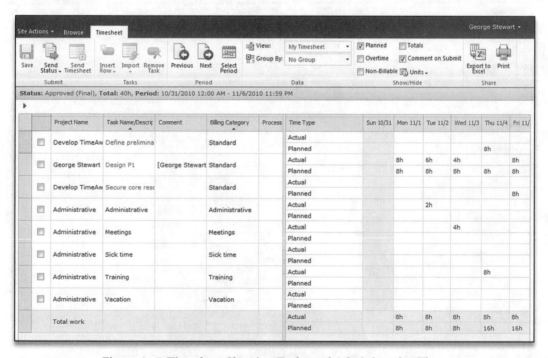

Figure 4 - 7: Timesheet Showing Tasks and Administrative Time

A final step for entering time on the *Timesheet* page may include adjusting the *Remaining Work* value according to your organization's methodology for submitting time. By default, the *Timesheet* view does not include the *Remaining Work* field. Instead, you should change your view to *My Work* to see this data column or have your administrator add this field to the *My Timesheet* view. The system displays the *Remaining Work* value according to the units you set as mentioned earlier in this section. Enter your remaining work for the task, if appropriate.

Warning: You can only edit the value in the *Remaining Work* column if your organization uses the *Only allow task updates via Tasks and Timesheets* option in Project Server 2010.

With this option enabled, you must enter all time and task progress in either the *Timesheet* page or the *Tasks* page. If your organization does not use this option, the system locks the *Remaining Work* column on the *My Timesheet* page.

Adding a New Line to a Timesheet

You may occasionally work on an assignment that is either not listed on your timesheet or is of a category of work that needs special tracking. Figure 4 - 8 shows the three kinds of work items that Project Server enables you to add to your timesheet. The *Timesheet Items Tracked* section of this document describes these items at a high level. Let us review an example of how to add each item type and the reasons for the addition.

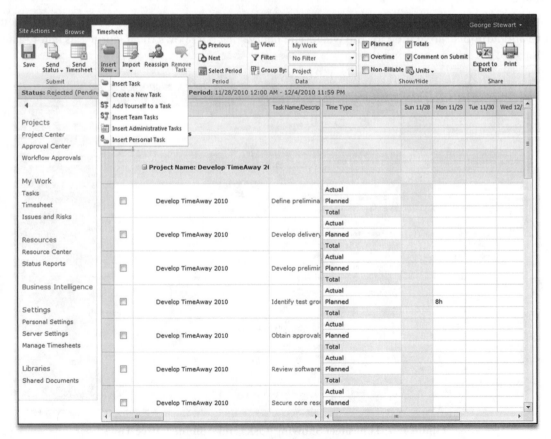

Figure 4 - 8: Timesheet Insert Row

For example, on Friday, November 12, George Stewart worked 2 hours on documenting "Lessons Learned" on the TimeAway 2010 project, as he wanted to include some lessons from recent issues. His assignment for this task is not for the current week. Because his organization requires resources to log all activities performed, George captures this time by adding a new line on his timesheet. To add a new timesheet line, click the *Add Lines* button. Project Server 2010 displays the *Select Task* dialog shown in Figure 4 - 9.

In the *Add an Existing Task* dialog, you can choose a task assignment from any project in which you have a current assignment. Click the *Project* pick list to select the project from which to retrieve the task. Click the *Task Hierarchy* pick list to narrow down the task selection. The *Task Hierarchy* field reads all Outline Level 1 tasks in the project plan as a fair number of Project Managers use these top-level tasks to denote project phases. Finally, select one of the tasks in the *Select from Existing Assignments* pick list. At the bottom of the dialog, you can add a comment as to why you are adding the task.

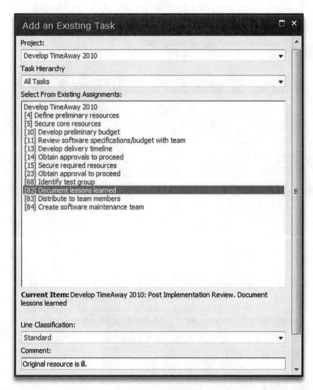

Figure 4 - 9: Add an Existing Project Task to Your Timesheet

George was an unplanned participant in a training class this week. His organization considers training as *Administrative* time ; therefore, he adds this time to his timesheet using the *Insert Administrative Tasks* option from the *Timesheets* ribbon. Figure 4 - 10 shows the dialog that appears once you select that option. You select the *Administrative Time* category on which to apply the time and add a description of the activity. Click the *OK* button to add it to the timesheet.

Figure 4 - 10: Add an Administrative Task to Your Timesheet

George Stewart also participates on a Merger System selection team as his company recently acquired another company. For tax accounting reasons, George's company tracks all merger activities. George attended a merger meeting for someone else and needs to account for this time. A personal task fulfills this need.

Selecting the *Insert Personal Task* option from the *Timesheet* ribbon yields the dialog shown in Figure 4 - 11. George types a name for this line, sets the category to *Merger* and adds a comment. Once he clicks the *OK* button, the line appears in his timesheet and he can enter time against this item.

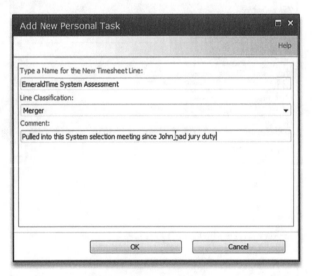

Figure 4 - 11: Add a Personal Task to Your Timesheet

Removing a Line from a Timesheet

When you need to remove a timesheet line, select the option checkbox at the left end of the line, and then click the *Remove Task* button. Project Server 2010 immediately removes the line from the timesheet.

You are not prompted prior to removing a timesheet line so use this option carefully.

If you accidentally delete a timesheet line, the only way to restore it is to delete the entire timesheet and recreate it. When you recreate the timesheet, the system restores the deleted line and restores all of the actual work hours you previously entered. I discuss how to delete a timesheet later in this section of the module.

Replacing Actual Work with Planned Work

Another method for entering time in your timesheet is to enter planned work as actual work for one or more selected tasks scheduled during the selected timesheet period. This feature enables you to enter your time rapidly on a large number of tasks. You then make manual adjustments only for those tasks where planned and actual values do not match. Since this feature works on the selected task, you can select the tasks upon which to perform this action. To perform it on all tasks, select the *Selector* column heading and select the *Select All* option prior to selecting the *Replace Actual with Planned* option. Figure 4 - 12 shows the *Timesheet* page showing the planned work for two tasks scheduled this week.

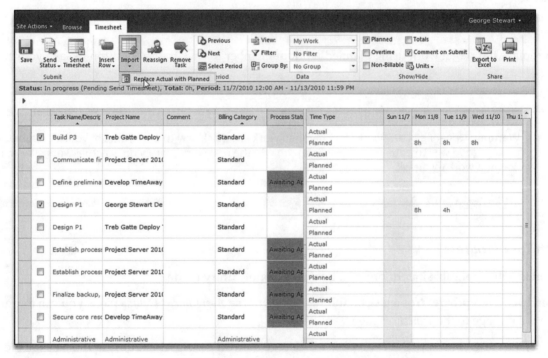

Figure 4 - 12: Timesheet shows Tasks Planned Work

To replace actual work with planned work, select the option checkbox to the left of each task you want to update and then click the *Replace Actual with Planned* button. The system updates the actual work using the planned work for each day, as shown in Figure 4 - 13. Note the *Information* bar will appear *Yellow* after performing this option and the *Process Status* values will change to *Not Submitted*, indicating that you have not yet submitted this information to the approver.

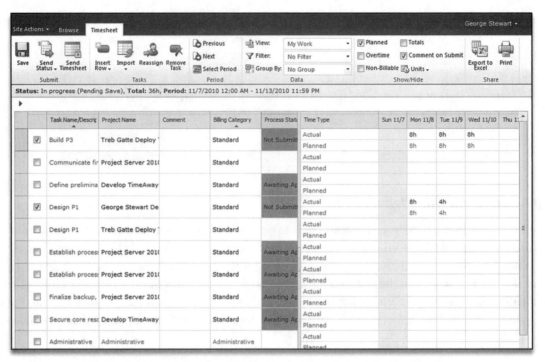

Figure 4 - 13: Replace actual work using planned work in the timesheet

After you replace the actual work using planned work, remember to click the *Save* button to save your timesheet.

Warning: Updating actual work from planned work is a quick way to enter time in your timesheet, but it is not a good way to enter accurate information. In the real world, rarely does actual work ever match planned work for a task.

Importing Task Progress

This section is only applicable if your organization uses Double Entry mode.

If you already entered progress for a task on the *Tasks* page or the *Assignment Details* page, you can import the progress from either page to the *Timesheet* page.

For example, Figure 4 - 14 shows the *Tasks* page for George Stewart's assignment during the week of November 7. Notice that George entered his daily Actual Work in the timesheet grid for the Design P1 task that week.

The *Imported Task Progress* function only works for Saved or Sent time entries on the *Tasks* page.

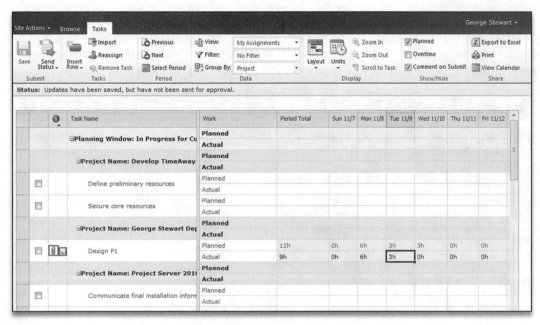

Figure 4 - 14: Actual Work entered in the Tasks page

Figure 4 - 15 shows George Stewart's timesheet for the week of November 7. Notice that the *Planned* work for the Design P1 task differs from the *Actual* work he entered on the *Tasks* page.

The *Import Task Progress* function only works on Saved timesheet entries on the *Timesheet* page. Attempting to import task progress on a modified but not saved timesheet entry will result in updated planning time but no change in actual time.

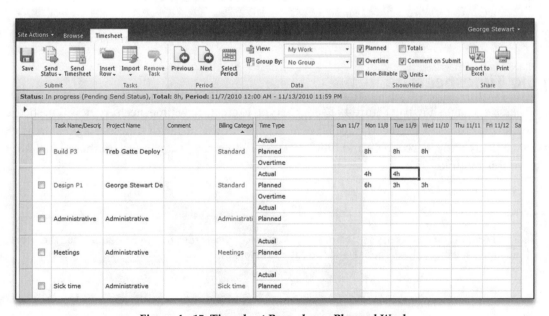

Figure 4 - 15: Timesheet Page shows Planned Work

To import task progress from the *Tasks* page or the *Assignment Details* page, select the option checkbox to the left of the task name in the *Timesheet* page and then click the *Import Task Progress* option on the *Import* menu button. The system imports the time from the *Tasks* (or *Assignment Details*) page as shown in Figure 4 - 16. Notice that the imported hours for the Design P1 task exactly match the hours on the *Tasks* page shown previously in Figure 4 - 14.

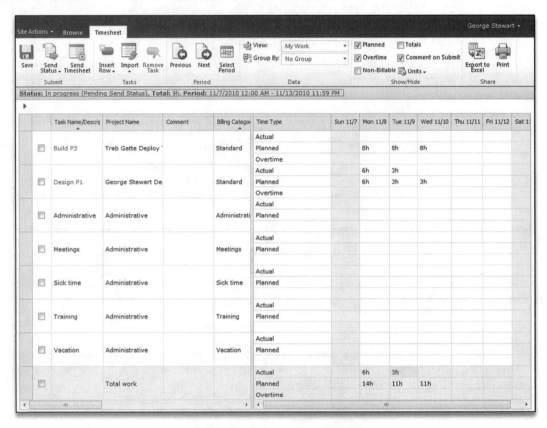

Figure 4 - 16: Timesheet after Task Import

After you import task progress to your timesheet, remember to click the *Save* button to save your timesheet.

Managing Timesheets

The *Manage Timesheets* page shown in Figure 4 - 17 enables you to create new timesheets, review timesheet submission status and delete your timesheets. The *Manage Timesheets* page shows the list of timesheets you already submitted, timesheets that are currently in-progress, and timesheets ready to create. I cover each of these functions in detail in later sections of this module.

The *Manage Timesheet* page lists timesheets in descending order by timesheet period. Therefore, your current timesheet always appears at the top of the page.

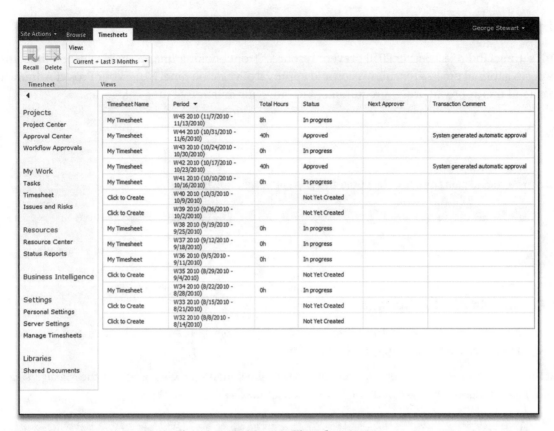

Figure 4 - 17: Manage Timesheets page

The *Manage Timesheets* ribbon includes a *View* pick list containing a list of views available for the page. The first time you access the *Manage Timesheets* page, the default view is *Current + Last Three Months*. If you click the *View* pick list, the system offers you the following views that control what timeframe the system uses to filter your list of timesheets:

- Current + Last 3 Months

- Next 6 Months + Last 3 Months

- Last 6 Months

- Last 12 Months

- All Timesheets

- Created and in progress

The view names explain each view, so further detail is not necessary. For most users, the default *Current + Last 3 Months* view suffices. The system reapplies this view if you navigate to another page in PWA and then return to the *Manage Timesheets* page.

The fastest way to create a new timesheet for a past or current time period is to click the *Click to create* link to the left of the timesheet period in the grid. Project Server 2010 creates your new timesheet using the default information specified by your Project Server administrator, which is set to display all tasks scheduled during the selected time period, plus any administrative tasks required by your organization.

Planning Time Away from Work

The default settings in Project Server 2010 prevent resources from booking unapproved vacation time. Instead, the system imposes a formal process for submission and approval of vacation time. Note, your Project Administrator can choose to extend this approval process requirement to other administrative time categories.

> You should plan administrative time categories that require approval.

Entering Planned Administrative Time

George decides to visit New York City from December 5 to December 11 to meet his brother and to do some holiday shopping. This requires George to request a week of vacation.

To submit his vacation time request for approval by his timesheet manager, George clicks the *Manage Timesheets* link on the *Quick Launch* menu. The system displays a screen similar to Figure 4 - 18.

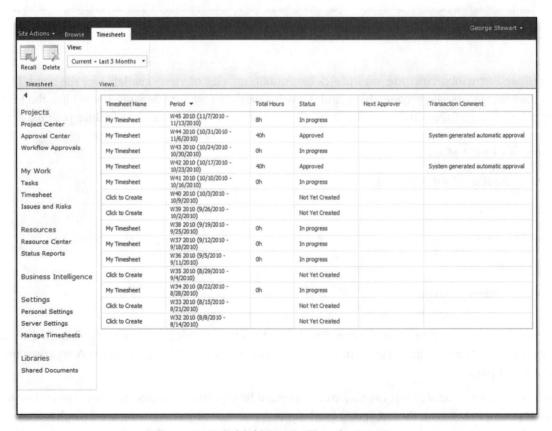

Figure 4 - 18: Initial Manage Timesheets page

George's timesheet for December 5 is not visible. George then selects the *Next 6 Months + Last 3 Months* value in the *Views* pick list to change the period. He clicks the *Click to Create* link to create the timesheet for the week of December 5 as shown in Figure 4 - 19.

Since the vacation time falls in a timesheet period for an uncreated timesheet, Project Server automatically sets the timesheet's status as *In Progress*. This status will not change until you submit actual time entries for that week.

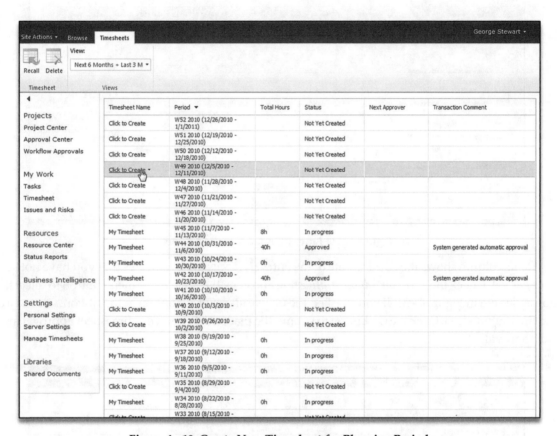

Figure 4 - 19: Create New Timesheet for Planning Period

Warning: Do not enter the planned vacation time on the *Actual* line. Doing so will mark this time as *Actual* work rather than *Planned* work.

George enters 8hrs for each workday for the week as shown in Figure 4 - 20. He also enters *"Off to New York"* in the *Comments* column so that his timesheet approval manager knows why he is requesting this time. You may need to move the splitter bar to see this column in the left grid.

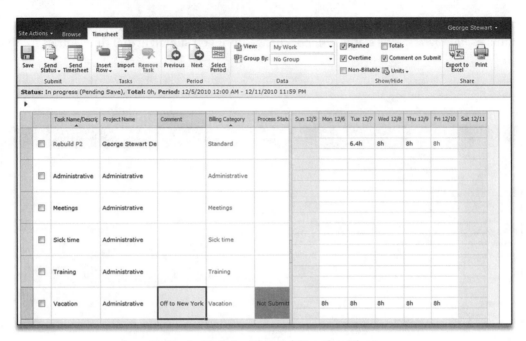

Figure 4 - 20: Enter Planned Vacation Time

The *Process Status* column shows the current state of the entry. *Not Submitted* indicates that you have not sent the status to a manager yet. Check the *Vacation Administrative* line and click the *Send Status* menu button to select the *Selected Tasks* option as shown in Figure 4 - 21. If you checked the *Comment on Submit* option in the ribbon, you see a comment box prior to final submission. Click the *OK* button to submit the planned time to your timesheet approval manager for review and approval.

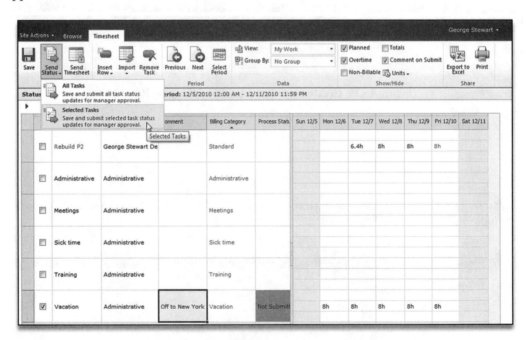

Figure 4 - 21: Send Status for Selected Tasks

Viewing the Submission Status

The *Process Status* column captures the current submission status of a *Timesheet* line. This column replaces the graphical status indicators of Project Server 2010 with an easier to understand text value. The field is blank normally when the current status requires no user action. When Project Server has a process status that requires user attention, the system adds a text status and color highlight to draw your attention.

To view the current approval status of the vacation request, click the *Manage Timesheets* link in the *Quick Launch* menu and click the link of the timesheet containing the vacation request. The system displays the timesheet for the selected period. Table 4 - 2 shows the *Process Status* values that indicate the current state of George's request.

Process Status Value	Color	What it means	User Action Required
[Blank]	None	Timesheet line is in an approved state.	None
Not Submitted	Red	You have not saved or submitted your change to this timesheet line.	Perform one of the following actions: Save Send Status Send Timesheet
Awaiting Approval	Red	Submission of the line by you is complete but the approval manager has not acted upon the entry.	Prompt the approval manager for action if this state persists.
Rejected	Red	The approval manager rejected your update.	Make changes to the entry and resubmit. OR Accept the rejection and remove the line.
Manager Updated	Red	The task manager changed the task properties.	Review the task.

Table 4 - 2: Process Status values

Hands On Exercise

Exercise 4-2

Enter time in a new timesheet.

1. Navigate to your *Timesheet* page by clicking the *Timesheet* link in the *My Work* section of the *Quick Launch* menu. If necessary, from the *Period* section of the *Timesheet* ribbon, click the *Next* button to advance to the period that includes tasks.

2. For the timesheet currently displayed, enter the following *Actual* work for the Design P1 task for your Deploy Training Advisor Software project:

3. Monday – 8 hours

4. Tuesday – 6 hours

5. Wednesday – 4 hours

6. Thursday – 0 hours

7. Friday – 8 hours

8. Enter 2 hours of time for *Administrative* work on Tuesday.

9. Enter 4 hours for meetings on Wednesday.

10. Delete the *Sick Time* timesheet line.

11. Enter 8 hours of training time for Thursday.

12. In the *Show/Hide* section of the *Timesheet* ribbon, select the *Totals* checkbox if it is not already selected. Examine the total hours entered in the *Total* field in the information bar under the ribbon.

13. Click the *Save* button to save your current timesheet information.

14. Click the *Browse* tab in the ribbon.

15. Click the Project Web App link to return to the home page.

Exercise 4-3

Plan and submit vacation time for a future time reporting period.

1. Click the *Manage Timesheets* link from the *Settings* section of the *Quick Launch* menu.

2. Change the view to *Next 6 Months + Last 3 Months*.

3. Click the *Click to Create* link for the topmost timesheet.

4. In the *Show/Hide* section of the *Timesheet* ribbon, select the *Planned* checkbox.

5. Enter 8 hours of planned time for each day of the week in the *Vacation* line item in the *Administrative* items at the bottom of the timesheet.

6. Click the *Send Timesheet* button. In the *Send Timesheet* dialog, click the *Browse* button to select Linda Erickson in the *Sent Timesheet to* field, if she is not the default recipient.

Submitting a Timesheet for Approval

After you enter your time for the week, you must submit your timesheet for approval to the person designated as your timesheet approver. Before you submit your timesheet, however, remember that you use the timesheet to submit actual hours worked on tasks and on hours spent on administrative time.

Project Server does not prevent you from entering actual time for tasks that you did not plan for this period. Life sometimes has a way of interfering with your plans and Project Server provides flexibility in these cases. It is the duty of the timesheet approver to approve or reject your timesheet entry.

George Stewart's car broke down on the way back to the office after a late lunch and he missed two hours of the workday. In Figure 4 - 22, he logs two hours of vacation time on his timesheet although there is no planned time for this activity.

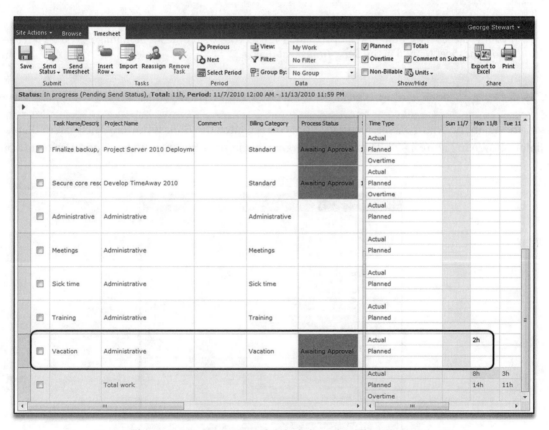

Figure 4 - 22: Unapproved Administrative Time Entry

 If your tracking routine includes importing time from your timesheet to the *My Tasks* page, import your time to the *My Tasks* page before you submit your timesheet.

To submit a timesheet, click the *Send Timesheet* button. Project Server 2010 displays the *Send Timesheet* dialog, shown in Figure 4 - 23. By default, the person shown in the *Send Timesheet to* field is the person designated as your timesheet manager by your organization's Project Server administrator.

Figure 4 - 23: Send Timesheet dialog

 If your Project Server administrator specified you as your own timesheet manager, you do not see the *Send Timesheet to* field in the *Send Timesheet* dialog.

If the person shown in the *Send Timesheet to* field is not correct, click the *Browse* button. The system displays the *Pick Resource* dialog shown in Figure 4 - 24. This dialog contains the names of users who have permission to approve your timesheet.

Figure 4 - 24: Pick Resource dialog

The *Pick Resource* dialog displays only twenty names at a time in the dialog. If your organization has more than twenty users who can approve timesheets, scroll to the bottom of the dialog and click the *Next* link in the lower right corner of the dialog to see more users.

In the list of possible timesheet approvers, double-click the name of your timesheet approver. The system enters the selected user's name in the *Send Timesheet to* field in the *Send Timesheet* dialog. Enter any additional comments about the timesheet in the *Comments* field and then click the *OK* button to complete your timesheet submission.

To view the current approval status of a timesheet, click the *Manage Timesheets* link in the *Quick Launch* menu. Project Server 2010 displays the *Manage Timesheets* page as shown in Figure 4 - 25. Refer back to Table 4 - 2 where I cover Process Status definitions.

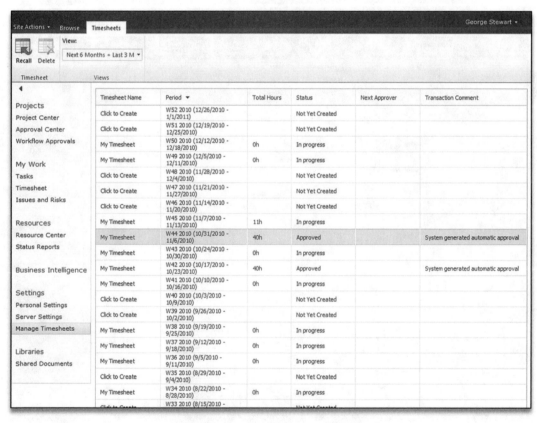

Figure 4 - 25: Manage Timesheets page

Responding to a Rejected Timesheet

In the normal flow of timesheet approvals, your timesheet manager approves your timesheets. However, a timesheet manager could reject a timesheet for a variety of reasons, such as:

- You submit a timesheet containing a factual error, such as when you fat finger the number 23 when you intended to type the number 3.

- You report work that totals greater than 24 hours in a single day.

- You create a new line of timesheet information to document time that does not fit into any of the tasks on your timesheet, but your timesheet manager needs you to add the time to the administrative task instead.

- You fail to report time on a day when you actually worked.

In situations like this, your timesheet manager may reject your timesheet and ask you to correct the troublesome information. For example, in the timesheet shown in Figure 4 - 26, George Stewart removed 20 hours of vacation time from his timesheet, but failed to enter any actual work in its place. Because his company requires resources to submit at least 40 hours of actual work each week results in the rejection of George Stewart's timesheet for the week of November 7.

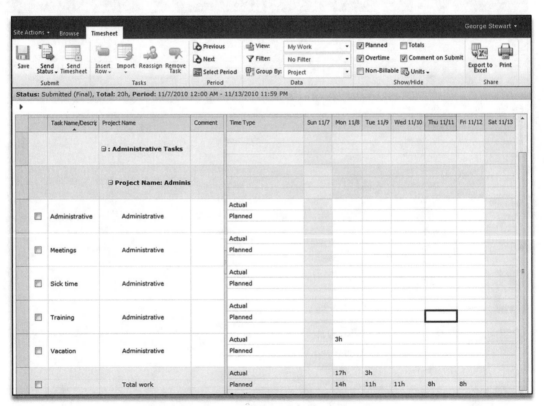

Figure 4 - 26: Timesheet with missing time entries

When a timesheet manager rejects a timesheet, Project Server automatically sends an e-mail message to notify the resource of the rejection, assuming your Project administrator enabled notifications. The system also shows the timesheet status as *Rejected* on the *Timesheets* page, as shown in Figure 4 - 27.

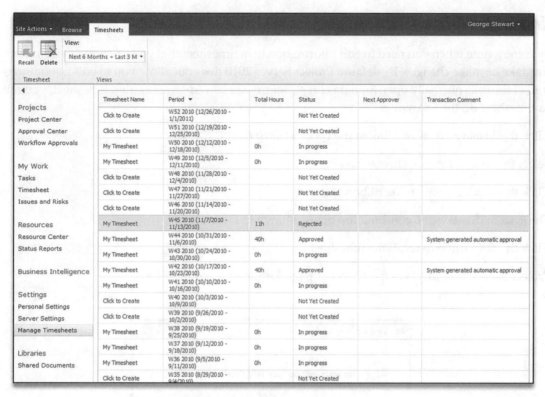

Figure 4 - 27: Rejected Timesheet

To respond to a rejected timesheet, click the *My Timesheet* link to the left of the rejected timesheet on the *Manage Timesheets* page. The system opens the *Timesheet* page for the rejected timesheet. Correct the timesheet information that shows a *Rejected* process status to address the reason for the rejection. Click the *Send Timesheet* button when you complete your entries.

Editing an Existing Timesheet

If you entered and saved your timesheet hours yesterday, you know that you must return to the timesheet today to add your actual work for the day. To edit the current time reporting period's timesheet, click the *Timesheet* link in the *Quick Launch* menu.

If the timesheet is not for the current time reporting period, click the *Manage Timesheets* link in the *Quick Launch* menu to access the *Manage Timesheets* page shown previously in Figure 4 - 27. Find the correct time reporting period and click the *My Timesheet* link for that timesheet.

Project Server 2010 loads the *Timesheet* page for the selected timesheet. Use any of the methods discussed previously to enter your actual work for today and then click the *Save* button. After the system saves your timesheet, click the *Manage Timesheets* link in the *Quick Launch* menu to return to the *Manage Timesheets* page.

New to Project Server 2010: If your Project Manager publishes a new task that is assigned to you for the current period, the system automatically adds the new task to your timesheet.

Recalling a Submitted Timesheet

There may come a time when you need to edit information on a timesheet that you previously submitted, such as to correct a mistake or make changes. By default, Project Server 2010 does not allow you to edit a submitted timesheet and locks all of the cells normally open for data entry. Before you can edit a submitted timesheet, you must recall it. To recall a timesheet do the following:

- Click the *Manage Timesheets* link in the *Quick Launch* menu.

- Select the row of the timesheet to recall.

- Click the *Recall* button on the ribbon.

- The system displays the confirmation dialog shown in Figure 4 - 28.

- Click the *OK* button to recall the timesheet.

- Project Server 2010 displays the *Timesheet* page for the selected timesheet.

Figure 4 - 28: Timesheet recall confirmation dialog

After recalling the timesheet, Project Server 2010 unlocks all data entry cells and resets the status of the timesheet to *In Progress*.

 You can recall timesheets with a *Submitted* or *Approved* status.

 Recalling and resubmitting your timesheet has no effect on any task progress you may have reported through this timesheet period.

Deleting a Timesheet

There may come a time when you need to delete an entire timesheet and recreate it. This can result from a variety of situations, such as when you totally "mess up" a timesheet and want to start over.

Do the following to delete a timesheet:

- Click the *Manage Timesheets* link in the *Quick Launch* menu.

- Select the row of the timesheet to recall.

- Click the *Delete* button on the ribbon.

- The system displays the confirmation dialog shown in Figure 4 - 29.

Figure 4 - 29: Confirmation dialog to delete a timesheet

- Click the *OK* button to delete the timesheet.

- Project Server 2010 deletes the timesheet and changes the timesheet name for that period to *Click to Create*.

- To recreate the timesheet, click the *Click to Create* link for the designated timesheet period.

Hands On Exercise

Exercise 4-4

Work with an existing timesheet.

1. Click the *Manage Timesheets* link from the *Settings* section of the *Quick Launch* menu. On the *Manage Timesheets* page, click the name of the timesheet you used in Exercise 4-1. Note that this timesheet shows an *In progress* value in the *Status* field and contains 40 hours of actual work.

2. Click the *Send Timesheet* button.

3. In the *Send Timesheet* dialog, notice the name listed in the *Send Timesheet to* field. Enter a comment in the *Comment* section, and then click the *OK* button.

4. From the *Settings* section of the *Quick Launch* menu, click the *Manage Timesheets* link and select the same timesheet that you just submitted, but do not click on the name.

5. In the *Timesheet* section of the *Timesheets* ribbon, click the *Recall* button and click the *OK* button in the confirmation dialog.

6. From the *Manage Timesheets* page, click the name of the timesheet that you just recalled. Then, on the *Timesheet* page click the *Send Timesheet* button.

7. Click the *Browse* tab on the ribbon and click the name of the Project Web App to return to the home page.

Tracking Task Progress in Project Web App

In most organizations, the purpose for tracking time in Project Server 2010 is to track task progress as well. Task progress information directly affects the enterprise projects in your Project Server 2010 database. The system offers your organization four methods for tracking task progress. The difference between each tracking method is the information that the system collects, as detailed below:

- **Percent of Work Complete** allows resources to enter % Work Complete and a Remaining Work estimate on each task assignment.

- **Actual Work Done and Work Remaining** allows resources to enter the cumulative Actual Work value and to adjust the Remaining Work estimate on each task assignment.

- **Hours of Work Done per Period** allows resources to enter the hours of Actual Work completed for the current time period and to adjust the Remaining Work estimate on each task assignment.

- **Free Form** allows resources to enter their work using whichever of the previous three methods is most convenient and Project Server calculates the requisite values.

Percent of Work Complete is the system default method of tracking progress unless your organization selects another method.

I discussed each of these tracking methods in Module 01 and demonstrated how each method controls how Project Server 2010 displays both the *Tasks* page and the *Assignment Details* page. Refer back to Module 01 to review this information.

Understanding the Tasks Page

To begin the process of tracking task progress, launch your Internet Explorer application and navigate to your Project Web App Home page. As you see in Figure 4 - 30, George Stewart has 30 new tasks assigned to him.

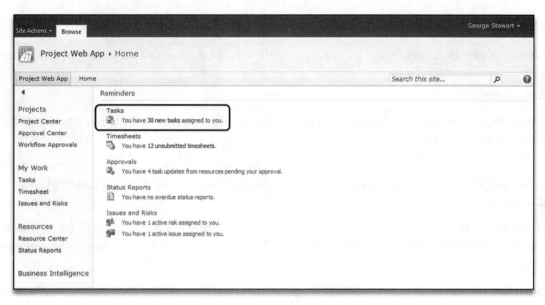

Figure 4 - 30: PWA Home Page Task Information

To navigate to the *Tasks* page, use any of the following methods:

- Click the *Tasks* link in the *My Work* section of the *Quick Launch* menu.

- Click the *Tasks* link in the *Reminders* section of the page.

- Click the ___ *new tasks* link in the *Reminders* section of the page (if available).

Project Server 2010 displays the *Tasks* page, shown in Figure 4 - 31.

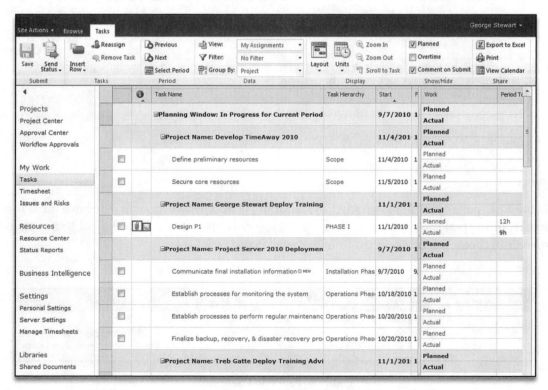

Figure 4 - 31: Tasks Page

Tasks Ribbon

The *Tasks* ribbon is new in Project Server 2010. This module covers all aspects of the *Tasks* ribbon functionality.

Show/Hide Options

The *Show/Hide* ribbon section also contains options that control the information presentation. Checking a box indicates you want to see that information.

The first two options relate to which time types the system displays. Each task includes two time types by default, which is *Actual* and *Planned*. You use the second line to enter actual work hours. The first line displays the planned or scheduled work hours for the task.

To add an additional time type to track overtime work for each project task, click the *Overtime* checkbox in the *Show/Hide* section of the *Tasks* ribbon as shown in Figure 4 - 32. All selected types now appear in the time phased entry grid on the right.

The *Comment on Submit* option determines whether a pop-up box where you enter timesheet level comments appears when you submit your timesheet. You can change the default option to show this dialog by unchecking the checkbox.

Figure 4 - 32: Tasks Show/Hide Options

 The default unit used for time (minutes, hours, days, weeks) entered in the time phased grid is controlled by the *Units* pick list on the *Tasks* ribbon.

Period Selectors

By default, the *Tasks* page opens in the current time reporting period. However, you may have cause to navigate to another time reporting period. As shown in Figure 4 - 33, you can either use the *Previous* and *Next* buttons to change periods <u>or</u> you can choose a specific period from the *Select Period* pick list.

Figure 4 - 33: Period Selectors

View Calendar

The *View Calendar* option enables the user to see their tasks visualized as a calendar. Clicking the *View Calendar* button as shown in Figure 4 - 34 takes you to the page shown in Figure 4 - 35.

Figure 4 - 34: View Calendar button

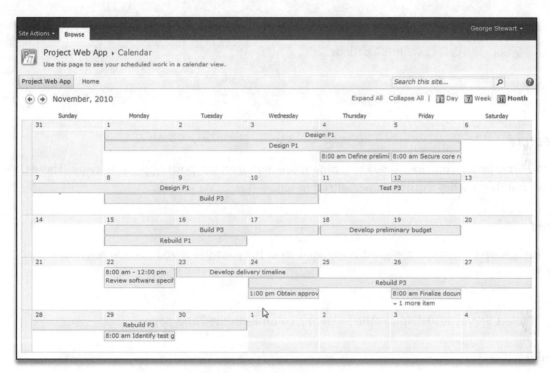

Figure 4 - 35: View Calendar page

The calendar can display by day, week or month. Clicking an individual task takes you to the *Assignment Details* page for that task.

Grouping and Views

By default, the system displays all tasks in the *Planning Window* grouping with tasks sorted by task start date. The *Planning Window* groups all of your tasks into four groups to facilitate your focus on the immediate tasks:

- In Progress for Current Period
- Near Future - Next x Periods
- Distant Future
- Completed

In Progress for Current Period

The *In Progress for Current Period* group includes all incomplete tasks which either have a task start date or task finish date less than or equal to the last day of the current period. Project 2010 no longer deems tasks as late; but rather is not currently complete. They appear at the top of the *Tasks* page to ensure they get proper attention.

Near Future – Next x Periods

The *Near Future – Next x Periods* group includes all tasks that have a task start date within the next x time reporting periods. Your Project Server administrator determines what number x will be. By default, this number is two.

> Your Project Server administrator specifies the number of periods that define the Near Future task group. The default value is 2 periods.

Distant Future

The *Distant Future* group contains all tasks starting more than x time reporting periods away. These tasks are your assignments but they do not require immediate attention.

Completed

The *Completed* group contains all assigned completed tasks for your use if you need to reference this information.

Fields

By default, Project Server 2010 displays the following columns in the *Tasks* page:

- Information
- Task Name
- Start
- Finish
- Remaining Work
- % Work Complete
- Work
- Actual Work
- Process Status

The *Information* column includes icons to denote task notes using a yellow note icon and a paperclip icon to denote linked issues, risks and documents.

Process Status

The *Process Status* column captures the current submission status of a *Task* line. This column replaces the graphical status indicators of Project Server 2010 with an easier to understand text value. The field is blank normally when the current status requires no user action. When Project Server has a Process Status that requires user attention, the system adds a text status and color highlight to draw your attention as shown in Table 4 - 3.

Process Status Value	Color	What it means	User Action Required
[Blank]	None	Timesheet line is in an approved state.	None
Not Submitted	Purple	You have not saved or submitted your change to this timesheet line.	Perform one of the following actions: • Save • Send Status • Send Timesheet
Awaiting Approval	Red	Submission of the line by you is complete but the approval manager has not acted upon the entry.	Prompt the approval manager for action if this state persists.
Rejected	Red	The approval manager rejected your update.	Make changes to the entry and resubmit. OR Accept the rejection and remove the line.
Manager Updated	Red	The task manager changed the task properties	Review the task.
Save Needed	Purple	You changed a task value but have not yet saved the change.	Save or exit without saving

Table 4 - 3: Process Status values

To rearrange the order of the fields, click and hold on the column header and drag the column to the desired location. The cursor changes to a four arrow cross to indicate the proper placement for dragging as shown in Figure 4 - 36.

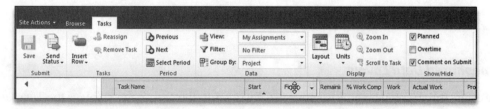

Figure 4 - 36: Example of Cursor Change for Column Rearrangement

Units

The *Units* pick list enables you to decide the display formats of *Work, Duration* and *Date* fields on the page as shown in Figure 4 - 37. For example, if you want to enter your updates as number of days, change the *Units* value for *Work* to *Days*.

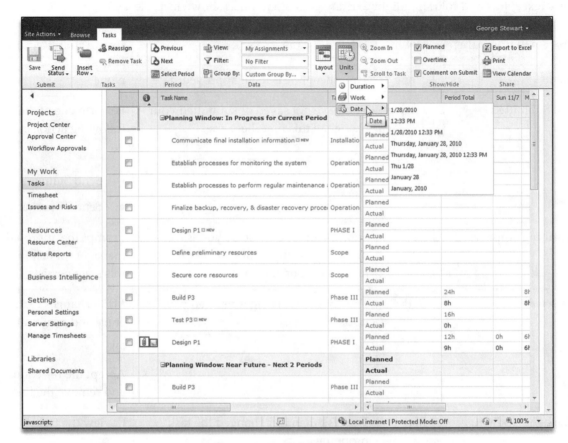

Figure 4 - 37: Units selector

 The default unit used for time (minutes, hours, days, weeks) entered in the time phased grid is controlled by the *Units* pick list in the *Task* ribbon.

Using the Timephased Data Layout

The *Tasks* page offers three screen layouts for your use. By default, the *Tasks* page displays the *Timephased Data* layout as shown in Figure 4 - 38. The right side of the page contains a data entry grid organized by day or week, where the user can enter actual and overtime data. This layout is best for hours per day or hours per week time entry.

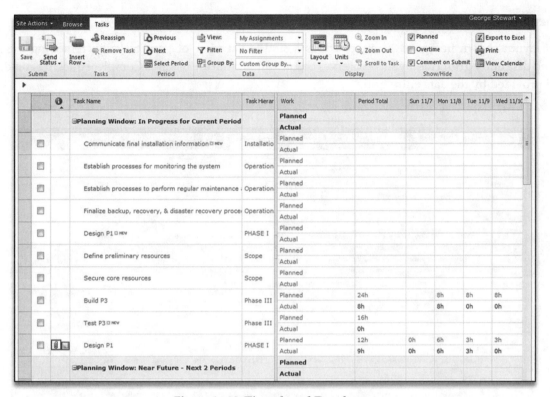

Figure 4 - 38: Timephased Data layout

Using the Gantt Chart Layout

The *Gantt Chart* layout, shown in Figure 4 - 39, provides the user with a way to visualize the relationships between their tasks. There are times where no graphics will show. Remember the current period is always the default so you may need to scroll to the appropriate place in the Gantt chart to see your tasks. The *Scroll to Task* button provides a quick way to do this. Select the desired task, then click the *Scroll to Task* button on the ribbon. The Gantt Chart graphics for that task come into view. The *Zoom In/Out* buttons also enable you to change the timescale used for the Gantt chart. By default, the view is at the day level. However, you can zoom out to see items at the month level.

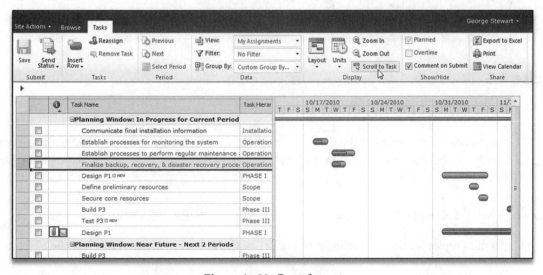

Figure 4 - 39: Gantt layout

Using the Sheet Layout

The *Sheet* layout shown in Figure 4 - 40, provides a simple list view of your tasks by removing the right side timephased data entry grid. This layout best serves organizations that are using % Complete tracking and do not need the detail provided by the data entry grid.

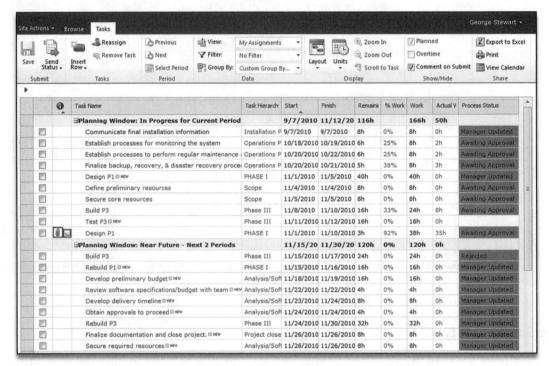

Figure 4 - 40: Sheet Layout

Hands On Exercise

Exercise 4-5

Understand progress reporting in the Tasks page.

1. In the *My Work* section of the *Quick Launch* menu, click the *Tasks* link. When the page displays, study the information shown in each of the default columns. If necessary, change the period display.

2. Click the triangle above the *Quick Launch* menu to collapse the menu.

3. In the *Display* section of the *Tasks* ribbon, click the *Layout* pick list and select the *Sheet* item.

4. Drag the *Process Status* column next to the task name.

5. Using the *Layout* pick list, change the layout to *Timephased Data*.

6. In the *Show/Hide* section of the *Tasks* ribbon, uncheck the *Planned Time* type.

7. In the *Display* section of the *Tasks* ribbon, click the *Units* pick list and select the *Duration* item and select *Days* from the fly out menu.

8. Use the *Layout* pick list to apply the *Gantt Chart* layout.

9. Select the row header for the third task in the *Display* section of the *Tasks* ribbon; click the *Scroll to Task* button.

10. In the *Share* section of the *Tasks* ribbon, click the *View Calendar* button and review the *View Calendar* page.

11. Close the calendar page when you complete your inspection.

Understanding the Assignment Details Page

To navigate to the *Assignment Details* page from the *Tasks* page, simply click the name of a task. Project Server 2010 displays the *Assignment Details* page for the selected task, shown in Figure 4 - 41.

The *Assignment Details* page displays complete information for the selected task assignment. Notice in Figure 4 - 41 that the *Assignment Details* page includes the following sections:

- **General Details** – Enter progress update information in this section, such as the Start date, Percent Complete, Remaining Work, or Finish date.

- **Recent Task Changes** – If your task spans more than the current time period, use this section to review the history of task changes, task updates, and comments that you or your project manager added.

- **Attachments** – From this section, you can view risks, issues, or documents associated with the task.

- **Contacts** – Use this section to see the names of your project manager, approval manager, and your fellow team members.

- **Related Assignments** – Use this section to see predecessor and successor tasks related to the selected task.

- **Notes** – From this section, you can add a note to the task.

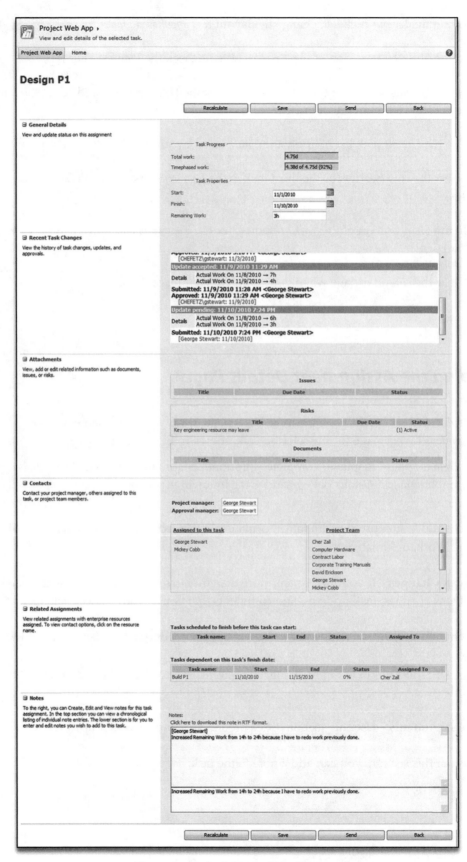

Figure 4 - 41: Assignment Details page

Hands On Exercise

Exercise 4-6

Report progress using the Assignment Details page.

1. Click the name of any task shown on the *Tasks* page.

2. On the *Assignment Details* page, study your organization's progress tracking method, as shown in the *General Details* section.

3. Click the *Back* button to return to the *Tasks* page.

Reporting Progress from the Tasks Page

As I stated earlier, Project Server 2010 offers your organization four different methods for tracking progress, one of which enables you to use any of the three described here. The information you enter on the *Tasks* page varies with the method of tracking your organization uses. Your organization can choose to use the default layout of the *Tasks* page, or can use a modified layout recommended by MSProjectExperts. Because of this flexibility, I discuss each method of tracking progress, using both the default layout and the custom MSProjectExperts layout of the *Tasks* page.

Using Percent of Work Complete

Although you can report progress from the *Tasks* page using the Percent of Work Complete method of tracking progress, Project Server 2010 accepts only a limited amount of information with the default layout of the *Tasks* page. If your organization requires you to enter task progress from the *Tasks* page, use the following methodology to report progress on a task using this method of tracking:

1. Click in the *% Work Complete* field and enter your estimate of the percentage of work completed to date on the task. The *Process Status* field value changes to *Save Needed* and the *Information* bar appears under the ribbon with the message: *Status: There are unsaved updates.*

> When you enter 100% complete on a task, Project Server 2010 assumes that you started and finished the task as **originally scheduled**. The system has no way of knowing that you started or finished a task early or late compared to the original schedule.

2. To adjust the remaining work (also known as the ETC or Estimated Time to Completion) for the task, click in the *Remaining Work* field and enter your remaining work estimate.

3. To add a note to the task, click on the task name and scroll to the bottom of the *Assignment Details* page as shown in Figure 4 - 42. Enter your note and click the *Save* button.

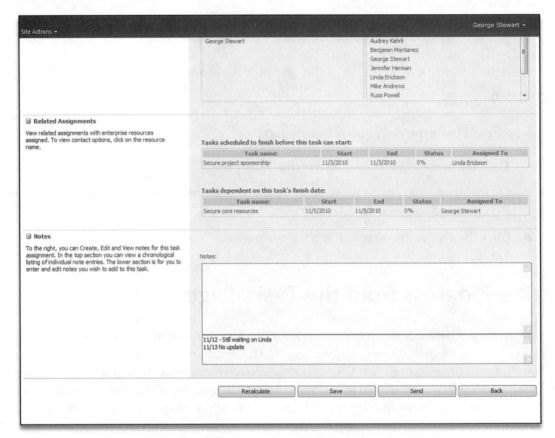

Figure 4 - 42: Add a Task Note

 If your project manager enters a note on a task in the actual Microsoft Project plan, the note text appears in the top half of the Project Web App *Assignment Notes* dialog. The top half of the dialog also contains notes that you previously submitted and which the project manager updated into the Microsoft Project plan.

 msProjectExperts recommends that you train team members to "date stamp" their notes text, as shown in the note in Figure 4 - 42. Project Server 2010 "name stamps" each note to show who submitted the note, but does not "date stamp" the note to show when the team member submitted the note.

Project Server 2010 displays your attached note with an indicator to the left of the task name, as shown in Figure 4 - 43.

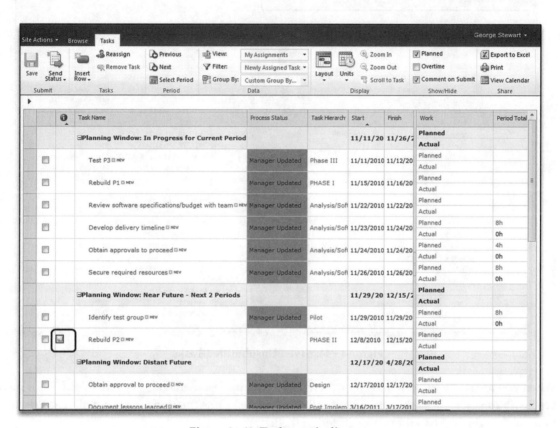

Figure 4 - 43: Task note indicators

To adjust the scheduled *Start* or *Finish* date for a future task, click in the *Start* or *Finish* field and change the date on the calendar date picker. This alerts your project manager that the actual start or finish is different from the current schedule in the project plan.

4. Click the *Save* button to save your task progress changes if you are not ready to submit them to your project manager for approval. When you save the changes, Project Server changes the line's *Process Status* value to *Not Submitted* and the *Information* bar shows the message: *Status: Updates have been saved, but have not been sent for approval* as shown in Figure 4 - 44.

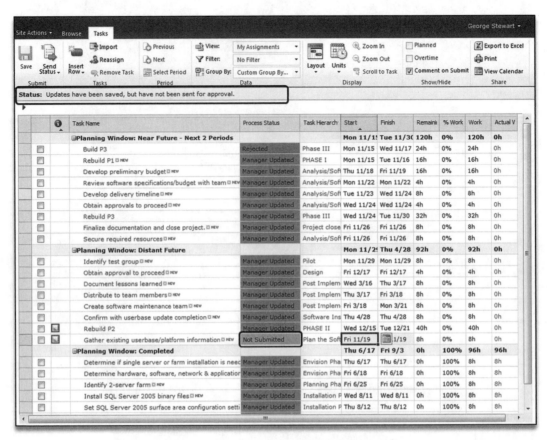

Figure 4 - 44: Saved Unsubmitted Tasks

5. When you are ready to submit the task changes to your project manager, select the *Send Status* menu button on the ribbon. The *All Tasks* option sends all changed tasks information for approval. The *Selected Tasks* option only sends the tasks that you selected in the list.

6. Project Server 2010 displays the *Submit Changes* dialog shown in Figure 4 - 45. Enter an optional comment about the update in the *Submit Changes* dialog and then click the *OK* button to submit the update to your project manager.

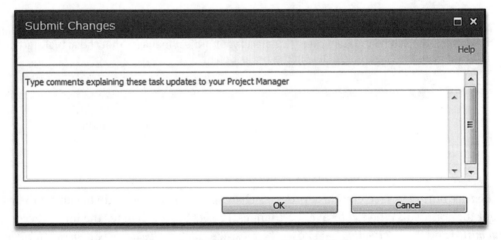

Figure 4 - 45: Comment on Submit dialog

Project Server 2010 displays the *Submit Changes* dialog as the *Show/Hide* option to *Comment on Submit* option is selected by default. To suppress the system prompt to add a comment each time you submit task progress, deselect the *Comment on Submit* option.

Project Server 2010 redisplays the *Tasks* page with a confirmation message in the *Information* bar indicating that the system submitted your updates for approval as shown in Figure 4 - 46.

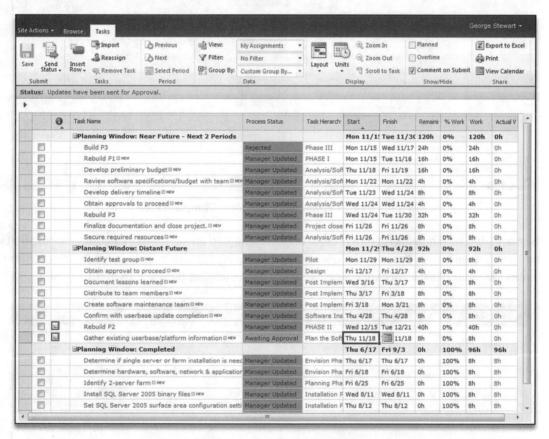

Figure 4 - 46: Submitted Tasks

Best Practice: Using Percent of Work Complete

MSProjectExperts recommends that your Project Server administrator create a custom view of the *Tasks* page to optimize your data entry experience. This view controls the data columns that are on the page; however you are in control of other aspects such as grouping.

The custom view contains the following columns: *Project Name, Task Name, Process Status, Task Hierarchy, Health, Actual Start, % Work Complete, Remaining Work, Actual Finish,* and *Resource Name*. Optional fields are *Start, Finish, Work* and *Comments*. These fields enable you to see the original dates as well as see any comments. I recommend the *Sheet* layout for this tracking method. The recommended grouping is by Project. Figure 4 - 47 shows the *Tasks* page with the custom view and MSProjectExperts recommended settings.

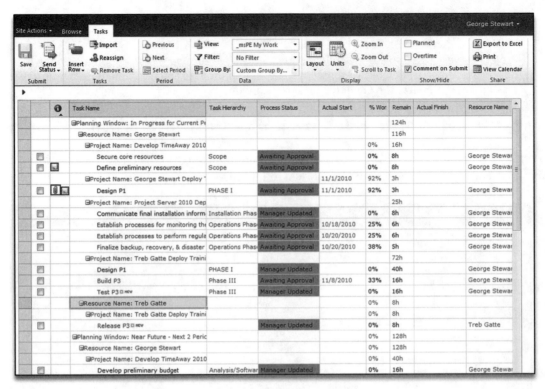

Figure 4 - 47: Recommended Percent Complete view

If you are the managing assignments for other resources, I recommend an alternative custom grouping that segregates your personal assignments from those of the resources you manage. In this particular case, your custom grouping values are set to *Planning Window, Resource Name, Project Name*, yielding the view in Figure 4 - 48.

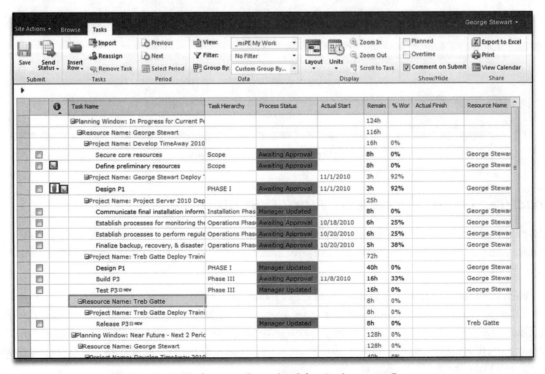

Figure 4 - 48: Tasks page Organized for Assignment Owners

To enter progress using the Percent of Work Complete method of tracking with the custom layout of the *Tasks* page, use the following methodology:

1. When you start a new task, click in the Actual *Start* field for the selected task and enter the date you began work on the task.

2. Click in the *%Work Complete* field and enter your estimate of the percentage of work completed to date on the task.

3. Enter your estimated amount of Remaining Work (or ETC) in the *Remaining Work* field.

4. When you complete a task, click in the *Finish* field for the selected task and enter the date you finished work on the task.

5. To add a note to the task, either:

6. Enter your note into the *Comments* field if it is present.

7. Enter your note on the *Assignment Details* page.

8. Save all changes.

9. Click the name of the task to navigate to the *Assignment Details* page.

10. Enter your note text at the bottom of the page.

11. Click the *OK* button.

12. Click the *Save* button to save your task progress changes if you are not ready to submit them to your project manager for approval.

13. When you are ready to submit the task changes to your project manager, select the option checkbox to the left of each task that you want to submit and click the *Submit Selected* button. Alternately, you can also click the *Submit All* button to submit all task changes automatically.

Although this method of tracking requires a little more work on the part of team members, entering an Actual Start and Actual Finish date gives the project manager much more accurate scheduling information. This helps the project manager to better forecast schedule slippage due to a late Actual Start date or late Actual Finish date on a task and all successor tasks.

Using Actual Work Done and Work Remaining

In this tracking method, you are entering the amount of time spent on the task and the amount of work remaining. This method of time accrual enables you and your management to gauge progress toward the task outcome and the quality of the initial work estimate. This method also minimizes the somewhat subjective nature of % Work Complete tracking by forcing focus on the level of effort expended versus planned.

In Project Server 2010, the layout of the *Tasks* page does not automatically reconfigure based on the tracking method. The assumption is that your Project Server administrator configured the view previously.

Best Practice: Using Actual Work Done and Work Remaining

MSProjectExperts recommends that your Project Server administrator create a custom view of the *Tasks* page to optimize your data entry experience as shown in Figure 4 - 49. This view ensures that data columns are on the page; however you are in control of other aspects such as grouping.

The custom view contains the following columns: *Project Name, Task Name, Process Status, Task Hierarchy, Health, Actual Start, Actual Work, Remaining Work, Actual Finish,* and *Resource Name.* Optional fields are *Start, Finish, Work* and *Comments.* These fields enable you to see the original dates as well as any comments.

I recommend the *Sheet* layout for this tracking method. The recommended grouping is by project.

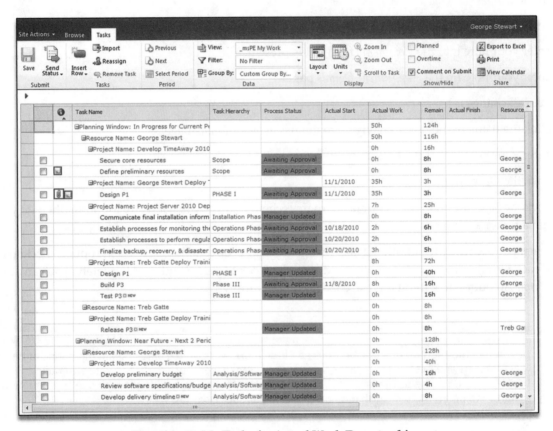

Figure 4 - 49: My Tasks for Actual Work Done tracking

As a courtesy, your Project Server administrator may also include the *Start* and *Finish* fields so that team members can see the scheduled dates for tasks to start and finish.

To enter progress using the Actual Work Done and Work Remaining method of tracking with the *Tasks* page custom layout, use the following methodology:

1. When you start a new task, click in the Actual *Start* field for the selected task and enter the date you began work on the task.

2. Click in the *Actual Work* field and enter the total amount of work completed to date (measured in hours) on the task.

> If you enter a total amount of work that equals the planned work on a task (indicating you completed the task), Project Server 2010 assumes that you started and finished the task as **originally scheduled**. The system has no way of knowing that you started or finished a task early or late compared to the original schedule.

3. Enter your estimated amount of Remaining Work (or Estimated Time to Completion/ETC) in the *Remaining Work* field.

4. When you complete a task, click in the *Finish* field for the selected task and enter the date you finished work on the task.

5. Click the *Save* button to save your task progress changes if you are not ready to submit them to your project manager for approval.

6. When you are ready to submit the task changes to your project manager, select the option checkbox to the left of each task that you want to submit and click the *Submit Selected* button. Alternately, you can also click the *Submit All* button to submit all task changes automatically.

> To adjust the scheduled *Start* or *Finish* date for a future task, click in the *Start* or *Finish* field and change the date on the calendar date picker. This alerts your project manager that the actual start or finish is different from the current schedule in the project plan.

7. If you see the *Submit Changes* dialog, enter an optional comment about the update and then click the *OK* button to submit the update to your project manager.

> Although this method of tracking requires a little more work on the part of team members, entering an Actual Start and Actual Finish date gives the project manager much more accurate tracking information. This helps the project manager to better forecast schedule slippage due to a late Actual Start date or late Actual Finish date on a task and their successor tasks.

Using Hours of Work Done per Period

Organizations that use the Hours of Work Done per Period method of tracking progress need the finer level of detail, typically to meet billing requirements or the more rigorous requirements of a mature Project Management process. The *Tasks* page typically requires the timephased data entry grid for entries by day using this tracking method.

The *Tasks* page shown in Figure 4 - 50 includes a scroll bar at the bottom of the data grid. On lower screen resolutions, such as my current 1024 x 768 resolution, the data grid is too wide to fit on the page, and the system displays the scroll bar. At higher screen resolutions, such as at 1280 x 1024, the system displays the entire data grid without a scroll bar.

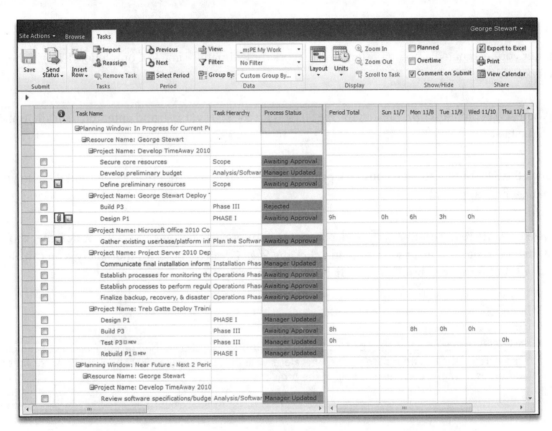

Figure 4 - 50: Tasks organized for Hours of Work Done Per Period tracking

Best Practice: Using Hours of Work Done per Period

MSProjectExperts recommends that your Project Server administrator create a custom view of the *Tasks* page to optimize your data entry experience as shown in Figure 4 - 51. This view ensures that data columns are on the page; however you are in control of other aspects such as grouping.

The custom view contains the following columns: *Project Name, Task Name, Process Status, Task Hierarchy, Health, Remaining Work, Actual Finish,* and *Resource Name.* Optional fields are *Start, Finish, Work* and *Comments.* These fields enable you to see the original dates as well as any comments.

I recommend the *Timephased Data* layout for this tracking method. The recommended grouping is by project.

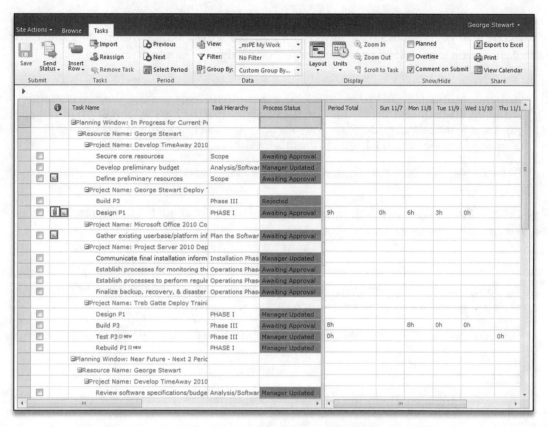

Figure 4 - 51: Tasks organized for Hours of Work Done tracking

To enter progress using the Hours of Work Done method of tracking with the custom layout of the *Tasks* page, use the following methodology:

1. On a daily basis, enter the hours you worked on each task in the timesheet grid.

2. Add notes as needed for each task, either:

3. Enter your note in the *Comments* field if it is present.

4. Enter your note on the *Assignment Details* page.

5. Save all changes.

6. Click the name of the task to navigate to the *Assignment Details* page.

7. Enter your note text at the bottom of the page.

8. Click the *OK* button.

9. Click the *Save* button to save your current progress at the end of each day.

10. On the last day of the reporting period, enter your estimated amount of Remaining Work (or Estimated Time to Completion/ETC) in the *Remaining Work* field for any tasks that require adjustment.

11. Add a note to any task that you adjust.

12. When you are ready to submit the task changes to your project manager, select the option checkbox to the left of each task that you want to submit and click the *Submit Selected* button. Alternately, you can also click the *Submit All* button to submit all task changes automatically.

To adjust the scheduled Start or Finish date for a future task, click in the *Start* or *Finish* field and change the date on the calendar date picker. This alerts your project manager that the actual start or finish is different from the current schedule in the project plan.

13. If you see the *Submit Changes* dialog, enter an optional comment about the update and then click the *OK* button to submit the update to your project manager.

As a best practice, MSProjectExperts recommends that you enter actual progress on a daily basis and update progress to your project manager on a weekly basis.

Hands On Exercise

Exercise 4-7

Enter and submit task progress from the Tasks page.

1. In the *My Work* section of the *Quick Launch* menu, click the *Tasks* link. In the *Data* section of the *Tasks* ribbon, use the *View* pick list to select the _msPE Work view. Pull the splitter bar to the right or apply the *Sheet* layout as you prefer.

2. For the Design P1 task, click the *Health* field for the in-progress task and select a value from the pick list.

3. Enter 40 hours in the *Actual Work* field and change the *Remaining Work* value to *24h*.

4. Click in the *Comment* field and enter a note on the task documenting a reason for the increase. (*Resource has to redo work previously done.*)

5. Click the *Save* button to save your task progress changes.

6. Notice the status message in the *Information* bar at the top of the tasks data grid.

7. Click the refresh button in your browser or press the **F5** key to refresh the screen. Select the option checkbox to the left of the in-progress task and then click the *Send Status* menu button, then select the *Selected Tasks* option.

8. Enter a comment about the update in the *Submit Changes* dialog and then click the *OK* button to submit the update to your project manager.

Reporting Progress from the Assignment Details Page

An alternate method for entering task progress is to use the *Assignment Details* page. Because this page contains so much more information about each task than the *Tasks* page, using the *Assignment Details* page is helpful if your organization uses the default layout of the *Tasks* page. That said, the *Assignment Details* page does not provide the same full update capabilities as the primary view. Depending on the tracking method, you can update the following values on the *Assignment Details* page as shown in Table 4 - 4.

Updatable Fields	% Complete	Actual Work / Remaining Work	Hours of Work Done
Completed Work		X	
Finish Date	X	X	X
Percent Complete	X		
Remaining Work	X	X	X
Start Date	X	X	X

Table 4 - 4: Updatable Fields on Assignment Details page

To access the *Assignment Details* page for any task, click the name of the task on the *Tasks* page. Figure 4 - 52 shows the layout of the *Assignment Details* page using the Percent of Work Complete method of tracking progress. Notice that the *Task Progress* section of the page includes the *Percent Complete* field.

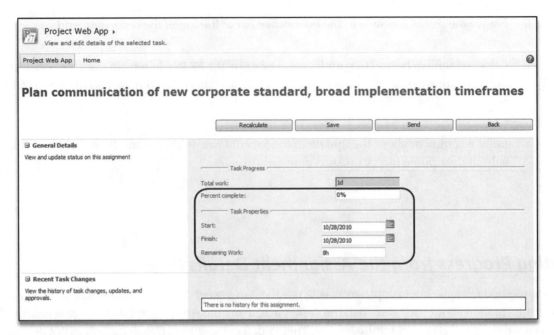

Figure 4 - 52: Assignment Details page using the % Work Complete method of tracking

Figure 4 - 53 shows the layout of the *Assignment Details* page using the Actual Work Done and Work Remaining method of tracking. Notice that the *Task Progress* section includes the *Completed work* field, measured in days.

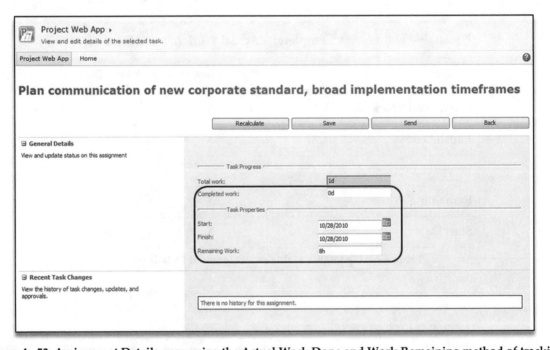

Figure 4 - 53: Assignment Details page using the Actual Work Done and Work Remaining method of tracking

Figure 4 - 54 shows the layout of the *Assignment Details* page using the Hours of Work Done per Period method of tracking. Note, in this tracking mode, you must use the primary *Tasks* view to enter time.

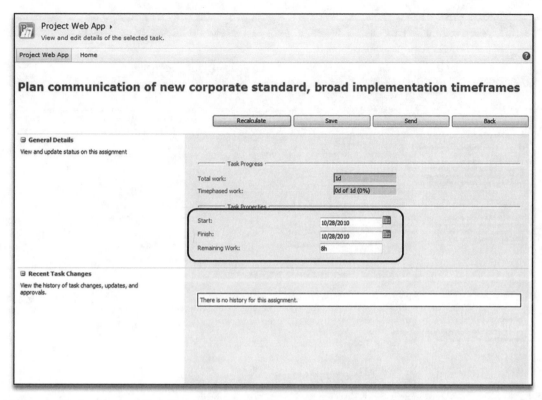

Figure 4 - 54: Assignment Details page using the Hours of Work Done per Period method of tracking

To report task progress from the *Assignment Details* page, use the same methodologies I presented earlier in this module for the method of tracking progress used by your organization. From this page, you can enter progress, adjust Remaining Work or add a note. When finished, click the *Save* button. From the *Tasks* page, submit the update to your project manager by clicking either the *Submit Selected* button or the *Submit All* button.

Importing Progress from the My Timesheet Page

Regardless of which hourly method your organization uses to track task progress, if you enter work hours in the *Timesheet* page, you can import the hours directly into the tasks shown on the *Tasks* page. To import timesheet hours, click the *Import* button on the *Tasks* page. Project Server 2010 displays the *Import Timesheet* page for the current time period, as shown in Figure 4 - 55.

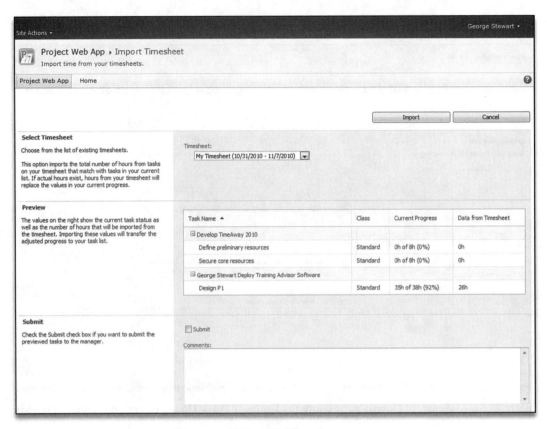

Figure 4 - 55: Import Timesheet page

To import a timesheet from a different time reporting period, click the *Timesheet* pick list at the top of the page and select the time reporting period you want to import. The system refreshes the page to show an updated *Import Timesheet* page. Click the *Import* button to import the timesheet data to the tasks shown on the *Tasks* page. When finished, add task comments as needed, and then submit the update to your project manager, following the methods detailed in the previous sections of this module.

Hands On Exercise

Exercise 4-8

Enter and submit task progress from the Assignment Details page.

1. If necessary, return to the *Tasks* page by clicking the *Tasks* link from the *My Work* section of the *Quick Launch* menu. On the *Tasks* page, click the Build P3 task assignment in the enterprise project used for this class.

2. On the *Assignment Details* page, enter a *Start* date that is two business days later than its currently scheduled *Start* date.

3. Mark the task as halfway complete using your organization's method of tracking progress.

4. For Percent Complete tracking method, update the *Percent Complete* field to *50%*.

5. For Actual Work / Remaining Work tracking method, update the *Completed Work* field with half the number of hours or days in the *Total Work* field.

6. For Hours of Work Done tracking method, skip this step, as this action is not possible on the *Assignment Details* page.

7. Expand the *Notes* section and add a note to document the reason for the late start.

8. Click the *Recalculate* button and notice the schedule changes in the *General Details* section.

9. Click the *Save* button.

10. Click the *Import* button on the *Tasks* ribbon to display the *Import Timesheet* page.

11. Click the *Timesheet* pick list and select the time reporting period under which you performed the timesheet exercises.

12. Click the *Import* button to import the timesheet entries to your *Tasks* page.

13. On the *Tasks* page, click the *Send Status* menu button and select the *All Tasks* item to submit all updates.

Managing Tasks

Along with reporting progress, other important task-related activities on the *Tasks* page include the following:

- Reassigning work to another resource
- Self-assigning Team tasks
- Creating new tasks
- Deleting tasks

I cover each activity in detail in the sections that follow.

Reassigning Work to another Resource

After a project manager assigns you to a task, Project Server 2010 offers you the option of reassigning the task to another resource. You might find this feature useful if you serve as a team leader to whom the project manager assigns tasks, and you are responsible for reassigning tasks to members of your team.

To reassign a task to another resource, navigate to the *Tasks* page, select one or more tasks to reassign and then click the *Reassign* button on the *Task* ribbon. Project Server 2010 displays the *Task Reassignment* page shown in Figure 4 - 56.

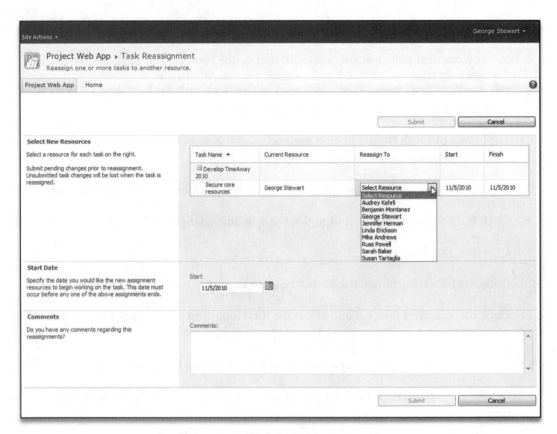

Figure 4 - 56: Task Reassignment page

The *Select New Resource(s)* section of the *Task Reassignment* page shows you a list of all your selected task assignments from the *Tasks* page. The *Reassign To* column in the data grid allows you to select the resource to which you want to reassign a task. Click the *Reassign To* field for the task you want to reassign and then click the pick list. The system displays the list of all resources that you have permission to see within the system.

> The default permissions in Project Server 2010 allow you to see only members of your project team. If you need to reassign a task to someone outside your project team, your project manager must first add the new resource to the project team in the project plan.

After you select the resources to which you want to reassign one or more tasks, click the *Start* pick list in the *Start Date* section of the *Task Reassignment* page. Select the date on which the system reassigns the selected tasks. The date in the *Start* field defaults to the current date. You must select a date that is before the *Finish* date of the selected tasks. Generally, you want the system to reassign the tasks immediately, which means you should keep the current date selected.

In the *Comments* field, enter any relevant comment text you want to add. When you complete your entries, click the *Submit* button. Project Server 2010 displays the *Tasks* page and removes the task(s).

The new resource can immediately enter time against the reassigned task. This enables team members to manage their own work to a certain extent in situations when the project manager is unavailable. However, the task reassignment is not final until the project manager approves the reassignment. When you click the *Submit* button, a task reassignment request automatically appears for the project manager to approve in the Approval Center.

Self-Assigning Team Tasks

A team resource acts as an assignment proxy for all members of your team. This enables project managers to assign tasks to teams without knowing the specific resource to assign initially.

There are two primary ways to use team tasks. The team lead, if properly configured, can reassign team tasks to specific team members. The second is that any member of the team can self-assign a team task. For example, if your team services work requests, then self-assignment of team tasks may be of interest.

If you are a member of a group of resources represented by a team resource, and the project manager assigns the team resource to a task, Project Server 2010 refers to the task as a team task. After the project manager publishes the enterprise project containing the team task, you can assign the team task to yourself by clicking the *Self-assign Team Tasks* button on the *Tasks* page. Project Server 2010 displays the *Team Tasks* page, as shown in Figure 4 - 57.

To self-assign a team task, select the *Insert Row* button on the ribbon and select the *Insert Team Tasks* option. You then see the page in Figure 4 - 57. Select a task and click the *Assign to me* button on the ribbon. Project Server removes the task from the list. Click the *Tasks* link in the *Quick Launch* menu to return to the *Tasks* page. When you self-assign a team task to you from an enterprise project, the system removes the task immediately from the *Team Tasks* page of all other resources.

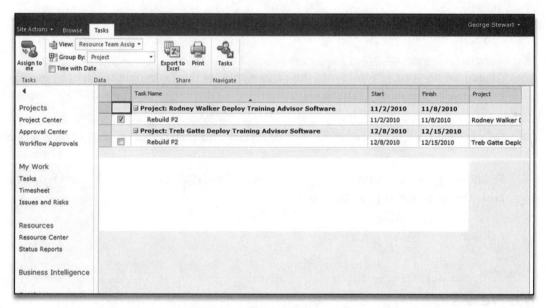

Figure 4 - 57: Team Tasks page

When you self-assign a team task, Project Server 2010 automatically approves the task reassignment.

Hands On Exercise

Exercise 4-9

Reassign work and self-assign team tasks from the Tasks page.

1. On the *Tasks* page, select the *Rebuild P1* task.

2. In the *Tasks* section of the *Tasks* ribbon, click the *Reassign* button.

3. Click the *Reassign To* pick list and select Cher Zall on the project team.

4. In the *Comments* field, add descriptive text to document the reason for the reassignment.

5. Click the *Submit* button.

6. (If enabled on your system) From the *Tasks* section of the *Tasks* ribbon, click the *Insert Row* pick list and select the *Insert Team Tasks* option.

7. Select the option checkbox for the *Rebuild P2* task and then click the *Assign task to me* button.

8. From the *My Work* section of the *Quick Launch* menu, click the *Tasks* link. Notice that the system adds the team task to your *Tasks* page.

Creating a New Task

In a collaborative project management environment, project team members may discover unplanned work and need to propose new tasks to their project manager. Proposed new tasks might include tasks related to tasks on which a resource is already working, but which were not included in the project plan, or future tasks that the team member anticipates.

To propose a new task, click the *Insert Row* menu button and select the *Create a New Task* option. Project Server 2010 displays the *New Task* page shown in Figure 4 - 58.

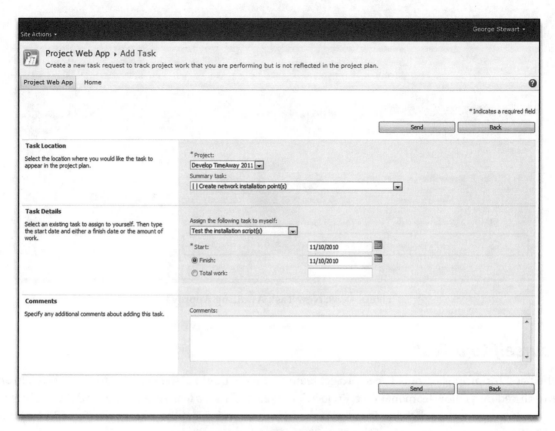

Figure 4 - 58: New Tasks page

To create the proposed task, begin by clicking the *Project* pick list and selecting the project in which to create the new task. The *Project* pick list contains only those projects in which you are a team member. Click the *Summary task* pick list and pick the level in the Work Breakdown Structure (WBS) at which to create the new task.

The first item on the *Subordinate to Summary task* pick list represents the highest level in the project. Selecting this item creates the new task at Outline Level 1, outside of any phase or deliverable sections in the project. The other items in the *Subordinate to Summary task* pick list include summary tasks that represent phase and deliverable sections in your project. Selecting one of these items creates the new task as a subtask of the selected phase or deliverable.

In the *Task Details* section of the *New Task* page, enter the new task name in *Task name* field. The *Start* field defaults to today's date but you should edit to reflect the actual anticipated start date. Lastly, either enter the anticipated finish date in the *Finish* field, the estimated work for the task in the *Total work* field or mark the task as a milestone.

After your project manager approves the new task request, Project Server 2010 adds the new task to the enterprise project and sets a Start No Earlier Than (SNET) constraint on the task using the date you enter in the *Start* field.

In the *Comments* field, add any additional documentation for your project manager. Additional comments might help your project manager to decide whether to approve the proposed task. Click the *Send* button when you finish. Project Server 2010 displays the *Tasks* page with the new proposed task added to the task list, as shown in Figure 4 - 59.

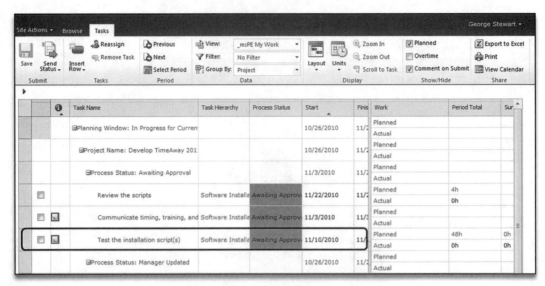

Figure 4 - 59: New Task Awaiting Approval

Add Yourself to a Task

Beyond the need for proposing new tasks, project team members might also need to add themselves to an existing task when enlisted by a fellow team member. Project Server 2010 allows a team member to add themselves to an existing task. To self-assign a task, click the *Insert Row* menu button and select the *Add Yourself to a Task* option. Project Server 2010 displays the *Add Task* page shown in Figure 4 - 60.

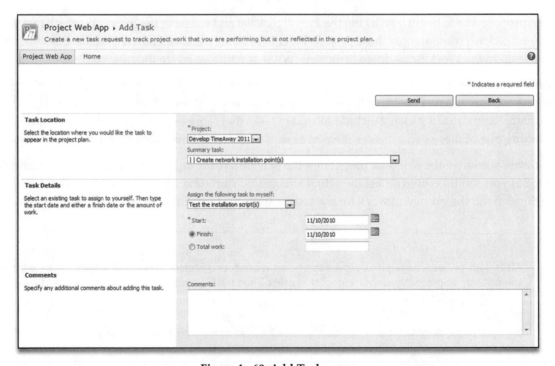

Figure 4 - 60: Add Task page

To begin, click the *Project* pick list and select the project containing the task you want to join. The *Project* pick list contains only those projects in which you are a team member. Click the *Summary task* pick list and pick the level in the

Work Breakdown Structure (WBS) to which the task belongs. Lastly, click the *Assign the following task to myself* pick list and select the appropriate task.

> The *Assign the following task to myself* pick list contains only those tasks that are contained by the summary task you selected in the *Summary task* pick list.

In the *Task Dates* section of the *Add Task* page, enter the anticipated start date of the new task in the *Start* field. Enter the anticipated finish date in the *Finish* field or enter the estimated work for the task in the *Total work* field. By default, the system sets dates in the *Start* and *Finish* fields to the current date.

> After your project manager approves the new task request, Project Server 2010 adds the new task to the enterprise project and sets a Start No Earlier Than (SNET) constraint on the task using the date you enter in the *Start* field.

In the *Comments* field, add any additional documentation for your project manager. Additional comments might help your project manager to decide whether to approve the proposed task.

Click the *Send* button when you finish. Project Server 2010 displays the *Tasks* page with the new proposed task added to the task list, as shown in Figure 4 - 61.

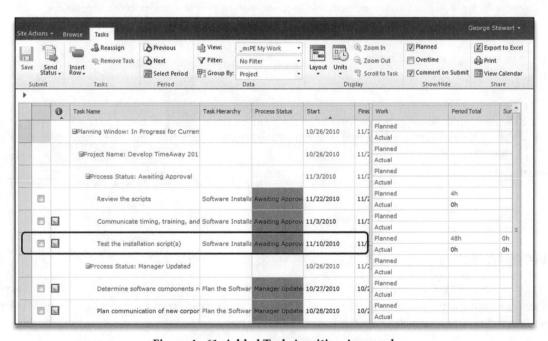

Figure 4 - 61: Added Task Awaiting Approval

When you click the *Send* button at the bottom of the *Add Task* page, Project Server 2010 immediately submits a new task request to your project manager for approval. If the project manager approves the proposed task, the task remains on the *Tasks* page and you can enter and submit progress for the task. If your project manager rejects the proposed task, the system changes the Process Status to *Rejected* as shown in Figure 4 - 62.

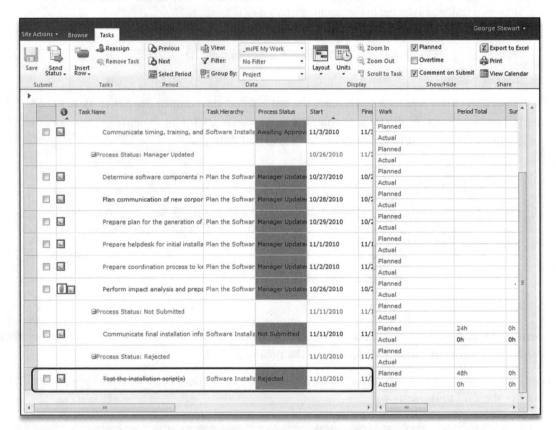

Figure 4 - 62: Tasks page shows rejected Add Task

If your project manager rejects your Add Task request, the system prevents you from entering progress against the task. Therefore, you should remove the rejected task from the *Tasks* page using the steps detailed below.

Removing Tasks

Project Server 2010 allows you to request removal of task assignments from the *Tasks* page. The *Remove* action creates a removal request that the project manager reviews and approves. Good targets for removal include rejected tasks, such as the rejected task shown previously in Figure 4 - 62.

Warning: Do not delete any other type of task from the *Tasks* page. If you attempt to delete a completed task, an in-progress task, or a future task, and your project manager accidentally approves your deletion request, the system **removes you from the task** in the Microsoft Project 2010 plan. You should delete future tasks only if your project manager gives you specific permission to do so, and intends to assign someone else to the tasks.

To remove tasks from the *Tasks* page, you and your project manager must follow a four-step process as follows:

1. You select and remove the tasks.

2. You submit the task removal request to your project manager.

3. Your project manager approves the removal.

4. Your project manager publishes the changes in the project.

To begin the task removal process, select the option checkbox to the left of each task to remove and then click the *Remove Task* button. Project Server 2010 displays the confirmation dialog shown in Figure 4 - 63.

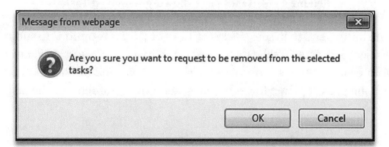

Figure 4 - 63: Task Removal confirmation dialog

Click the *OK* button to complete the task removal process on the *Tasks* page. The system refreshes the *Tasks* page and does the following:

- Changes the task Process Status to *Save Needed*.

- Strikes through the task name.

- Retains the selection status of the task

Notice in Figure 4 - 64 that the system formats the removed task with strikethrough text.

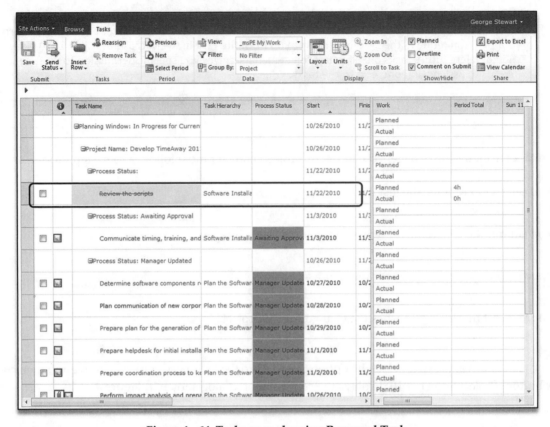

Figure 4 - 64: Tasks page showing Removed Task

Click the *Send Status* menu button and then select *Selected Tasks* or *All Tasks* options to submit the removal request to your project manager. Project Server 2010 sends your project manager a *Remove Assignment* request for each of the tasks you select. After your project manager approves the task removal and publishes the changes to the project, the task no longer appears on the project plan. However, the system does not remove the tasks from the *Tasks* page.

Hands On Exercise

Exercise 4-10

Create and submit a new task to your project manager. Remove one of your tasks.

1. If necessary, from the *My Work* section of the *Quick Launch* menu, select the *Tasks* link to return to the *Tasks* page. Click the *Insert Row* pick list and select the *Create a New Task* item.

2. Click the *Project* pick list and select your *Deploy Training Advisor Software* project.

3. Click the *Summary task* pick list and select the *Phase III* item.

4. Enter *Rebuild P3* as the name for the task in the *Task Name* field.

5. In the *Task Dates* section, enter dates in the *Start* and *Finish* fields. Use a start date later than the current time period you are working with.

6. Enter a comment.

7. Click the *Send* button. The system redisplays the *Tasks* page.

8. On the *Tasks* page, select the row selection check box for the *Build P3* task.

9. Click the *Remove Task* button.

10. Click the *OK* button in the confirmation dialog.

11. Click the *Send Status* menu button, and then select the *All Tasks* item to send your updates.

12. Click the *OK* button in the *Submit Changes* dialog.

Exercise 4-11

Assign yourself to a new task.

1. From the *Tasks* page, click the *Insert Row* menu button and select the *Add Yourself to a Task* item.

2. Click the *Project* pick list and select the Deploy Training Advisor project.

3. Click the *Summary task* pick list and select the *Phase III* summary task.

4. Click the *Assign the following task to myself* pick list, and select the *Test P3* task from the pick list.

5. In the *Comments* field, add descriptive text to explain why you assigned yourself to an existing task.

6. Click the *Send* button.

Updating tasks through Outlook

If your Project Server administrator configured Exchange synchronization for your system, your resources can update their tasks through Outlook. Each time that you publish task assignments, the system kicks off a synchronization job for tasks in your project, synchronizing Project Server assignments with the Outlook tasks list for each user in the schedule that has the *Synchronize Tasks* option selected in their Project Server user record. The synchronization process supports synchronization to the Outlook task list only, and your resources can enter percent complete only. Exchange synchronization does not support collecting time against tasks. Figure 4 - 65 shows a project assignment displayed in an Outlook task form.

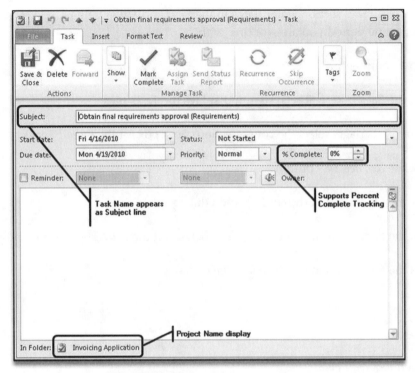

Figure 4 - 65: Project assignment as Outlook 2010 task

Notice in the figure that the task name appears as the *Subject* in the task form. Notice also that the task contains the planned start and end dates and the project name displays in the *In Folder* space at the lower left hand area of the task form. To report progress on the task, enter a percentage of completion in the *% Complete* field to show partial completion or use the *Mark Complete* button in the *Manage Task* section of the *Task* ribbon and adjust your dates accordingly. To commit your change click the *Save & Close* button on the ribbon. When you save your change, the system sends the update to Project Server via Exchange Server.

Exchange synchronization runs a full synchronization job nightly. In addition, a range of events trigger point synchronizations, including adding, deleting and modifying tasks in Outlook; modifying tasks in the *Tasks* page; and accepting and rejecting task updates in the Approval Center. Project actions such as deleting a published project, deleting a resource, activating or deactivating resources, and enabling and disabling the site-level exchange setting also trigger a synchronization event. Exchange synchronization supports users who work with the Outlook desktop client as well as Outlook Web App.

Module 05

Managing Personal Settings

Learning Objectives

After completing this module, you will be able to:

- Set e-mail Alerts and Reminders for yourself

- Set e-mail Alerts and Reminders for resources that you manage

- Manage Queued jobs

- Set Delegations for yourself

- Act as a Delegate

Inside Module 05

Personal Settings Overview

Depending on your permissions within the system, Project Server 2010 offers you a number of personal settings that you can modify to suit your needs. Click the *Personal Settings* link in the *Quick Launch* menu to change your personal settings. The system displays the *Personal Settings* page shown in Figure 5 - 1.

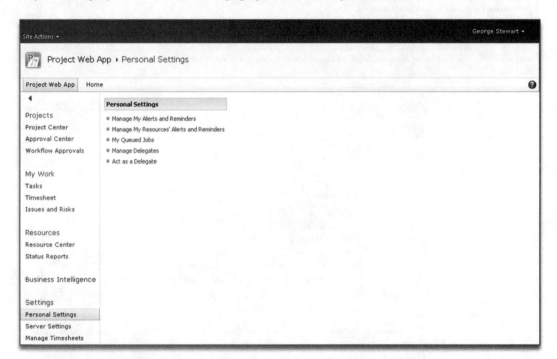

Figure 5 - 1: Personal Settings page in Project Web App

Depending on your permissions in Project Server 2010 and your method of authentication, the *Personal Settings* page may offer you some or all the following options:

- Manage My Alerts and Reminders

- Manage My Resource's Alerts and Reminders

- My Queued Jobs

- Manage Delegates

- Act as a Delegate

I discuss each of these options individually except for managing jobs in the queue.

Managing Alerts and Reminders for Yourself

Project Web App allows you to set up a subscription to receive e-mail Alerts and Reminders from Project Server 2010. An Alert is an e-mail message that the system sends immediately when an event occurs, such as when the project manager publishes a new project in which you are a team member. A Reminder is an e-mail message that the system sends on a periodic cycle, usually once a day at midnight, to remind you of upcoming or overdue responsibilities, such as an overdue Status Report.

To manage your subscription for Alerts and Reminders, click the *Manage My Alerts and Reminders* link on the *Personal Settings* page. Project Server 2010 displays the *Manage My Alerts and Reminders* page shown in Figure 5 - 2.

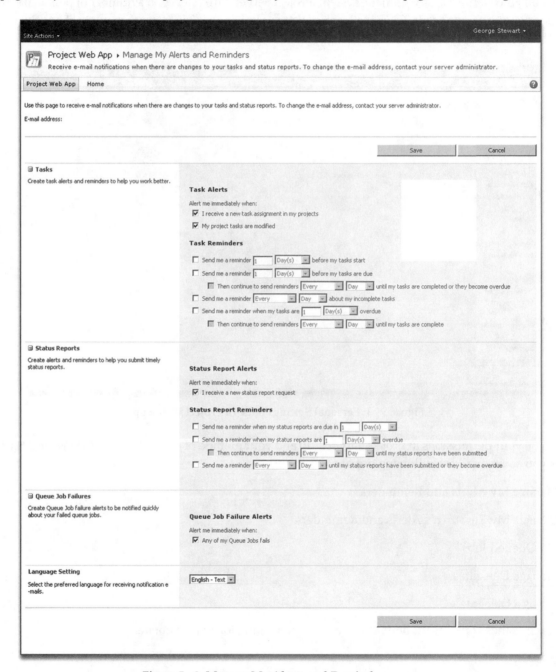

Figure 5 - 2: Manage My Alerts and Reminders page

Notice that the *Manage My Alerts and Reminders* page includes options in four sections. You set your alerts and reminders in the *Tasks* section and the *Status Reports* section. In the *Tasks* section, the default options trigger the system to send you an e-mail message whenever the following occurs:

- A project manager publishes a new project containing a task assigned to you, or the project manager assigns you to a new task in an existing project and then publishes the project.

- The schedule changes for one or more of your task assignments in an existing project.

Between the two default e-mail subscriptions for Alerts on tasks, the first is most valuable because you should always notify team members about new task assignments. The second e-mail subscription is problematic, however, because it can lead to a large number of e-mail messages sent to team members every time the project schedule changes. If team members receive too many e-mail messages from Project Server 2010, they may treat these messages as "spam" and create an Outlook rule to filter out all messages originating with Project Server.

To reduce the number of e-mail messages that users receive from Project Server 2010, msProjectExperts recommends that all project managers and team members deselect the *My project tasks are modified* option on the *Manage My Alerts and Reminders* page.

The second set of options in the *Tasks* section allows you to subscribe to e-mail reminders related to specific task criteria for project work. Each night the system tests your criteria and generates an email message containing the task reminders for your subscriptions. You receive an email only if you set reminder criteria and the system finds an appropriate match between your tasks in the system and your specified criteria. Think of these criteria as triggering conditions, which include each of the following:

- Before a task starts

- Before a task is due

- Until a task is complete or becomes overdue

- When you have an incomplete task

- When you have an overdue task

- Until an overdue task is complete

Notice in Figure 5 - 2 that the default settings include none of these options. If you select any of these options, you should also specify the frequency, as you do not have to receive these messages every day unless you prefer daily delivery.

The options in the *Status Reports* section are similar to those in the *Tasks* section. The default permission for alerts on Status Reports causes the system to send you an e-mail message immediately when a manager includes you in a new Status Report request. The second set of options allows you to subscribe to reminders for Status Reports.

The *Queue Job Failures* section of the *Manage My Alerts and Reminders* page includes only a single option. This option causes Project Server 2010 to send you an e-mail message immediately if any job you send to the Queue fails in the queuing process. For example, if you submit a timesheet or a task update, each of these constitutes a job sent to the Queue for processing. If the job fails, the system immediately sends you an e-mail message.

The *Language Setting* section contains a single option that allows you to set your language preference for e-mail messages sent to you by Project Server 2010. Select the language you want, if necessary, and then click the *Save* button to save the selections you specify.

Managing Alerts and Reminders for Your Resources

In addition to managing e-mail subscriptions for Alerts and Reminders for yourself, Project Server 2010 also allows you to manage e-mail subscriptions for your team members and your resources. The system defines "your team members" as those resources who are a team member in your projects and assigned to at least one task. The system defines "your resources" as any resource included in a Status Report request. To set e-mail subscriptions for your team members and resources, click the *Manage My Resource's Alerts and Reminders* link on the *Personal Settings* page. Project Server 2010 displays the *Manage My Resource's Alerts and Reminders* page shown in Figure 5 - 3.

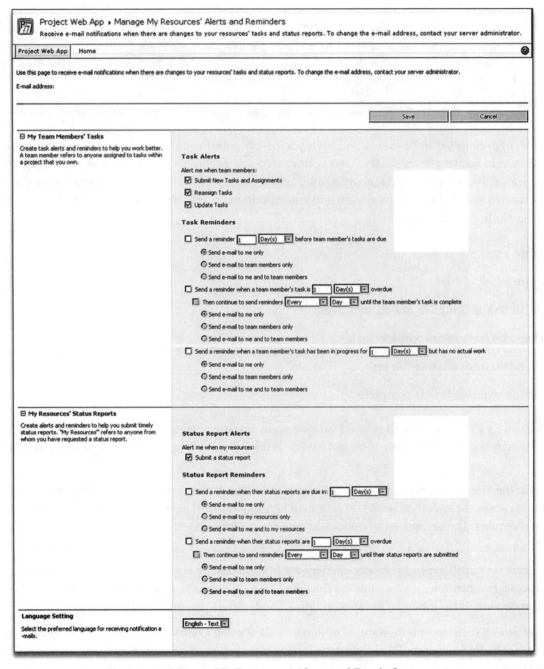

Figure 5 - 3: Manage My Resources' Alerts and Reminders page

Notice in Figure 5 - 3 that the *Manage My Resource's Alerts and Reminders* page layout is similar to the *Manage My Alerts and Reminders* page. In this case, the page consists of only three sections, with sections for My Team Member's Tasks, My Resource's Status Reports, and Language Settings. Notice also that the default options in the *Task Alerts* section of the page cause Project Server 2010 to send you an e-mail alert immediately when one of the following triggering events occurs:

- A team member submits a New Task request or a New Assignment request to you.

- A team member reassigns (delegates) a task to another team member.

- A team member submits task progress to you.

Because these three default options can lead to a high volume of e-mail messages sent to you by Project Server 2010, you may wish to deselect one or more of these options. Of the three, the *Update Tasks* option causes the system to send the most e-mail messages.

The *Task Reminders* section of the page allows you to set up subscriptions for e-mail reminders for your team members about their project work. When you set up reminder subscriptions for your team members, you may choose to have the reminder sent to you only, to the team members only, or to both you and your team members. Set the reminders for your team members and specify who receives the e-mail reminders.

The *Status Report Alerts* section contains only a single option, selected by default. This option causes Project Server 2010 to send you an e-mail alert immediately when a resource submits a Status Report to you. Again, because this option can lead to a flurry of e-mail messages, you may wish to deselect it.

The *Status Report Reminders* section allows you to set up subscriptions for e-mail reminders for those resources assigned in Status Report requests you create. Again, you may choose to have the reminders sent to you only, to the resources only, or to both you and your resources.

> If one of your team members or resources deselects a reminder option on the *Manage My Alerts and Reminders* page, and you select the same reminder option for your team members or resources on the *Manage My Resource's Alerts and Reminders* page, your selection overrides the user's selection and sets the reminder.

In the *Language Setting* section, specify your language preference and then click the *Save* button to save your settings.

Hands On Exercise

Exercise 5-1

Set Alerts and Reminders for yourself, and for your team members and resources.

1. Launch your Internet Explorer and navigate to your organization's Project Web App Home page.

2. Click the *Personal Settings* link in the *Quick Launch* menu.

3. Click the *Manage My Alerts and Reminders* link on the *Personal Settings* page.

4. Set your options and then save your changes.

5. Click the *Manage My Resource's Alerts and Reminders* link on the *Personal Settings* page.

6. Set your options and then save your changes.

Managing My Queued Jobs

Every time you stand in line at a fast food restaurant, you are waiting in a "queue." In Project Server 2010, the Queue is a waiting line that is necessary whenever the number of service requests to the system is greater than the system's optimum serving capacity. When you save and submit a timesheet or a task update, the system places your job in the Queue for processing.

Project Server 2010 allows you to view the jobs in the Queue by clicking the *My Queued Jobs* link on the *Personal Settings* page. The system displays the *My Queued Jobs* page shown in Figure 5 - 4.

Figure 5 - 4: My Queued Jobs page

The *My Queued Jobs* page should normally appear blank, as shown previously in Figure 11-5. A blank page means, "no news is good news." This indicates that the Project Server 2010 system is running without errors. If you see a Queue job on the *My Queued Jobs* page, you can watch the job's progress in the system by clicking the *Refresh Status* button occasionally.

In addition to being able to view jobs currently processing in the Queue, Project Server 2010 also allows you to view the history of processed jobs. Click the *View* pick list in the *View* ribbon and select one of the following views:

- In Progress and Failed Jobs in the Past Week (the default view)

- All In Progress and Failed Jobs

- Successful Jobs in the Past Week

- All Successful Jobs

- All Jobs in the Past Week

- All Jobs

For example, Figure 5 - 5 shows the *My Queued Jobs* page with the *Successful jobs in the Past Week* view selected. Notice that the page shows a number of different job types.

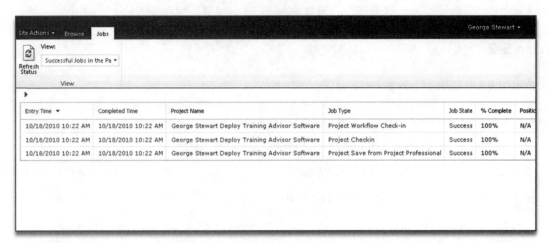

Figure 5 - 5: My Queued Jobs page shows the Successful jobs in the Past Week view

If you notice a job that the system simply does not process, or a job that failed, you should contact your Project Server administrator immediately for assistance. To help the Project Server administrator, you should click the *Click to view the error details* link in the *Error* column. The system displays the *Queue Job Error Details* dialog as shown in Figure 5 - 6.

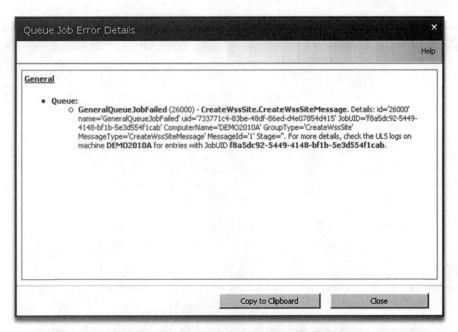

Figure 5 - 6: Queue Job Error Details dialog

The *Queue Job Error Details* dialog contains information valuable to help your Project Server administrator to diagnose and solve the Queue errors. To share the error information with your Project Server administrator, click the *Copy to Clipboard* button and paste the error contents into an email message.

Hands On Exercise

Exercise 5-2

Explore the *My Queued Jobs* page.

1. Click the *Personal Settings* link in the *Quick Launch* menu.

2. Click the *My Queued Jobs* link on the *Personal Settings* page.

3. Click the *View* pick list and study the Queue information shown for several different views.

4. Return to the *Home* page in Project Web App.

Manage Delegates

Project Server 2010 allows you to designate delegates who can act on your behalf in the system, such as when you know you will be away when timesheets are due. Using delegation in Project Server allows you to appoint a coworker to submit your timesheet for you. Click on the *Manage Delegates* link on the *Personal Settings* page and the system opens the *Manage Delegates* page shown in Figure 5 - 7.

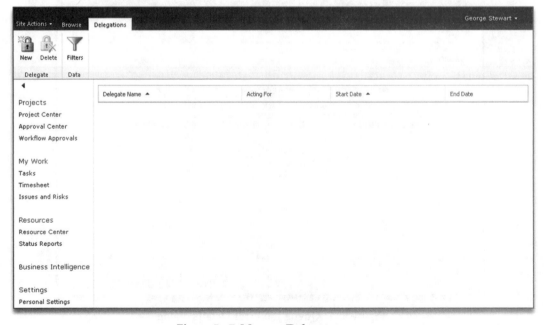

Figure 5 - 7: Manage Delegates page

To create a new delegation, click the *New* button in the *Delegate* section of the *Delegations* ribbon. The system displays the *Add Delegation* page shown in Figure 5 - 8.

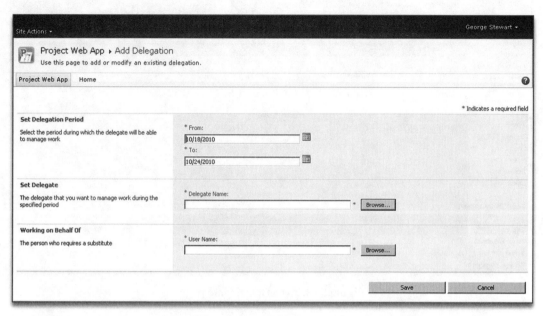

Figure 5 - 8: Add Delegation page

To add a new delegation, begin by setting a date range during which the delegation is effective using the *From* and *To* fields. Next, select the person who you would like to act as your delegate by clicking the *Browse* button and selecting the username from the list. Finally, use the *Browse* button in the *Working on Behalf of* section to select yourself from the list. Click the *Save* button when you complete your entries.

> Administrators and others who have *Manage Resources' Delegates* permission can create delegations for themselves and anyone else who has the the *Act as Delegate* permission. Non-administrators may only create delegations for themselves unless an Administrator gives them additional permissions.

Act as Delegate

When another user selects you as a delegate by creating a delegation, you can act on behalf of that person to perform most functions within Project Web App. To act as a delegate, select the *Act as a Delegate* link from the *Personal Settings* page. The system displays the *Act as a Delegate* page shown in Figure 5 - 9.

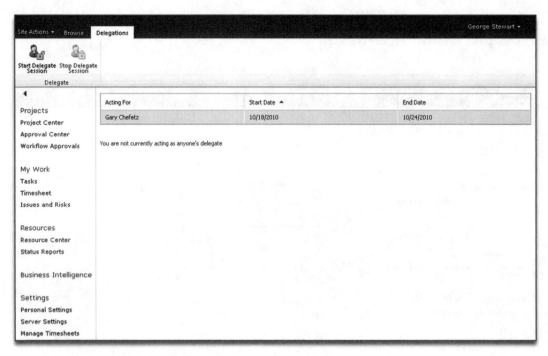

Figure 5 - 9: Act as a Delegate page

If another user or an administrator created a delegation for you to act on behalf of another user, the *Act as a Delegate* page displays those delegations. Notice in Figure 5 - 9 that George Stewart has a delegation for Gary Chefetz effective October 18 through October 24, 2010. To start a delegate session, select the delegation you want to use by highlighting the row, and then click the *Start Delegate Session* button from the *Delegate* section of the *Delegations* ribbon. The page changes to indicate that the delegation session is active as shown in Figure 5 - 10.

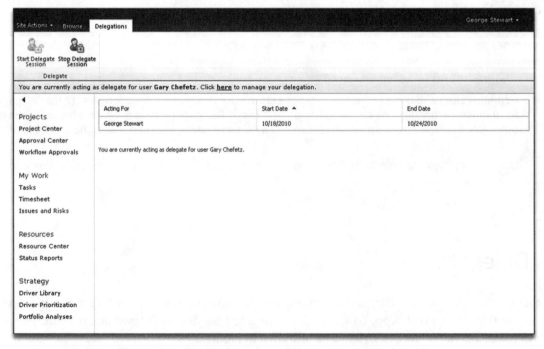

Figure 5 - 10: Act as Delegate page with delegation session in progress

Notice in Figure 5 - 10 that the screen changes by displaying a band across the page just beneath the ribbon indicating that the delegation session is active. This warning band remains across every page in Project Web App while you are acting as a delegate to remind you that you are now looking at Project Web App through someone else's eyes. After you complete your work on behalf of the other user, you end your delegate session by returning to the *Act as Delegate* page by clicking on the *Click here* link in the information band, or by navigating to the page from the *Personal Settings* page. Click the *Stop Delegate Session* button from the *Delegate* section of the *Delegations* ribbon. The system exits the delegate session and the page displays *You are not currently acting as anyone's delegate* in the message section.

Warning: Delegaton does not appy to all features. For instance, features supported by SharePoint only, such as Project Sites and the BI Center, are not included in delegation. Delegation does not apply to Project Professional 2010 or editing project schedules with Project Professional 2010.

Module 06

Collaborating with Project Sites

Learning Objectives

After completing this module, you will be able to:

- Understand the features available in a Project Site
- Track and manage project Risks
- Track and manage project Issues
- Share and manage project Documents
- Track and manage Action Items
- Track and manage Calendar events

Inside Module 06

Understanding Project Sites

When you publish a new enterprise project, Project Server 2010 automatically provisions a new Project Site in Windows SharePoint Services if your system options are set to automatic workspace creation. Project team members and other project stakeholders can collaborate using Project Site tools to do the following depending upon their permissions:

- Manage risks, issues, documents, and deliverables associated with the project.

- View a calendar of events and announcements related to the project.

- Create and/or work on tasks associated with the project but not included in the actual enterprise project plan.

- Participate in a discussion related to the project.

- Restore a deleted object from the Recycle Bin.

Once you open a Project Site, you are working mostly with the native capabilities of Windows SharePoint Services 3.0. The *Project Document* library contains customizations that handle linking documents to Project objects. The *Issues* and *Risks* lists feature custom web parts embedded in standard SharePoint lists to provide connectivity to Project Server. The *Deliverables* list also contains custom capabilities specific for use with Project Server. All of the other features that you encounter in your Project Sites are available to any SharePoint site. The skills you learn in this section apply to general SharePoint usage, not just Project Server. To access a *Project Site* for any project, from the Project Center, select the row header for the project and from the *Navigate* section of the *Projects* ribbon click the *Project Site* button. The system displays the homepage for your project site shown in Figure 6 - 1.

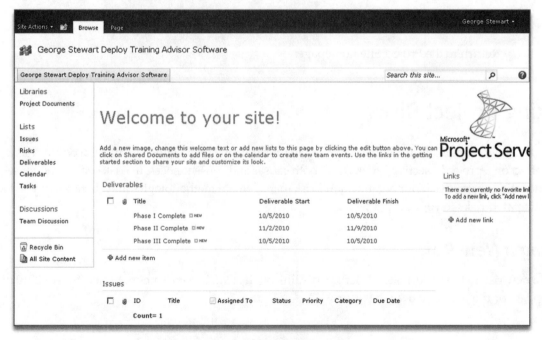

Figure 6 - 1: Project Site homepage

Notice in Figure 6 - 1 that the Project Site contains the following features:

- The *Quick Launch* menu on the left side of the page offers links that allow you to work with documents, issues, risks, deliverables, calendar events, tasks, and team discussions.

- The main content area in the middle of the page displays announcements and calendar events.

- The sidepane on the right side of the page displays links to additional information.

Hands On Exercise

Exercise 6-1

Navigate to and explore your Project Site.

1. From the *Project Center* page, select the row header for your Deploy Training Advisor Software project and from the *Navigate* section of the *Projects* ribbon click the *Project Site* button. The system displays the homepage for your Project Site.

2. Notice that the deliverables display in the *Deliverables* list near the center of the page.

3. Visit the *Project Documents* library, the *Risks* list, and the *Issues* list.

4. Return to the Project Site homepage.

Tracking Project Risks

The Project Management Institute defines a risk as "an uncertain event or condition that, if it occurs, has a positive or negative effect on a project objective." Risks have both causes and consequences. If a risk occurs, the consequence can be either negative or positive. Your organization's risk management methodologies may dictate that you log and document anticipated risks to your project work.

Creating a New Risk

To create a new risk in the Project Site, click the *Risks* link on the *Quick Launch* menu. Project Server 2010 displays the *Risks* list page for the project shown in Figure 6 - 2.

Figure 6 - 2: Risks page for the Deploy Training Advisor Software project

Click the *Add new item* link in the page. The system displays the *New Item* dialog for risks partially shown in Figure 6 - 3.

Figure 6 - 3: New Item dialog for risks

The *New Item* page for risks contains fields into which you can enter relevant information about the risk. The system requires you to enter information into only four fields: *Title, Status, Probability*, and *Impact*. Notice that the *Status* field defaults to a pick list entry "Active." This field determines the status of the risk for display in your reminders on the homepage, the Project Server reminder email, and on the *Issues and Risks* page. Project Server 2010 requires probability and impact entries to determine the *Exposure* value for the risk, which it calculates by multiplying the two numbers.

Project Server 2010 displays the *Exposure* field on the *Risks* page. You can use the exposure value to rank risks in descending order by severity. For example, your organization might establish a risk management methodology that requires you to create a risk management plan for the top four risks ranked by exposure.

Warning: Do not change the values for the *Status* field or you break some of the integration with Project Server.

In the *Title* field, enter a brief description. In the *Owner* field, enter the name of the individual who owns the new risk. If you manually type the name of the individual, click the *Check Names* button to the right of the field to confirm a valid name. If you enter an incorrect name, the system displays warning text below the *Owner* field. If you want to pick the name of the owner from a list, then click the *Browse* button to the right of the *Owner* field. Project Server 2010 displays the *Select People and Groups* dialog shown in Figure 6 - 4. Enter a full or partial name in the *Find* field and then click the *Search* button at the right end of the *Find* field. Select a name from the list and click the *OK* button.

Figure 6 - 4: Select People and Groups Webpage dialog

In the *Assigned To* field, enter the name of the person responsible for managing the risk. This is the person assigned to monitor risk conditions and enact a backup plan if the risk occurs. You may use the *Check Names* button and the *Browse* button to the right of the field, to assist your data input.

Click the *Status* pick list and select the status. This defaults to *Active* for new risks. The options include *Active, Postponed,* and *Closed.* The *Category* field is a field your organization should edit to display risk management information specific to your organization or your particular project. The default values in this field do not contain relevant identifiers, so unless you or your Project Server administrator modifies these values, you may ignore this field.

In the *Due Date* field, enter either the date on which you anticipate the risk may occur, or the date on which the *Assigned To* person must complete the risk management plan. Because this field is optional, your organization may use it any way you deem appropriate. You may also select a date and time for the *Due Date* field using the *Calendar* button and the *Time* pick lists to the right of the field.

In the *Probability* field, enter a percentage value between 0 and 100, representing the likelihood that the risk may actually occur. In the *Impact* field, enter a number between 1 and 10 to describe the magnitude of the consequences in the project should the risk occur. Remember that Project Server 2010 multiplies these two numbers to determine the *Exposure* value for the risk. In the *Cost* field, enter any additional cost incurred to the project if the risk occurs.

Entering a value of 0% in the *Probability* field makes no sense. If there is no chance of risk there is no risk. Entering a value of 100% makes no sense either. If the risk is absolutely certain, it is not a risk, it is an issue.

Click into the *Description* field to activate the text editing buttons at the top of the field. Enter additional information about the risk, such as causes of the risk and consequences to the project, should the risk occur. Format the text using the formatting buttons at the top of the field.

Click into the *Mitigation Plan* field and enter your plan for reducing the likelihood of the risk occurring, or to reduce the impact of the risk should it occur. Click in the *Contingency Plan* field and enter your backup plan for action should the risk actualize.

Click into the *Trigger Description* field and enter the description of what triggers the risk and determines whether it is about to occur, is currently occurring, or has already occurred. If you want to enter additional trigger information, click the *Trigger* pick list button and select an item from the list. Alternately, you may also select the *Specify your own value* option and enter text in the accompanying field.

If you want to link the new risk to one or more project objects, scroll to the top of the page. To link the new risk to an existing file, click the *Custom Commands* tab to expose the *Custom Commands* ribbon. Click the *Link Items* button on the ribbon. The system displays the *Link Items* dialog shown in Figure 6 - 5.

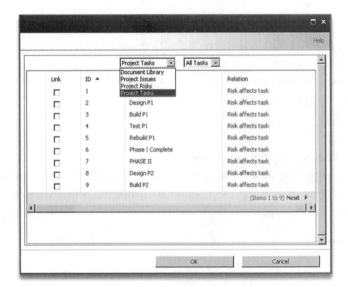

Figure 6 - 5: Link Items dialog

Notice in the figure that I expanded the *Object Type* pick list to display the various objects for which you can create links. These links drive the display of icons next to task rows in Project drilldown views and in the Project Center. Notice the *View* pick list next to the *Object Type* pick list. You use this context-sensitive pick list to limit the number of items displayed in the view. The list varies by object type and does not display when you select *Document Library* from the list.

To link the new risk to tasks, other risks or issues, or to documents in the document library associated with the project, select the check boxes for the linked items in the *Link* column, which behaves like a yes/no toggle, as shown previously in Figure 6 - 5.

In the RTM release of Project Server 2010, the *Link Item* dialog lacks control labels as well as a dialog label. The *Link Items* button in the *New Item* dialog is a leftover placeholder as well. This might be changed in later builds.

Figure 6 - 6 shows the completed *New Item* dialog for a risk scrolled to the bottom of the page. Notice at the bottom of the page that I linked the new risk to the Design P1 task in the project. Click the *Save* button to save the new risk.

Warning: Your Project Server administrator can configure SharePoint to also use web pages instead of popup dialog forms like the *New Item* dialog shown in this section. If your Project Server administrator changed this setting, your experience with the screens in this module will vary.

Figure 6 - 6: New Item dialog showing link information

Hands On Exercise

Exercise 6-2

Create a new risk and link it to a task.

1. From your Deploy Training Advisor Software Project Site homepage select the *Risks* link from the *Quick Launch* menu. The system displays the *Risks* homepage.

2. Click the *Add new item* link to launch the *New Item* dialog for risks. In the *New Item* dialog enter a name for your risk in the *Title* field. Enter or select your own user account in both the *Owner* and *Assigned To* pick lists by clicking on the *Browse* icon to the right of the field. In the *Select People and Groups Web Page* dialog, type a name into the *Find* field, click on the *Search* icon, select the name you typed in the field, and click the *OK* button.

3. Leave the default *Active* selection for the *Status* field and the default selection for the *Category* field. Set a value in the *Due Date* field for 10 days from today.

4. Enter 50% in the *Probability* field and enter 5 in the *Impact* field.

5. Enter a cost, description, optional mitigation plan, contingency plan, and trigger information in their respective fields.

6. Select the *Custom Commands* tab to display the *Custom Commands* ribbon and click the *Link Items* button. The system displays the *Link Items* dialog.

7. Select the check box for the Design P1 task. Select the *Risk affects task* item in the *Relation* pick list and click the *OK* button to link the risk to the task.

8. In the *New* Item dialog click the *Save* button to create your new risk.

9. Repeat this process at least two more times to define several risks for your project.

Working with Existing Risks

While working with existing risks, the system allows you to do the following:

- Apply a view to the *Risks* page.

- Sort the risks by the data in any column.

- View a risk.

- Edit a risk.

- Delete a risk.

- Subscribe to e-mail alerts about changes to a risk.

I cover each of these topics individually. Figure 6 - 7 shows the *Risks* page for the Deploy Training Advisor Software project. Notice the three active risks associated with the project.

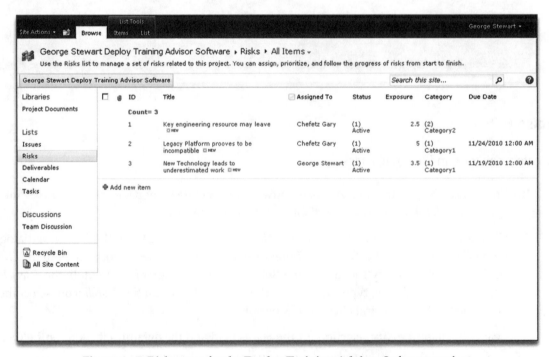

Figure 6 - 7: Risks page for the Deploy Training Advisor Software project

Working with Risk List Views

To apply a view to the *Risks* page, select the *List* tab, and from the *Manage Views* section, click the *Current View* pick list button and then select an available view as shown in the expanded pick list in Figure 6 - 8.

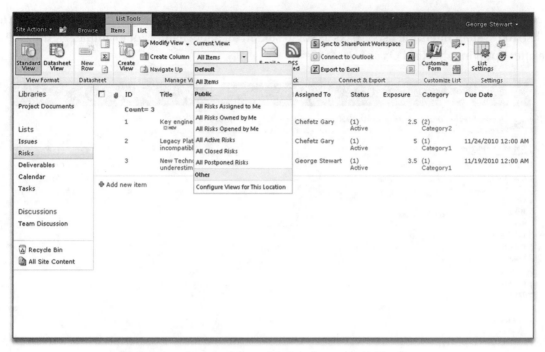

Figure 6 - 8: Current View pick list shows available views

The *Current View* pick list for the *Risks* page offers seven pre-defined *Public* views, including the following:

- All Items (the default View)

- All Active Risks

- All Closed Risks

- All Postponed Risks

- All Risks Assigned to Me

- All Risks Opened by Me

- All Risks Owned by Me

You use the *Configure Views for This Location* selection in the *Other* section when you use the *Locations* feature in SharePoint. For more information on this topic, see Microsoft's TechNet site.

Project Server 2010 also allows you to modify views and to create new views. After you apply a view from the *Current View* pick list, the system filters the list of risks as suggested in the view name. For example, Figure 6 - 9 shows the *Risks* page after applying the *Risks Owned by Me* view.

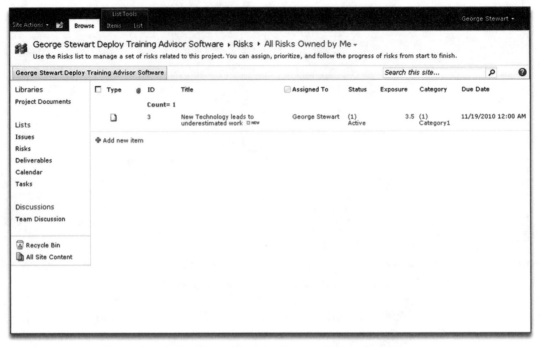

Figure 6 - 9: Risks Owned by Me view applied to the Risks page

Notice in Figure 6 - 9 that I am the owner for only one of the three risks for this project. To view all risks, reapply the *All Items* view. To sort the risks, click the name of the column header on which to sort the data. The system applies default sorting on the ID number column, sorted in the order users created the risks. For example, Figure 6 - 10 shows that you can change the sort order by floating your mouse pointer over the column header to reveal the pick list control, then select either the *Ascending* or *Descending* item from the pick list.

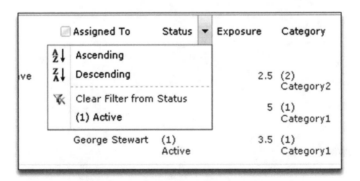

Figure 6 - 10: Selecting a sort order

Notice the downward-pointing arrow indicator to the right of the *Exposure* column name, indicating sorting in descending order in Figure 6 - 11. You can also see the list of *AutoFilter* options. Notice that the pick list for the *Exposure* column contains every value in the column, plus the options to sort in *Ascending* (Smallest on Top) or *Descending* (Largest on Top) order. Select an item from the pick list to AutoFilter the risks based on data contained in that column.

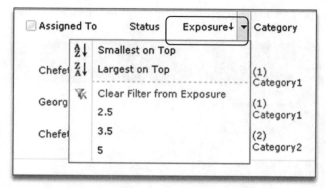

Figure 6 - 11: Sort order for the Exposure column

When you apply AutoFiltering to a column, Project Server 2010 indicates the AutoFiltered column by displaying a funnel indicator to the right of the column name. To remove AutoFiltering from a column, click the pick list button and select the *Clear Filter from* _____ item on the list

Viewing and Editing Existing Risks

To work with an existing risk, such as to view or edit it, float your mouse pointer over the name of the risk. Project Server 2010 displays a pick list button to the right of the risk name. Click the pick list button and the system displays the menu shown in Figure 6 - 12.

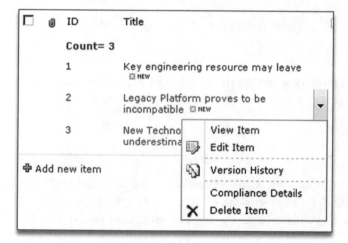

Figure 6 - 12: Pick list button and pick list for an existing risk

Notice that the menu allows you to select from *View Item*, *Edit Item*, or *Delete Item*, and view the *Version History* and *Compliance Details* for the list items. These concepts apply when using both the *Risks* list and the *Issues* list, and any other SharePoint list you work with. The *Version History* item applies only when you have this feature enabled in the system. The *Compliance Details* feature is something you use when your system employs advanced types of Share-Point document management features including, among others, records compliance, content retention policies and content validation. These features are beyond the scope of this book.

Click the *View Item* item from the pick list to open a risk in view-only mode, as shown in Figure 6 - 13.

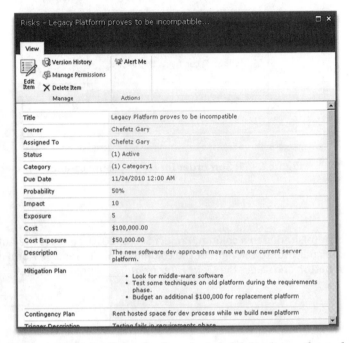

Figure 6 - 13: Risks dialog for the selected risk in view-only mode

You can also display a risk in view-only mode by clicking the name of the risk in the *Title* field.

To subscribe to e-mail alerts about changes to a risk or other list type item, from the *Actions* section of the *View* ribbon, click the *Alert Me* button. If you choose to receive e-mail messages about the risk, the system displays the *New Alert* dialog shown in Figure 6 - 14.

On the *New Alert* page, specify your options in each section of the page and then click the *OK* button. Notice that the *New Alert* page allows you to determine what type of change triggers the system to send an e-mail message to you, and that you can determine this change when the system sends the message.

Warning: Your SharePoint Server must be configured for email to use the *Alerts* feature in SharePoint.

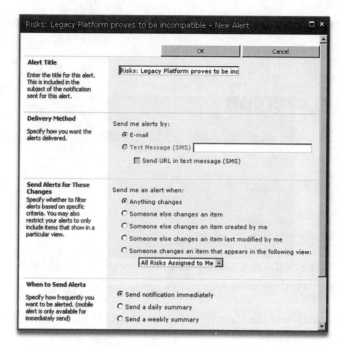

Figure 6 - 14: New Alert dialog

To edit the selected risk, from the *Manage* section of the *View* ribbon, click the *Edit Item* button or select the *Edit Item* option from the pick list menu shown previously in Figure 6 - 12. The system opens the risk for editing in the *Risk* dialog as shown in Figure 6 - 15.

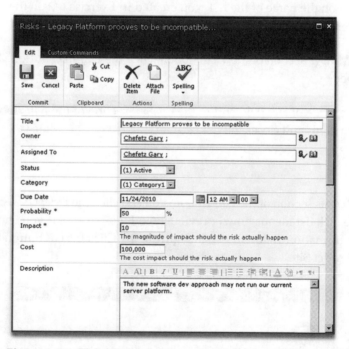

Figure 6 - 15: Risks dialog for the selected risk in editing mode

Notice that the system hides the *View* ribbon and displays the *Edit* ribbon. Edit the data in any of the fields, or use item linking to update your risk. Click the *Save* button to save your changes or click the *Cancel* button to discard your changes. Notice that the menu provides you with clipboard functionality to support the rich editing tools in the text field areas.

Hands On Exercise

Exercise 6-3

Edit and work with an existing risk.

1. Click on the name of the risk you created in Exercise 6-2 on the *Risk* list homepage. The system opens the risk in read-only mode.

2. In the *Actions* section of the *View* ribbon, click the *Alert Me* button. The system opens the *New Alert* dialog.

3. In the *New Alert* dialog, explore the various options for configuring an alert. When finished, click the *Cancel* button unless your instructor guides you differently. The system closes the *New Alert* dialog and returns to the *Risks* homepage.

4. Again, click on the name of the risk you created in Exercise 6-2 on the *Risk* list homepage. The system opens the risk in read-only mode.

5. From the *Manage* section of the *View* ribbon, click the *Edit Item* button. The system opens the risk in edit mode.

6. Change the value of any field and in the *Commit* section of the *Edit* ribbon, click the *Save* button. The system saves and closes the risk.

Deleting a Risk

To delete a risk, from the *Actions* section of the *Edit* ribbon, you can click the *Delete Item* button or you may select the *Delete Item* option from the pick list menu shown previously in Figure 6 - 12. If you choose to delete a risk, Project Server 2010 displays the confirmation dialog shown in Figure 6 - 16. Click the *OK* button to delete the risk and send it to the Recycle Bin for the Project Site.

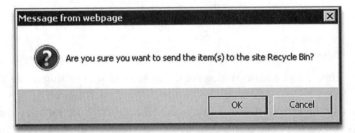

Figure 6 - 16: Confirmation dialog to delete a Risk

Restoring a Deleted Risk from the Recycle Bin

When you delete a risk, Project Server 2010 transfers the record to the Recycle Bin for the Project Site. If you accidentally delete a risk, Project Server 2010 allows you to restore it easily. Click the *Recycle Bin* link in the *Quick Launch* menu to begin the restoration process. The system displays the *Recycle Bin* page shown in Figure 6 - 17.

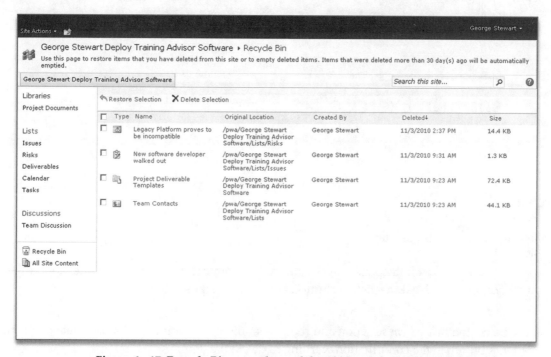

Figure 6 - 17: Recycle Bin page shows deleted items of various types

On the *Recycle Bin* page, select the option checkbox to the left of the item you want to restore, such as the deleted risk, and then click the *Restore Selection* link above the content area. Project Server 2010 displays the confirmation dialog shown in Figure 6 - 18.

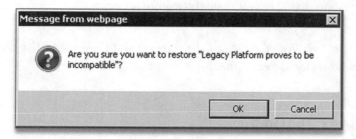

Figure 6 - 18: Restore item confirmation

Click the *OK* button and the system restores the deleted risk item from the Recycle Bin to the *Risks* list. You can delete and restore items in SharePoint lists and libraries using the same techniques. You can permanently delete an item by selecting it on the *Recycle Bin* page and then clicking the *Delete Selection* link next to the *Restore Selection* link.

SharePoint systems also have an administrative Recycle Bin that captures all deletions in the system. Therefore, it may be possible for your system administrator to restore items that you permanently delete from the user Recycle Bin depending upon the retention policies enforced by your organization.

Hands On Exercise

Exercise 6-4

Delete and restore a risk list item.

1. On the *Risks* list homepage, hover your mouse pointer over the name of one of your risks in the *Title* field to reveal the pick list button and click to expose the pick list.

2. Select the *Delete Item* selection and the system displays a confirmation to delete the item. Click the *OK* button in the confirmation warning to delete the item.

3. Click on the *Recycle Bin* link at the bottom of the *Quick Launch* menu. The system displays the *Recycle Bin* page.

4. Select the checkbox next to the item that you just deleted and then click the *Restore Selection* link above the content area. The system displays a restore item confirmation. Click the *OK* button in the confirmation dialog to complete the restore action.

5. Click the *Risks* link from the *Quick Launch* menu and the system displays the *Risks* list page. Confirm that your restored item appears on the page.

Managing Project Issues

An issue is any type of problem or concern you might experience and need to manage during the life of the project. Another way to think of an issue is to consider it a realized risk. Whether or not you predicted their occurrence through proactive risk management, issues are events that cause problems that require management. The issues management features in Project Server allow you to identify, track, and manage issues in collaboration with your project team and stakeholders. Examples of project issues include a shortage of resources or an unanticipated hardware upgrade requirement.

Creating a New Issue

The process for creating a new issue is nearly identical to creating a new risk, although the fields in the custom web parts for these are different. Click the *Issues* link in the *Quick Launch* menu of your Project Site and Project Server 2010 displays the *Issues* page, as shown in Figure 6 - 19.

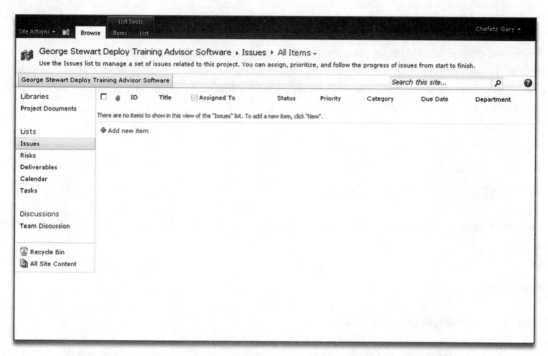

Figure 6 - 19: Issues page for the Deploy Training Advisor Software project

Click the *Add New Item* link on the page. The system displays the *New Item* dialog for issues shown in Figure 6 - 20.

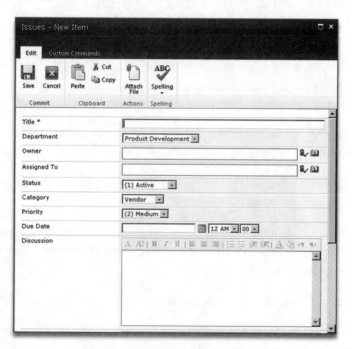

Figure 6 - 20: New Item dialog for Issues

165

The *New Item* dialog for issues contains only two required fields, the *Title* field and *Status* field. Enter a descriptive name for the issue in the *Title* field. The same caution about the *Status* field for risks applies to the *Status* field for issues. You must not alter the values in this field or you break the display of issue status in Project Web App. Use the same process described in the Creating a New Risk topical section of this module to enter data in the *Owner*, *Assigned To*, *Status*, and *Category* fields.

Click the *Priority* pick list and select an item from the list. Notice that the system allows you to set the priority of an issue as High, Medium, or Low. Enter a date in the *Due Date* field. In the *Discussion* field, enter preliminary discussion details to describe the issue, including potential resolutions for the issue. Do not enter any information in the *Resolution* field, unless you already have an idea about ways to resolve the issue. You use the same process described in the Creating a New Risk topical section to link your new issue to a file or to other issues, tasks, risks, and documents. Click the *Save* button to save and complete your new issue.

Hands On Exercise

Exercise 6-5

Create a new issue and link it to a risk.

1. From your Deploy Training Advisor Software Project Site homepage select the *Issues* link from the *Quick Launch* menu. The system displays the *Issues* homepage.

2. Click the *Add new item* link to launch the *New Item* dialog for issues. In the *New Item* dialog, enter a name for your issue in the *Title* field that closely relates to one of the risks you created earlier. Enter or select your own user account in both the *Owner* and *Assigned To* pick lists.

3. Leave the default *Active* selection for the *Status* field and the default *Category 2* selection for the *Category* field. Select a priority value in the *Priority* field. Set a value in the *Due Date* field for 10 days from today.

4. Enter an opening discussion in the *Discussion* field and assume that there is nothing to enter into the *Resolution* field at this time.

5. Select the *Custom Commands* tab to expose the *Custom Commands* ribbon and click the *Link Items* button. The system displays the *Link Items* dialog.

6. Select the *Project Risks* item from the *Item Type* pick list then select the risk that closely relates to your issue to create a "risk realized" issue. Click the *OK* button to link your new issue to your previously created risk.

7. In the *New Item* dialog click the *Save* button to create your new risk.

8. Repeat this process at least two more times to define several issues for your project linking them to other items rather than risks.

Viewing and Editing Existing Issues

Figure 6 - 21 shows the *Issues* page for my Deploy Training Advisor Software project. Notice that there are three active issues associated with the project. Notice also that I customized the values for the *Category* field.

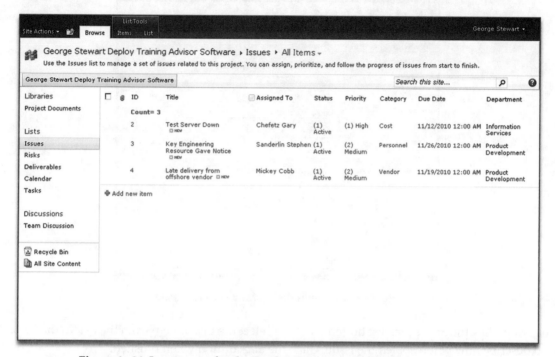

Figure 6 - 21: Issues page for the Deploy Training Advisor Software project

Similar to risks, the system allows you to do the following with existing issues:

- Apply a view to the *Issues* page.

- Sort the issues by the data in any column.

- AutoFilter the issues using the data in any column.

- View an issue.

- Edit an issue.

- Delete an issue.

- Subscribe to e-mail alerts about changes to an issue.

Because I described how to do each of these in the Working with Existing Risks topical section of this module, I do not repeat this information here except for editing an existing issue, because you need to know how to close an issue when it is resolved. I also cover viewing issue version history because I did not cover that in the risk topics.

To edit an existing issue, float your mouse pointer over the issue in the *Title* field, click the pick list button, and select the *Edit Item* option on the pick list. Project Server 2010 displays the *Issues* dialog for the selected issue, as shown in Figure 6 - 22.

Figure 6 - 22: Issues dialog for a selected Issue

To close the issue, click the *Status* pick list button and then select the *Closed* item from the list. In the *Resolution* field, enter text to describe how you resolved the issue. Click the *Save* button when finished.

Hands On Exercise

Exercise 6-6

Edit and close an issue.

1. Float your mouse pointer over one of the new issues you created in Exercise 6-5, and then click the pick list button.

2. Select the *Edit Item* item on the pick list menu. The system opens the *Issues* dialog.

3. Click the *Status* pick list button and select the *Closed* item from the list.

4. Enter text in the *Resolution* field to describe how you resolved the issue.

5. Click the *Save* button to save the closed issue.

6. Close the Internet Explorer application window for the *Project Site* page and return to the *Home* page in Project Web App.

Working with Version History

If your issues list, or any SharePoint list you may work with, has version control enabled, the system automatically creates a new version of list items each time someone edits them. To view the item history for a list item, you can select the *Version History* item by floating your mouse pointer over the *Title* field / column? for your issue, and selecting it from the pick list. The system displays the *Version History* dialog shown in Figure 6 - 23.

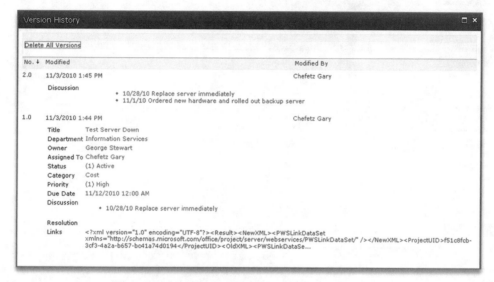

Figure 6 - 23: Version History dialog for a list item

Notice that the system creates a version record when you first create the item and then creates a version record every time someone edits the item, which displays the details for the version. To close the *Version History* dialog, click the *Close* **X** button.

Viewing Your Assigned Issues and Risks

Project Server 2010 offers you a quick way to view and manage the risks and issues assigned to you. Navigate to any page in Project Web App that displays the *Quick Launch* menu, and then click the *Issues and Risks* link in the *My Work* section. The system displays the *Issues and Risks* page, shown in Figure 6 - 24. The page displays issues and risks for George Stewart to whom the software assigned one active issue and one active risk, each of which belongs to its own project.

Warning: This page confuses many users. Notice the large gap between the two data table sections and the lack of header labels for data grid. Many users need to scroll to see the *Risks* section at the bottom of the page and leave the page before discovering this. You must remember that the software presents this page with issues in the top section and risks listed at the bottom. Your Project Server administrator can customize this page to make it more user-friendly.

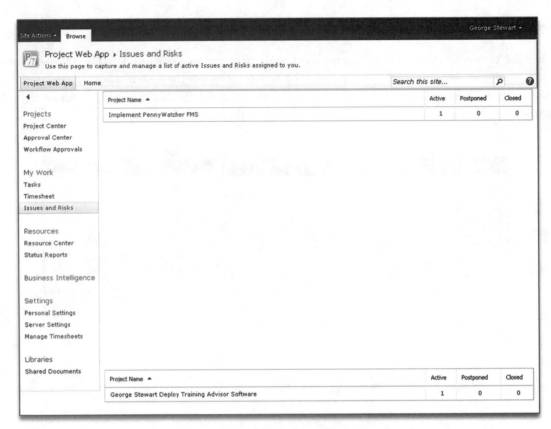

Figure 6 - 24: Issues and Risks page for George Stewart

To access either the *Risks* page or the *Issues* page for one of the listed projects, click the project name in the *Issues* or *Risks* section of the page. Project Server 2010 displays the *Risks* or *Issues* page for the selected project applying the *All Risks Assigned to Me* view. Figure 6 - 25 shows George Stewart's *Risks* page for the Deploy Training Advisor Software project.

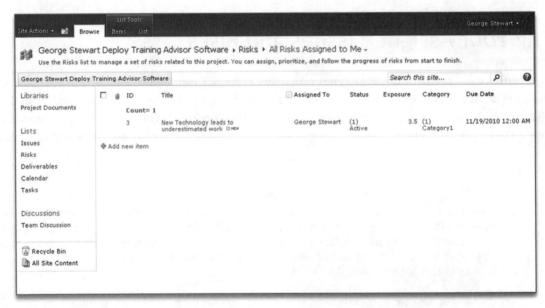

Figure 6 - 25: Risks page for George Stewart for the Deploy Training Advisor Software project

Notice that the page defaults to the *All Risks Assigned to Me* view. You can change the view by clicking on the pick list button next to the view name in the *Browse* area. You can apply any public view to this page by switching to the *List* ribbon and using the *View* selection tools from the ribbon.

Hands On Exercise

Exercise 6-7

View risks and issues assigned to you.

1. From any page that displays the *Quick Launch* menu in Project Web App, click the *Issues and Risks* link in the *My Work* section.

2. On the *Issues and Risks* page, notice the names of any projects containing issues or risks assigned to you.

3. Click the name of a project containing an issue or risk assigned to you.

4. Examine the *Issues* page or the *Risks* page for any items assigned to you.

5. Click the *Navigate Up* icon ![icon] and use the bread crumb menu to return to the Project Web App homepage.

Managing Project Documents

During the typical project life cycle, you and your team create multiple documents associated with the project. During project definition, you might create a project charter and a statement of work document. During the execution stage of the project, you might create change control documents and expense reports. At project closure, you might create a lessons learned document to capture the knowledge gained during the project. Regardless of which type of project documents you create, each document is a part of your project's "electronic paper trail" and you can manage these documents within Project Server 2010 Project Sites.

Viewing and Creating Document Libraries

You learned in your introduction to Project Sites that each site contains a project document library for storing individual documents. Each Project Web App instance also has a general document library provided for the shared use of all Project Web App users, not just for members of specific projects. You can open the *Shared Documents* library by clicking the *Shared Documents* link from the *Libraries* section at the bottom of the standard *Quick Launch* menu. When you select the *Libraries* link, the system displays the *All Site Content* page listing all available document libraries in the PWA site as shown in Figure 6 - 26. Every PWA instance contains a single *Shared Documents* library for general use and a number of others that support other functionality in the system.

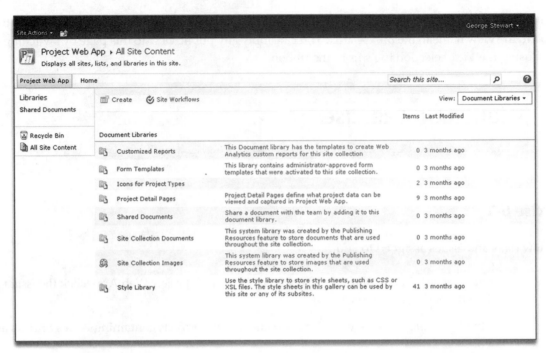

Figure 6 - 26: All Site Content page showing all PWA site Document libraries

When you click the same link from the homepage of your Project Site, the system displays the same page for your specific site as shown in Figure 6 - 27.

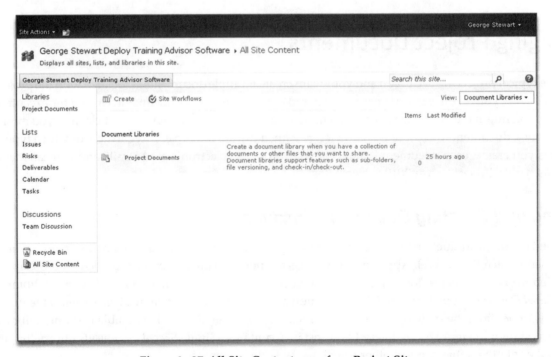

Figure 6 - 27: All Site Content page for a Project Site

Notice that the site contains a single *Project Documents* library.

If you enable the versioning feature in a document library, the system creates a new version of a document every time a user edits and saves the document. If you need to reverse the changes made to a document, you can restore the previous version and then continue working with the document.

Uploading Documents to a Document Library

To begin the process of uploading an existing document to a document library, click the name of the library in the *Libraries* section of the *Quick Launch* menu. The system opens the *Project Document* library for the Deploy Training Advisor Software project as shown in Figure 6 - 28.

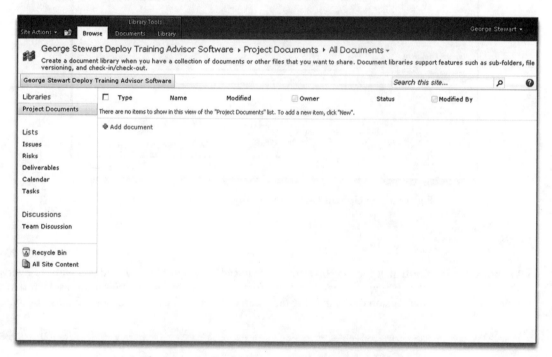

Figure 6 - 28: Project Documents library homepage

Project Server 2010 offers you three ways to upload documents to a document library:

- Upload one document at a time.

- Upload a batch of documents in a single operation.

- Use the Explorer view to copy documents from local folders and network shares.

To upload one document at a time, click the *Add document* link on the page, or click on the *Documents* tab to reveal the *Documents* ribbon, then click on the *Upload Document* pick list button and select the *Upload Document* item from the pick list. Project Server 2010 displays the *Upload Document* dialog for the selected document library, as shown in Figure 6 - 29 with version control enabled, and in Figure 6 - 30 with version control disabled. Notice that the option in the *Upload Document* section below the *Name* field changes based on the version control setting.

With Version Control: If your document library uses version control, leave the *Add as new version to existing files* option selected. Click the *OK* button.

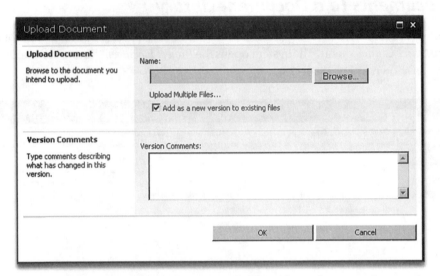

Figure 6 - 29: Upload Document dialog with version control

Without Version Control: If the file currently exists in the document library, and you want to overwrite the existing file with the new file, then leave the default *Overwrite existing files* option selected. If you want to create a new version of the existing file, then deselect the *Overwrite existing files* option.

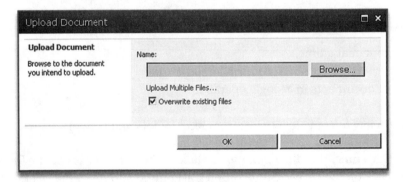

Figure 6 - 30: Upload Document dialog without version control

Click the *Browse* button. The system displays the *Choose File* dialog shown in Figure 6 - 31.

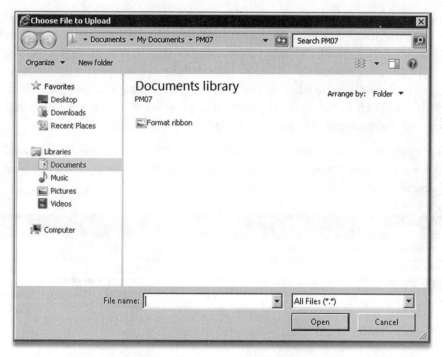

Figure 6 - 31: Choose File dialog

Navigate to the folder containing the file you want to upload, select the file, and then click the *Open* button. Project Server 2010 lists the path to the file in the *Name* field in the *Upload Document* dialog shown previously in Figure 6 - 29 and in Figure 6 - 30. The system may display a *Processing* message window as it uploads a copy of the selected document and then displays the *Edit Item* dialog shown in Figure 6 - 32.

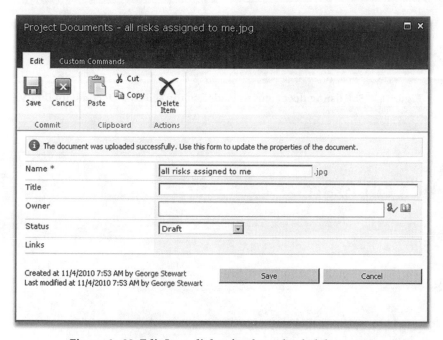

Figure 6 - 32: Edit Item dialog for the uploaded document

On the *Edit Item* page, the only required field is the *Name* field. You can rename the document by changing the text in the *Name* field. If you want to add a title for the document, enter a title in the *Title* field. Enter the name of the docu-

175

ment owner in the *Owner* field, and use the *Check Names* and *Browse* buttons at the right end of the field, to locate names if necessary. Click the *Status* pick list button and select the status of the document. The default *Status* options include *Draft*, *Ready for Review*, and *Final*. From the *Commit* section of the *Edit* ribbon, click the *Save* button to complete the document upload process or click the *Cancel* button to cancel the upload. Notice that these buttons appear at the bottom of the dialog as well. Just like the *Edit Item* dialog for list items that you worked with earlier in this module, you can delete a document from this dialog, use clipboard tools, and select the *Custom Commands* ribbon to access the *Link Items* button and link the document to issues, risks, tasks and other documents.

Project Server 2010 displays the newly uploaded document in the document library, as shown in Figure 6 - 33. You can apply ribbons, views, sort, and AutoFilter the list of documents in the library the same way you can with risks, issues and other SharePoint lists.

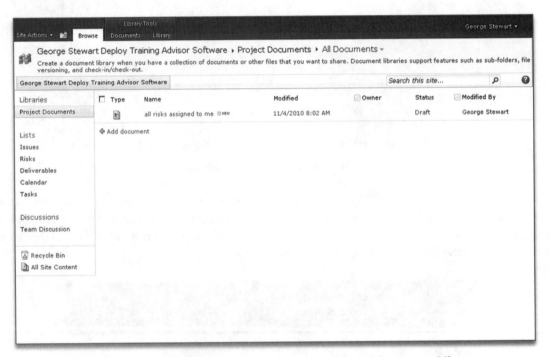

Figure 6 - 33: Existing document uploaded to the selected Document Library

Hands On Exercise

Exercise 6-8

Upload a document to the Project Documents library.

1. Navigate to your Deploy Training Advisor Software Project Site homepage and click the *Project Documents* link in the *Quick Launch* menu.

2. Click on the *Documents* tab and in the *New* section click the *Upload Document* pick list button, then select the *Upload Document* item from the pick list. Alternately, click the *Add Document* link in the content area of the page. The system displays the *Upload Document* dialog.

3. Click the *Browse* button and the system displays the *Choose File to Upload* dialog. Select a Microsoft Word document from your PC's hard drive or from a network folder and click the *Open* button, then click the *OK* button. The system displays a processing message and then displays the *Edit Item* dialog.

4. In the *Edit Item* dialog, enter a unique title for the document in the *Title* field, enter your name in the *Owner* field, and specify a status for the document in the *Status* field. Click the *Save* button and the system returns to the library homepage.

5. Examine your new document in the *Project Documents* library.

You can upload multiple files as a batch from the *New* section of the *Document* ribbon by clicking the *Upload Document* pick list button and selecting the *Upload Multiple Documents* item from the pick list. If you have Office 2010 installed on your computer, Project Server 2010 displays the *Upload Multiple Documents* dialog shown in Figure 6 - 34.

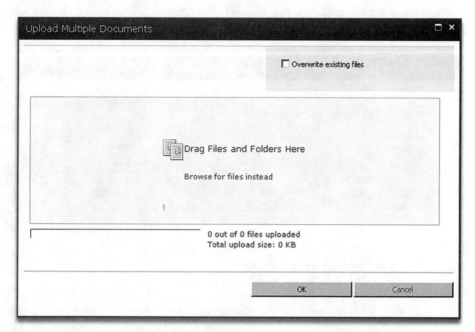

Figure 6 - 34: Upload Multiple Documents dialog with Office 2010

If you have Office 2007 installed, the system displays the *Upload Multiple Documents* dialog shown in Figure 6 - 35.

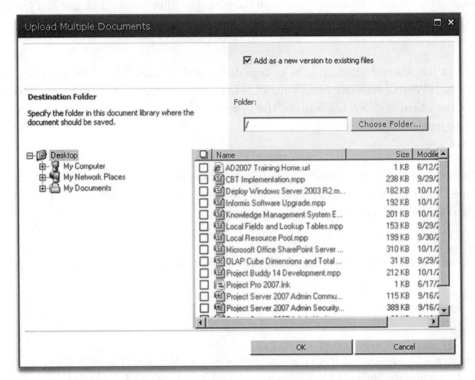

Figure 6 - 35: Upload Multiple Documents dialog with Office 2010

The dialog you see when using Office 2010 provides two methods for selecting files: **Drag and Drop** which allows you to drag files from an Explorer window or other location that supports file dragging or **File Select** which allows you to use a standard *Open* dialog to choose your files. I do not demonstrate the latter technique here. Figure 6 - 36 shows the *Upload Multiple Documents* dialog after dragging documents to the *Drag Files and Folders Here* area. Notice that you can remove files by clicking the *Remove* link in the *Status* column.

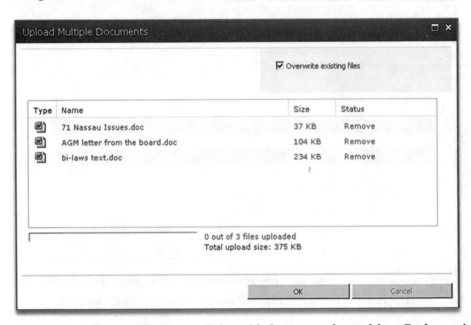

Figure 6 - 36: Upload Multiple Documents dialog with documents dragged from Explorer window

On the *Upload Multiple Documents* page, click the *OK* button when you complete your file selections. The system displays progress information in the dialog and updates the status of each document as shown in Figure 6 - 37.

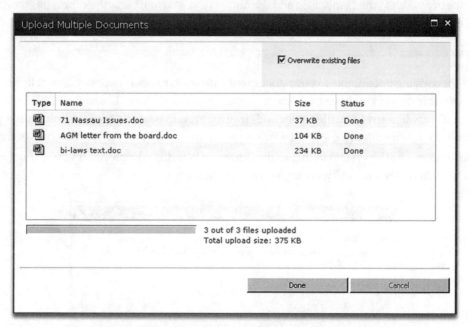

Figure 6 - 37: Upload Multiple Documents dialog with upload status updated

Click the *Done* button to close the dialog and return to your Project Site library homepage. When the system uploads the batch of files, it does not select a name in the *Owner* field for each document, and it sets the *Status* field value to *Draft* for each document. You can see this for the four uploaded documents in Figure 6 - 38. When you upload multiple files, the system does not present an *Edit Item* dialog for each item as it does for single file uploads.

Figure 6 - 38: Project Documents library includes four newly-uploaded documents

To specify values in the *Owner* field and the *Status* field, you must edit the properties for each document.

The third method for copying documents to your documents library is to open your document library using Windows Explorer. You can do this only if you have the correct SharePoint permissions. Using the *Explorer* view allows you to treat the document library like any local file folder and drag, copy, and paste documents into it. To open the library in *Explorer* view, select the *Library* tab to expose the *Library* menu. In the *Connect &Export* section of the ribbon click the *Open with Explorer* button. The system launches the library in Windows Explorer. If you do not have permission to take this action, the system displays the warning shown in Figure 6 - 39.

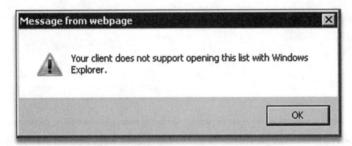

Figure 6 - 39: Explorer View prohibited

 Hands On Exercise

Exercise 6-9 for Office 2010 Users

Upload multiple documents to the Project Documents library.

1. Navigate to your Deploy Training Advisor Software Project Site homepage and click the *Project Documents* link in the *Quick Launch* menu.

2. Click on the *Documents* tab and in the *New* section click the *Upload Document* pick list button and select the *Upload Multiple Documents* item from the pick list. The system displays the *Upload Multiple Documents* dialog.

3. You can upload documents in one of two ways:

- Size your browser window so that you can drag files into the *Drag Files and Folders Here* area of the dialog from your desktop or Windows Explorer, and then click the *OK* button after dragging your selected files. After you click the *OK* button in the *Upload Multiple Documents* dialog, the system reports its progress in the dialog.

- Click the *Browse for files instead* link and the system displays the *Open* dialog. Select multiple documents from your PC's hard drive or from a network folder and click the *Open* button. Click the *OK* button in the *Upload Multiple Documents* dialog, the system reports its progress in the dialog.

4. When the system completes the upload, the *OK* button becomes a *Done* button. Click the *Done* button to close the dialog and return to the library.

5. Examine your new documents in the *Project Documents* library and verify the new additions.

Exercise 6-9 for Office 2007 Users

Upload multiple documents to the Project Documents library.

1. Navigate to your Deploy Training Advisor Software Project Site homepage and click the *Project Documents* link in the *Quick Launch* menu.

2. Click on the *Documents* tab and in the *New* section click the *Upload Document* pick list button and select the *Upload Multiple Documents* item from the pick list. The system displays the *Upload Multiple Documents* dialog.

3. Use the folder navigation tool to the left of the file selection pane to navigate to your source folder. After selecting a source folder, select multiple documents from that location by clicking the checkboxes next to the file names. Click the *OK* button and if the system prompts you with a confirmation dialog click the *Yes* button to continue. The system uploads your documents and then returns to the *Project Documents* library.

4. Examine your new documents in the *Project Documents* library and verify the new additions.

Creating a New Folder in a Documents Library

In addition to uploading existing documents to a document library, Project Server 2010 also allows you to organize your content by creating folders within the library.

When you use folders to organize content in SharePoint libraries, you are not taking full advantage of the power of SharePoint. Always consider using content types and metadata with views and filters to organize content in SharePoint libraries and lists.

To create a new folder in your document library, display the *Documents* ribbon and in the *New* section click the *New Folder* button. The system displays the *New Folder* dialog shown in Figure 6 - 40.

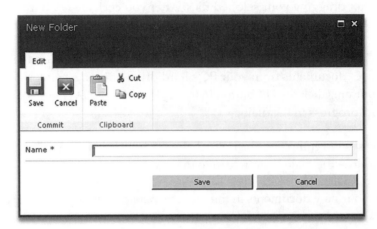

Figure 6 - 40: New Folder page

Enter the name of the new folder in the *Name* field and then from the *Commit* section of the *Edit* ribbon, or at the bottom of the dialog, click the *Save* button. Project Server 2010 displays the folder in your document library, as shown in Figure 6 - 41. Notice that I created a new folder called Archive.

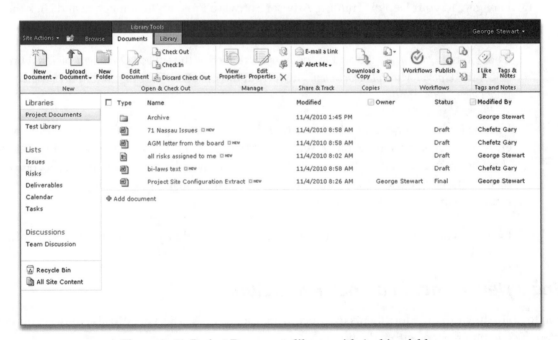

Figure 6 - 41: Project Documents library with Archive folder

 When you add folders to SharePoint libraries, various SharePoint tools become aware of the folders. For instance, the *Upload Documents* dialog prompts for a *Destination Folder* value when it detects the presence of folders in the library.

Hands On Exercise

Exercise 6-10

Create a new folder in a document library.

1. In your *Project Documents* library, display the *Documents* ribbon and in the *New* section of the ribbon, click the *New Folder* button. The system displays the *New Folder* dialog.

2. Enter the name **Archive** for the new folder and click the *Save* button.

3. Notice your new folder in the *Project Documents* library.

Working with Existing Documents in a Documents Library

Depending on your permissions in the system, Project Server 2010 allows you to do the following to work with an existing document:

- View the document properties.

- Edit the document properties.

- Edit the document in the Office application used to create it.

- Check out the document.

- View compliance details (configuration dependent)

- Set alerts on the document

- Send the document to another location or application.

- Delete the document.

To perform any of the above actions with an existing document in a document library, float your mouse pointer over the name of the document and then click the pick list button, as shown in Figure 6 - 42.

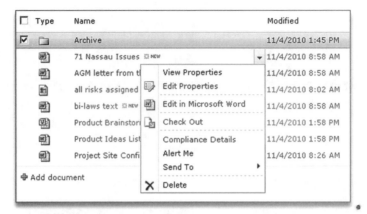

Figure 6 - 42: Options for working with an existing document

Viewing and Editing Document Properties

To view the properties for any document, float your mouse pointer over the name of the document, click the pick list button, and then click the *View Properties* item on the pick list. Project Server 2010 displays the *View Item* dialog for the selected document, as shown in Figure 6 - 43.

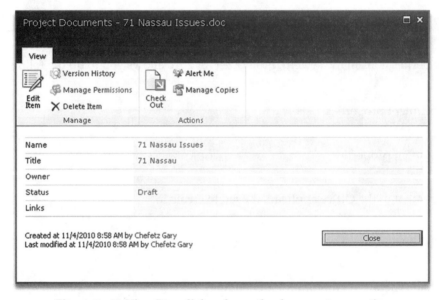

Figure 6 - 43: View Item dialog shows the document properties

Like the *View Item* dialog for list items, when you click to view only, you cannot edit any fields in the dialog until you click the *Edit Item* button in the ribbon. Notice that you can check out the item before you edit it.

Whe a document library does not have version control enabled, it is up to the user to decide whether to check out the document prior to editing it. When you enable version control in a SharePoint library, the system enforces check out and check in rules for editing.

From the *Manage* section of the *View* menu in the *View Item* dialog, click the *Edit* button. Alternately, select the *Edit Properties* item from the pick list shown previously in Figure 6 - 42. The system displays the *Edit Item* dialog for documents shown in Figure 6 - 44.

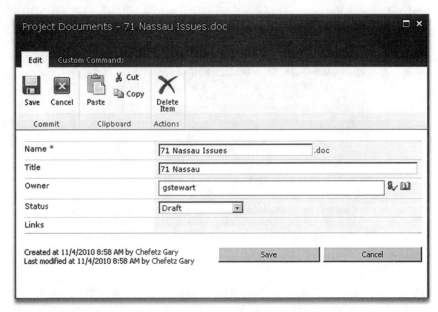

Figure 6 - 44: Edit Item dialog for a document

The editable properties for any document include *Name, Title, Owner, Status,* and *Links*. Just as you did with list items, you apply the *Custom Commands* ribbon to use the *Link* button. Notice that you can also delete a document from the dialog; however, there are more expedient ways to access this feature. Click the *Save* button to save your changes and close the dialog or click the *Cancel* button to close the dialog without saving.

Hands On Exercise

Exercise 6-11

View and edit properties for an existing document in the Project Documents library.

1. Float your mouse pointer over the name of a Microsoft Word document in the *Project Documents* library, click the pick list button, and select the *View Properties* item on the pick list.

2. Examine the properties for the selected document in the *View Item* dialog.

3. In the *Manage* section of the *View* ribbon, click the *Edit Item* button. The system opens the *Edit Item* dialog.

4. Enter your account in the *Owner* field and verify your entry.

5. Click the *Save* button at the bottom of the dialog to save your change

Checking Out a Document Manually

If you are using a Microsoft Office application earlier than the 2007 version, you cannot check out the document from within the Office application. Instead, you must manually check out the document from the document library. To check out a document, float your mouse pointer over the name of the document, click the pick list button, and then select the *Check Out* item on the pick list shown previously in Figure 6 - 42. Project Server 2010 displays the confirmation dialog shown in Figure 6 - 45.

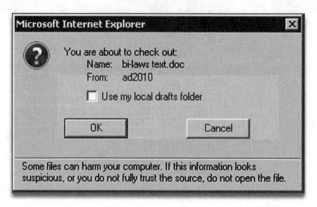

Figure 6 - 45: Confirmation dialog for check out

Click the *OK* button in the confirmation dialog to complete the check out. The system displays the checked-out status of the document by adding a green and white arrow logo to the lower right corner of the indicator for the selected document. Float your mouse pointer over the indicator to determine who currently has the document checked out, as shown in Figure 6 - 46. Alternately, you can modify the view to show the check-out information for each document.

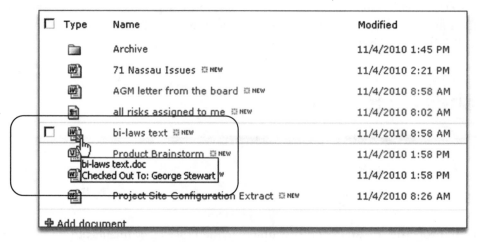

Figure 6 - 46: Selected document checked out to George Stewart

When you close the document after editing, you must manually check in the document by floating your mouse pointer over the name of the document, clicking the pick list button, and then selecting the *Check In* item on the pick list. After you check out a document, the selections on the item pick list change as shown in Figure 6 - 47.

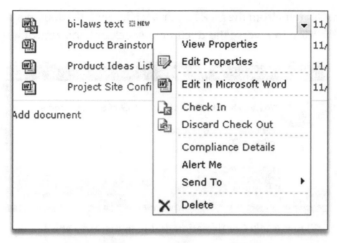

Figure 6 - 47: Pick list after document check out

Notice that you can choose from two options: *Check In* or *Discard Check Out*. Select the *Discard Check Out* option if you have not made any changes to the document; otherwise, select the *Check In* option on the menu and the system displays the *Check In* dialog shown in Figure 6 - 48.

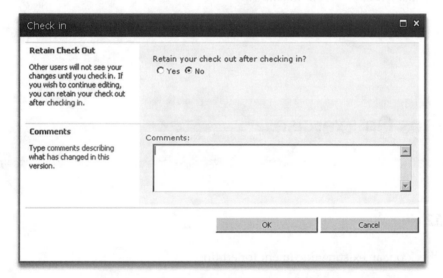

Figure 6 - 48: Check In dialog for a document

Enter information in the *Comments* field in the *Check In* dialog about your latest editing session and select whether to retain the checkout after checking in the current version, and then click the *OK* button. The system checks in the document and adds your comments to the *Version History* for the document if your document is version control enabled.

When you use document check out in a SharePoint library, any user who opens your document sees the document version in the state in which it was when you checked it out, even if you upload more current versions. MSProjectExperts recommends that you periodically check in interim versions of your document when editing over long periods, so that others can access the changes.

If you select the *Discard Check Out* item from the pick list, Project Server 2010 displays the confirmation dialog shown in Figure 6 - 49. Click the *OK* button to reverse the document check out and return it to a checked-in state.

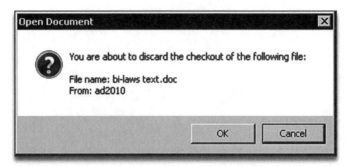

Figure 6 - 49: Confirmation dialog to discard a check out

 If you check in a document after accidentally checking it out, the system creates an additional version of the document if you have versioning enabled. If you discard the check out, the system does not create an additional version of the document.

 Hands On Exercise

Exercise 6-12

Open and check out an existing document for editing.

1. Float your mouse pointer over the name of a Microsoft Word document in the *Project Documents* library, click the pick list button, and select the *Check Out* item from the list.

2. When the system prompts, click the *OK* button to check out the document.

3. Float your mouse pointer over the name of the same Microsoft Word document in the *Project Documents* library, click the pick list button, and select the *Check In* item from the list.

4. Add a comment and click the *OK* button to check in your document.

Working with Document Copies

You can manage copies of a document from the *View Item* dialog for a document shown previously in Figure 6 - 43. In your project management environment, you might wish to create and manage multiple copies of a single document. For example, you might have a draft copy of a document, a copy that is in revision and a final completed copy as well.

To manage additional copies of a document, from the *Actions* section of the *View* ribbon click the *Manage Copies* button. The system displays the *Manage Copies* dialog shown in Figure 6 - 50.

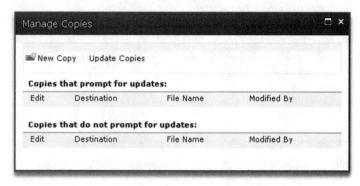

Figure 6 - 50: Manage Copies dialog for a document

To create a new copy of the selected document, click the *New Copy* button at the top of the page. The system displays the *Edit Copy* dialog shown in Figure 6 - 51.

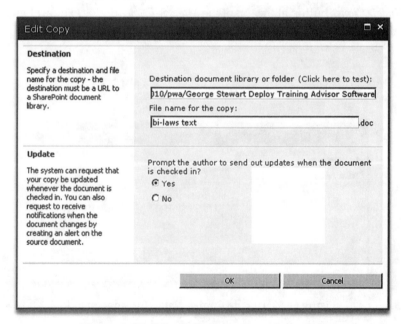

Figure 6 - 51: Edit Copy dialog for a document

Using the *Edit Copy* page, optionally enter an alternate location for the document in the *Destination document library or folder* field. Enter a name for the new copy of the document in the *File name for the copy* field. In the *Update* section of the page, select the *Yes* or *No* option to determine whether the document editor must send an update after editing and checking in the document copy. Click the *OK* button. Project Server 2010 redisplays the *Manage Copies* dialog as shown in Figure 6 - 52.

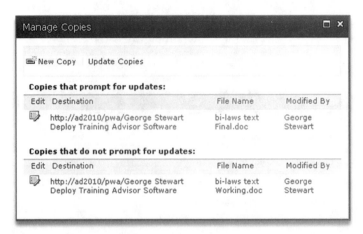

Figure 6 - 52: Manage Copies dialog shows two copies of a document

Notice that the *Manage Copies* dialog shows two new copies of the document. One copy represents the in-progress working copy of the document, and requires an update by the editor when checking in the edited document. The other copy represents the final draft of the presentation and does not require an update from the editor. To update one or more copies, click the *Update Copies* button at the top of the *Manage Copies* dialog. The system displays the *Update Copies* dialog shown in Figure 6 - 53.

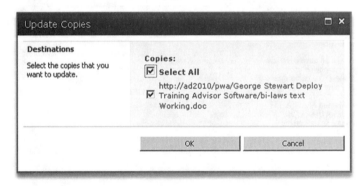

Figure 6 - 53: Update Copies dialog for a document

On the *Update Copies* dialog, select the option checkbox to the left of each copy you wish to update, or click the *Select All* option to select all copies. The system displays the *Copy Progress* dialog shown in Figure 6 - 54.

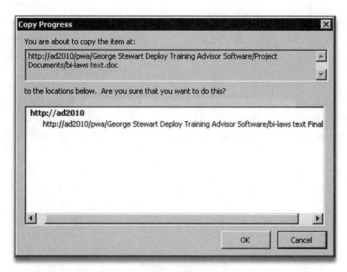

Figure 6 - 54: Copy Progress dialog for document copies

Click the *OK* button to complete the update process. After updating the copy, the system closes the *Manage Copies* dialog, unless you encounter an error.

Editing a Document

To edit a document in a document library, float your mouse pointer over the name of the document, click the pick list button, and then select the *Edit in Microsoft* _____ item on the pick list. The system opens the document for editing in the application used to create it, such as Microsoft Word 2010 shown in Figure 6 - 55.

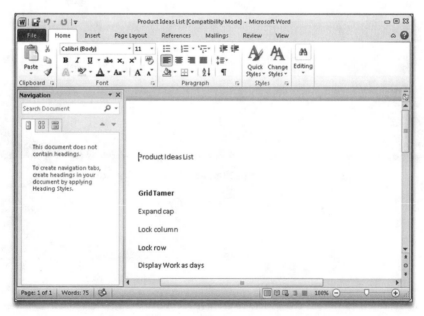

Figure 6 - 55: Document open in Microsoft Word

In an environment where multiple users may need to edit a document in a *Document* library, you should always check out the document after opening it for editing. When you check out a document, Project Server 2010 prevents all other users from opening the document for editing, thus preventing multiple unwanted versions of a document.

To check out a document using any Microsoft 2010 application, click the *File* tab and then select the *Info* tab on the left hand side of the *Backstage* as shown in Figure 6 - 56. At the bottom of the main area of the page, click the *Manage Versions* button to open the pick list shown in the figure. Select the *Check Out* item to check out the document.

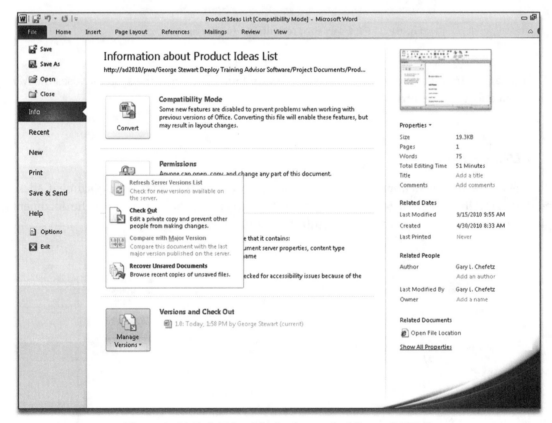

Figure 6 - 56: Info Tab of the backstage in Microsoft Word

The system checks out the document and closes the *Backstage*. To verify that the system checked out your document form the SharePoint library, return to the *Info* tab in the *Backstage* and your information display should appear like the one shown in Figure 6 - 57.

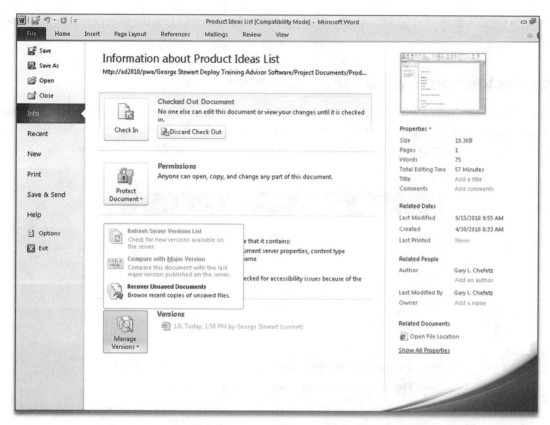

Figure 6 - 57: Backstage with checked out document information

Notice in the figure that the system displays *Checked Out Document* information at the top of the page with a prominent *Check In* button and a somewhat less prominent *Discard Check Out* button. Notice also that the *Manage Versions* pick list changes to reflect the current state of the document.

After you edit your document and save your changes, you must check in the document before others can view the changes. To check in a document using any Microsoft 2010 application, click the *Edit* button and select the *Info* tab in the *Backstage* to reveal the page shown previously in Figure 6 - 57. Click the *Check In* button and the system displays the *Check In* dialog shown in Figure 6 - 58.

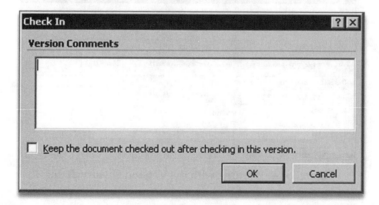

Figure 6 - 58: Check In dialog for a document

In the *Check In* dialog, enter information in the *Version Comments* field about your latest editing session and then click the *OK* button. The system checks in the document and adds your comments to the version history for the document if your system is version control enabled. After you check in the document, close the document and exit the Microsoft application.

Viewing the Version History for a Document

If you enabled versioning in your SharePoint document library, you can view the version history of each document. Float your mouse pointer over the name of the document, click the pick list button, and then select the *Version History* item on the pick list. Project Server 2010 displays the *Version History* dialog shown in Figure 6 - 59.

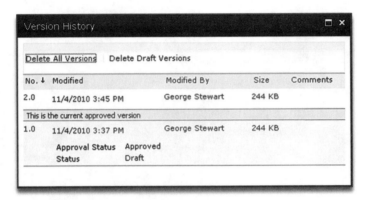

Figure 6 - 59: Version History dialog for a document

The *Version History* dialog shows you the running history for all versions of a document, sorted in descending order so that the latest version appears at the top of the list. Notice in Figure 6 - 59 that there are two versions of the selected document. Notice that the records include comments that users enter while checking in the document. These comments are very useful when people make a habit of entering them.

To manage the versions of the selected document, float your mouse pointer over the date and time of the version you wish to manage and then click the pick list button and select an action item as shown in Figure 6 - 60.

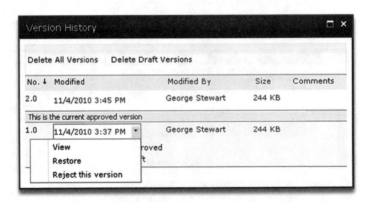

Figure 6 - 60: Working with the Version History dialog

The system offers you three options for managing a document version. Using these options, you can view, restore, or reject any version. If you select the *View* item from the pick list menu, the system displays the *View Item* dialog for the selected version, as shown in Figure 6 - 61. Notice that the dialog contains tools for working with versions.

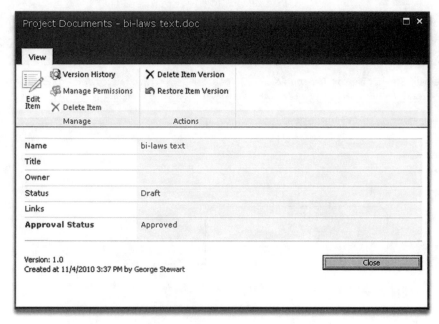

Figure 6 - 61: View Item page for a selected version of a document

Use the buttons in the *Actions* section of the ribbon to delete the selected version, restore it, or return to the *Version History* dialog. If you click the *Close* button, the system returns you to the *Document Library* page. You can restore any previous version and make it the current version of any document. To restore any previous version, select the *Restore* item from the pick list menu or click the *Restore Item Version* item on the ribbon. The system displays the confirmation dialog shown in Figure 6 - 62.

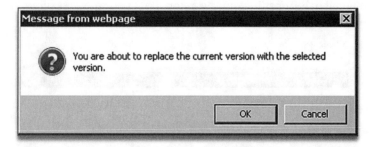

Figure 6 - 62: Confirmation dialog for restoring a previous version

Click the *OK* button to complete the process of restoring a previous version and make it the current version of any document. The system creates a new current version from the previous version, as shown in Figure 6 - 63.

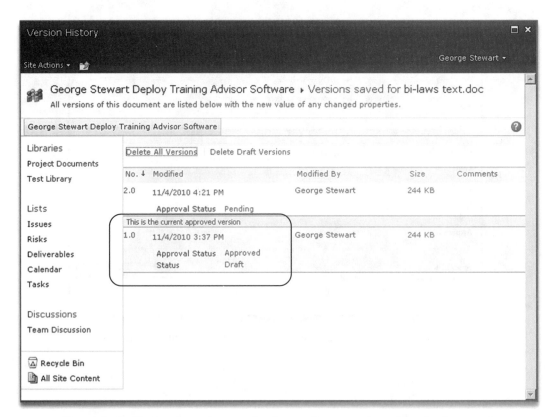

Figure 6 - 63: Restored previous version is now the current version of a document

The system always opens the current version of a document when you select the *Edit in Microsoft* _____ item for any document in a *Document* library.

Project Server 2010 also allows you to deny any version of a document if you no longer want it to be active in the *Document* library but want to retain it in history. To deny a version, float your mouse pointer over the version you want to deny and then click the *Reject this Version* item from the pick list menu. The system displays the confirmation dialog shown in Figure 6 - 64.

**Figure 6 - 64: Confirmation dialog
to delete a document version**

Click the *OK* button to deny the version.

Deleting Documents and Document Versions

Notice at the top of the *Version History* dialog shown previously in Figure 6 - 63, that you can also delete versions. The system allows you to delete only draft versions of the document or delete all versions of the document except the current document version and send them to the recycle bin. To delete versions of a document in a *Document* library, click either the *Delete All Versions* link or the *Delete Draft Versions* link at the top of the page. The system prompts you with a warning similar to the one shown in Figure 6 - 65.

Figure 6 - 65: Warning about deleting versions

 The system does not delete a document that is checked out.

To delete the current version of a document and delete all the previous versions along with it, on the *Document Library* page, float your mouse pointer over the name of the document, click the pick list button, and then select the *Delete* item on the pick list. The system displays the confirmation dialog shown in Figure 6 - 66.

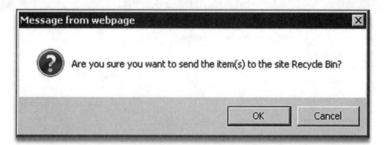

Figure 6 - 66: Confirmation dialog to delete a document

Click the *OK* button to complete the deletion. The system removes the deleted document and all of its versions from its *Document* library and transfers them to the Project Site Recycle Bin.

Sending a Document to another Location or Application

Project Server 2010 allows you to send a document and document information from a *Document* library to another location or application using the following methods:

- Send a copy of the document to the location of existing copies of the document.

- Send a copy of the document to a new folder in the WSS folder system.

- Send the URL of the document to others in an e-mail message.

- Download a copy of the document to your hard drive or to a network drive.

To send a document or document information to another location, float your mouse pointer over the name of the document, click the pick list button, and then select the *Send To* item on the pick list. The system displays the *Send To* submenu shown in Figure 6 - 67.

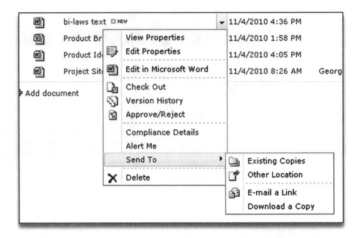

Figure 6 - 67: Send to submenu for a selected document

Select the *Existing Copies* submenu item to send the selected document to the location where you previously saved copies of the document. The system displays the *Update Copies* page shown previously in Figure 6 - 53. Select the *Other Location* submenu item to send the document to another location or to create additional copies of the document. The system displays the *Update Copies* page shown in Figure 6 - 68.

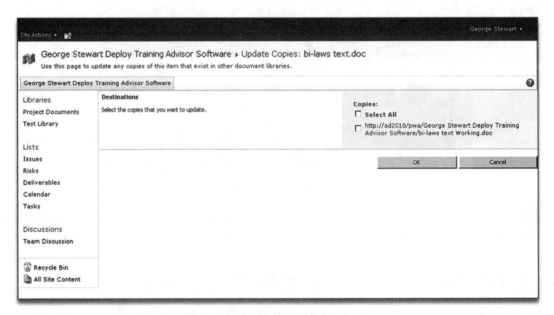

Figure 6 - 68: Update Copies page

The *Update Copies* page is similar to the *Update Copies* dialog you learned about previously. Refer to the Managing Document Copies section of this module for more information about creating and managing copies of a document. Select the *E-mail a Link* submenu item to send the URL for the document to others in an e-mail message. The system launches your default e-mail application, creates a new e-mail message, and then inserts the URL for the document in the body of the message. In the outgoing e-mail message, enter one or more addresses in the *To* field, enter a subject in the *Subject* field, and add additional information in the body of the message.

Warning: Depending on your operating system and security settings, the system may prompt you to allow access to your e-mail application.

Select the *Download a Copy* submenu item to download a copy of the document to your hard drive or to a network drive. Project Server 2010 displays the *File Download* dialog shown in Figure 6 - 69.

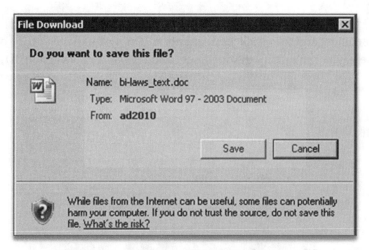

Figure 6 - 69: File Download dialog

Click the *Save* button to save the selected document. The system displays the *Save As* dialog shown in Figure 6 - 70.

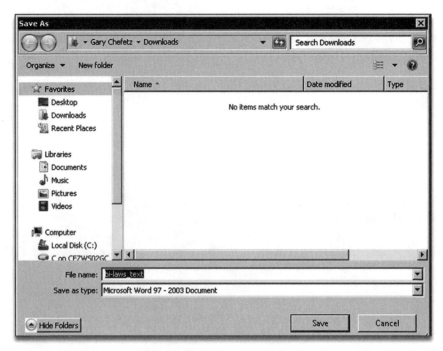

Figure 6 - 70: Save As dialog

Select a location for the document and then click the *Save* button. The system saves a copy of the document to the designated location. From there, you can modify the document and upload a new version of the document into the *Document* library.

Subscribing to E-Mail Alerts about a Document

As with risks and issues, Project Server 2010 allows you to subscribe to e-mail alerts whenever a user changes a selected document in a *Document* library. To subscribe to e-mail alerts, float your mouse pointer over the name of the document, click the pick list button, and then select the *Alert Me* item on the pick list. The system displays the *New Alert* dialog shown in Figure 6 - 71.

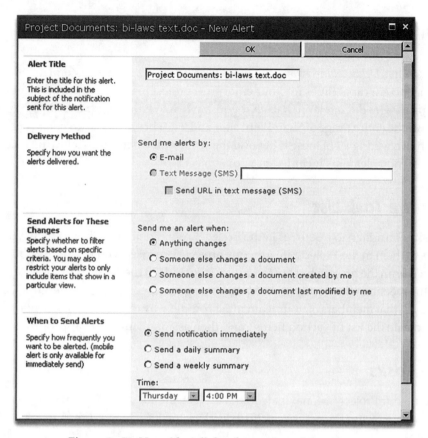

Figure 6 - 71: New Alert dialog for a selected document

In the *New Alert* dialog, specify your options in each section of the page and then click the *OK* button. Notice that the *New Alert* dialog allows you to determine what type of change triggers the system to send an e-mail message to you, and you can determine when the system sends the message.

Hands On Exercise

Exercise 6-13

Subscribe to an e-mail alert about changes to a document in the Project Documents library.

1. Float your mouse pointer over the name of a Microsoft Word document, click the pick list button, and then select the *Alert Me* item on the pick list.

2. In the *New Alert* dialog, select your options for the new e-mail alert.

3. Click the *OK* button to subscribe to the e-mail alert.

Working with other SharePoint Lists

While the *Issues* list, *Risk* list, *Deliverables* list and the *Project Document Library* are customized SharePoint elements that provide specific management capabilities for your enterprise project management system, your Project Site also includes a number of provisioned SharePoint lists that you can use to enhance your team's collaboration experience. Additionally, you have the entire range of SharePoint sites and list types available to you in creating your own collaboration solutions. While covering all of these is beyond the scope of the book, the following sections teach you how to use the common SharePoint elements included in your Project Site.

Working with the Task List

In addition to the tasks you assign to resources in the Project Professional 2010 project plan, you can also create tasks and assign resources to them in the Project Site for your project. Typically, you use the *Tasks* list in the Project Site to define work associated with the project, but are too trivial to include in the actual project plan. For example, you have a weekly project status meeting with your project team. During this meeting, you generate a list of "action items" associated with the project that members of your team must complete by the next status meeting. Use the *Tasks* feature in the Project Site to create the list of "action items" and then assign them to the appropriate team members.

Creating New Tasks

To use the *Tasks* list in your Project Site, navigate to the Project Site for your project. Click the *Tasks* link in the *Lists* section of the *Quick Launch* menu. Project Server 2010 displays the *Tasks* page shown in Figure 6 - 72. Note that I selected the *Items* ribbon.

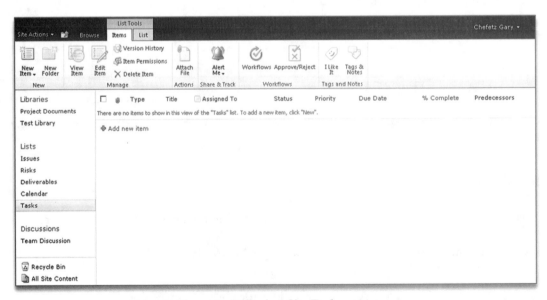

Figure 6 - 72: Project Site Tasks page

To create a new task, from the *New* section of the *Items* ribbon, click the *New Item* pick list button and select the *Task* item from the list. Notice that you can create a task or a summary task. The system displays the *New Item* dialog for the *Tasks* list shown in Figure 6 - 73.

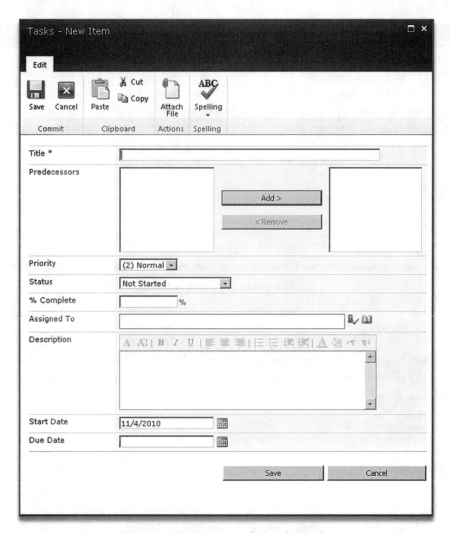

Figure 6 - 73: New Item dialog for Tasks

To create the new task, begin by entering a name for the task in the *Title* field, which is the only required field. Select a priority for the task from the *Priority* pick list. Your options in the *Priority* pick list include *High, Normal,* and *Low*. Leave the value in the *Status* pick list set to *Not Started,* because the resource assigned to the task must change the value in the pick list while performing the work. Items available in the *Status* pick list include *Not Started, In Progress, Completed, Deferred,* and *Waiting on Someone Else*. Leave the *% Complete* field blank because the resource assigned to the task must enter this information. Notice that you can define other tasks in the list as predecessors; however, this is the first entry in the list.

Enter the resource assigned to the task in *Assigned To* field, and use the *Check Names* and *Browse* buttons to the right of the field to locate or verify resource names. Enter additional information about the task in the *Description* field. In the *Start Date* field, enter the date that the resource must begin work on the task. In the *Due Date* field, enter the date the resource must complete the work on this task. From the *Actions* section of the *Edit* ribbon, click the *Attach File* button to optionally attach a file to the task. Click the *Save* button to finish. The system creates the new task and displays it on the *Tasks* list as shown in Figure 6 - 74.

Figure 6 - 74: Tasks page shows three Tasks

Notice that the *Tasks* list shown in Figure 6 - 74 contains three tasks, one summary task and two individual tasks assigned to members of the project team. The system represents *Summary* tasks as folder items and you create subtasks by drilling down into the folder.

Warning: Do not confuse tasks that you create in the Project Work Space with tasks in the enterprise project. The tasks you create in the Project Site are not part of the reporting cycle in Project Web App, they do not affect resource loading, and you cannot use any of the system's scheduling capabilities with these tasks.

Working with Existing Tasks

When a team member begins working on a task assigned in the Project Site, he or she must edit the task and enter progress. When complete, the team member must edit the task to indicate that it is complete. Working with an existing task is very similar to working with an existing risk or issue. Float your mouse pointer over the name of the task, click the pick list button, and select an item from the pick list menu, as shown in Figure 6 - 75.

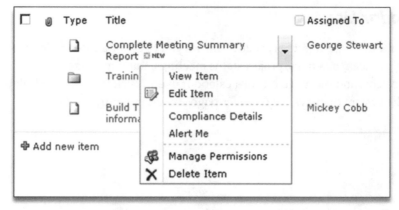

Figure 6 - 75: Working with an existing task

Notice on the pick list that Project Server 2010 allows you to view the task, edit the task, delete the task, or subscribe to e-mail alerts about changes to the task. Because I discussed these concepts previously in this module, I do not repeat this information here. Refer to previous sections in this module concerning risks and issues to review this information.

Hands On Exercise

Exercise 6-14

Create new tasks in the Project Site and assign them to project team members.

1. From your Project Site homepage, click the *Tasks* link in the *Lists* section of the *Quick Launch* menu. The system displays the *Tasks* list for your Project Site.

2. Select the *Items* tab and from the *New* section, click the *New Item* pick list button and select the *Task* item from the list. The system opens the *New Item* dialog.

3. Enter a name for the new task in the *Title* field, leave the *Predecessors* field blank, select a priority for the task in the *Priority* field, leave the *Status* and *% Complete* fields at their default values, and then enter your own name in the *Assigned To* field.

4. Enter a description for the task in the *Description* field, a *Start Date* value and a *Due Date* value, and then click the *Save* button.

5. Repeat steps #2-4 again and create two additional tasks, and assign each of them to another member of your project team.

Using the Calendar List

In the Project Site for your project, Project Server 2010 allows you to create a calendar of events related to the project. These events might include team meetings, project status meetings, training classes, client consultations, and perhaps even a project closure celebration party. To create a calendar event, click the *Calendar* link in the *Lists* section of the *Quick Launch* menu. The system displays the *Calendar* page shown in Figure 6 - 76.

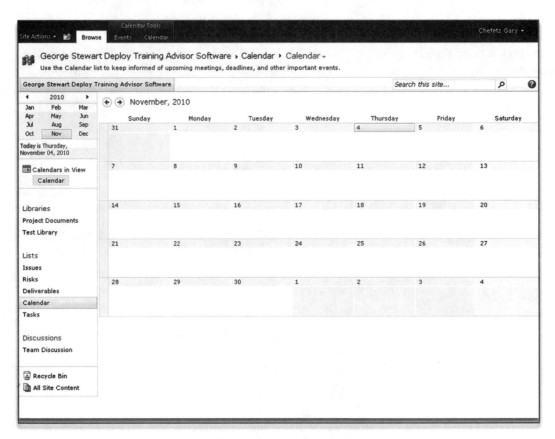

Figure 6 - 76: Calendar List homepage

Creating a New Calendar Event

To create a new calendar event, click on the *Events* tab to display the *Events* ribbon. In the *New* section click the *New Event* button and select the *Event* item from the list. The system displays the *New Item* dialog for the calendar, as shown in Figure 6 - 77.

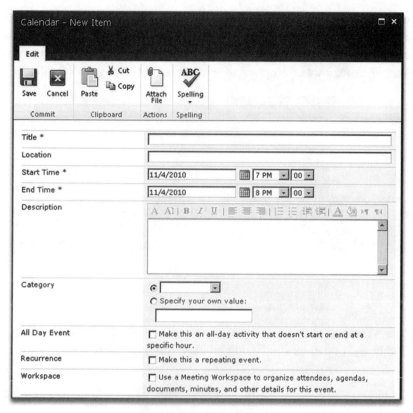

Figure 6 - 77: New Item dialog for the Calendar

The *New Item* dialog for the calendar contains three required fields: the *Title, Start Time,* and *End Time* fields. Enter the name of the event in the *Title* field and the event location in the *Location* field. Enter the time of the event in the *Start Time* and *End Time* fields. Enter optional event description information in the *Description* field. To set the event as an all-day event, select the *Make this an all-day activity that doesn't start or end at a specific hour* option. When you select this option the system removes the time information from the *Start Time* and *End Time* fields. To make the event a recurring event, select the *Make this a repeating event* option. Project Server 2010 redisplays the *New Item* dialog to include recurrence information, as shown in Figure 6 - 78.

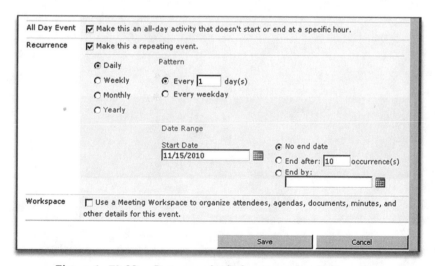

Figure 6 - 78: New Item page includes recurrence information

In the *Recurrence* section of the page, select the options necessary to define how your event recurs. Be sure to enter a date in the *Start Date* field and to specify how many events to create by selecting the *No end date* option, the *End after ___ occurrence(s)* option, or the *End by* option. If you want to use a Meeting Workspace to help organize the event, select the *Use a Meeting Workspace to organize...* option at the bottom of the page. Click the *OK* button to finish.

While creating a new event, if you select the *Use a Meeting Workspace to organize...* option at the bottom of the page, the system creates a New Meeting Workspace.

Project Server 2010 displays the new calendar event(s) as shown in Figure 6 - 79. Notice that I created a weekly Team Meeting event every Friday and one individual event on November 15, 2010.

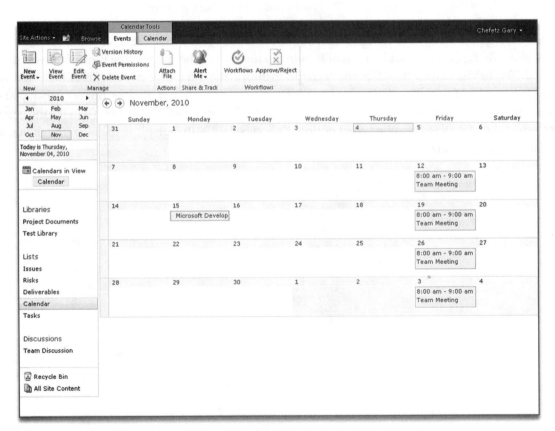

Figure 6 - 79: November events in the Project Site Calendar

Hands On Exercise

Exercise 6-15

Create Calendar events in the Project Site.

1. Click the *Calendar* link in the *Lists* section of the *Quick Launch* menu.

2. On the *Calendar* page, click the *Events* tab to display the *Events* ribbon and click the *New Event* pick list button and select the *Event* item from the list. The system displays the *New Event* dialog.

3. Enter a name for the event in the *Title* field, enter a location in the *Location* field, and enter date and time information in the *Start Time* and *End Time* fields. Ignore the remaining five fields.

4. Click the *Save* button to create the new event.

5. Repeat steps #2-4 to create another event, but make it a recurring event that occurs weekly every week on Wednesday, and ends after 12 occurrences.

6. Click the *Save* button to create the new recurring event.

7. Navigate through your *Calendar* page and examine your new events.

8. Click on the *Calendar* tab to display the *Calendar* ribbon and explore the *Manage Views* section. Explore the views selections in the *Scope* section on the left.

Creating a Meeting Workspace for an Event

When you create a new event and select the *Workspace* option at the bottom of the *New Item* dialog as shown previously in Figure 6 - 78, the system launches the *New Meeting Workspace* page, shown in Figure 6 - 80, after you click the *Save* button in the *New Item* dialog. I want to create a meeting workspace in which to plan the details of the Microsoft Developer Learning event that I am sending half my team to attend.

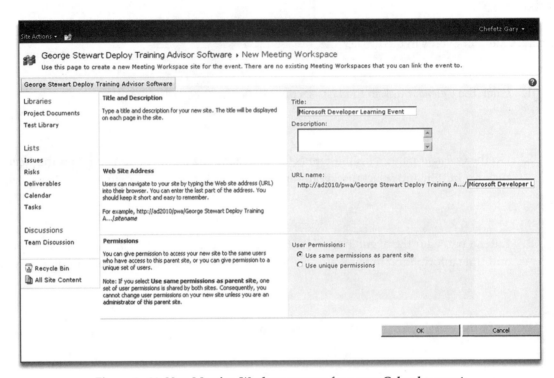

Figure 6 - 80: New Meeting Workspace page for a new Calendar event

In the *New Meeting Workspace* page, edit the information in the *Title* field and enter description information in the *Description* field. Project Server 2010 automatically enters a URL for the meeting workspace in the *URL name* field. In the *Permissions* section of the page, select the *Use same permissions as parent site* option to keep the same security as your Project Site. The *Permissions* option you specify determines what users can do in the Meeting Workspace site. The system allows you to specify the same permissions as the Project Site (the parent site) or to specify unique permissions.

Warning: Project Server 2010 does not allow you to create a Meeting Workspace site if you have only Project Manager permissions in the system. Therefore, if you attempt to create a Meeting Workspace, the system generates a Windows SharePoint Services error message. If you need to create a Meeting Workspace site, contact your Project Server administrator for assistance before you attempt to create it.

Click the *OK* button to finish. Project Server 2010 displays the *Template Selection* page shown in Figure 6 - 81.

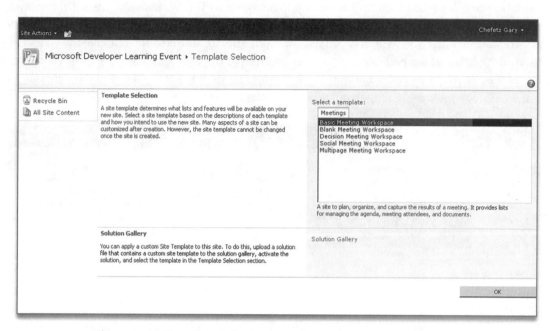

Figure 6 - 81: Template Selection page for a new Meeting Workspace

Select an appropriate site template from the list shown in the *Template Selection* field and then click the *OK* button. The system creates a new Meeting Workspace as a collaboration area for all users involved with the event, such as the Meeting Workspace shown in Figure 6 - 82.

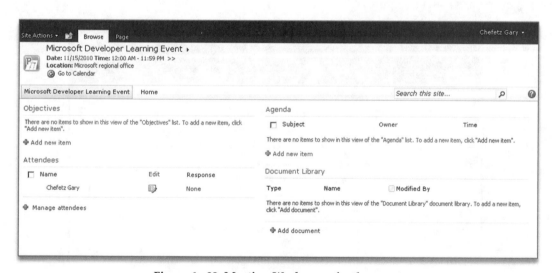

Figure 6 - 82: Meeting Workspace for the event

In the Meeting Workspace, you and your fellow users can collaborate to create a variety of items in the workspace, such as a list of event attendees, directions to the event, and a list of things to bring to the event. To return to the *Calendar* page in the Project Site, click the *Go to Calendar* link at the top of the page.

Working with Existing Calendar Events

Project Server 2010 provides a number of ways for you to navigate within the *Calendar* page. To display a particular month on the *Calendar* page, click the link for the name of the month in the list of months at the top of the *Quick Launch* menu. To move from period to period you use the navigation tools that appear above the *Quick Launch* menu. These vary according to the value you select in the *Scope* section of the *Calendar* ribbon. To apply a daily, weekly, or monthly view of the *Calendar* page, click the *Day, Week,* or *Month* button to set the scope of the *Calendar* page. For example, Figure 6 - 83 shows a weekly scope applied to the *Calendar* page.

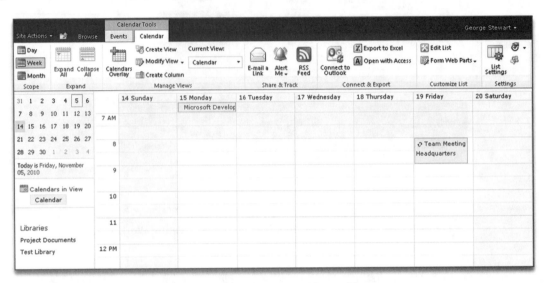

Figure 6 - 83: Calendar page with weekly scope

To view the information for any calendar event, click the link for the event. The system displays the information page for the selected event, as shown in Figure 6 - 84.

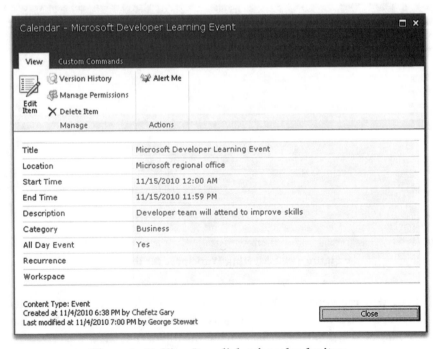

Figure 6 - 84: View Item dialog for calendar item

Notice in the figure that it displays the event information for the Microsoft Developer Learning Event. The *View Item* dialog contains all of the information for this event, including an optional *Workspace* link at the bottom for a Meeting Workspace if one is available. To edit the event, from the *Manage* section of the *View* menu, click the *Edit Item* button. The system displays the *Edit Item* dialog for the calendar item shown in Figure 6 - 85. To delete the event form the *View Item* dialog, click the *Delete Item* button. To subscribe to e-mail alerts about changes to the event, in the *Actions* section of the ribbon, click the *Alert Me* button.

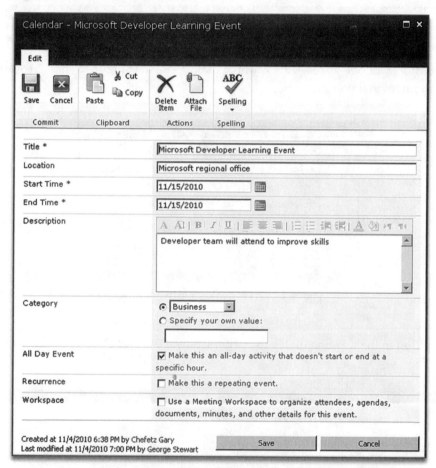

Figure 6 - 85: Edit Item dialog for calendar item

Using the *Edit Item* dialog is identical to using the *New Item* dialog and similar to editing the other types of list items that you worked with earlier in this module.

Connecting SharePoint Calendars to Outlook

You can display SharePoint calendar lists in Microsoft Office Outlook just as you can display shared Outlook calendars that belong to other people. Once you connect your SharePoint calendar list to Outlook, you can work the calendar items using the appointment tools in Outlook. You can share events between calendars by copying and pasting, or dragging and dropping.

You connect your SharePoint calendar to Outlook by selecting the *Calendar* tab and from the *Connect & Export* section of the ribbon, click the *Connect to Outlook* button as shown in Figure 6 - 86.

Figure 6 - 86: Calendar ribbon

When you click the button, Outlook displays the warning dialog shown in Figure 6 - 87. The warning advises you to connect only to data sources that you trust.

Figure 6 - 87: Outlook security warning

Click the *Advanced* button in the warning dialog to open the *SharePoint List Options* dialog shown in Figure 6 - 88.

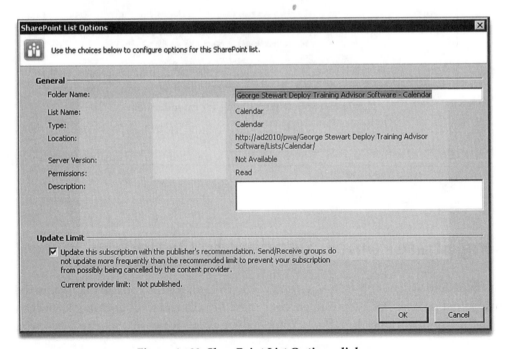

Figure 6 - 88: SharePoint List Options dialog

In the *SharePoint List Items* dialog, you can change the display name for the calendar and add a description. Notice the *Update Limit* section in the dialog. This option, selected by default, allows you to determine whether your copy of Outlook polls the SharePoint calendar each time it executes a send and receive action, or whether it respects a polling limit set for the SharePoint calendar administratively. Normally, you want to respect polling limits set in the source system. Click the *OK* button and the system transfers focus to Microsoft Outlook displaying your newly connected calendar as shown in Figure 6 - 89.

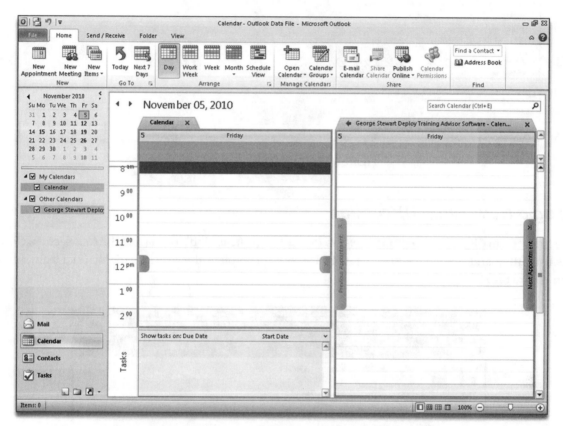

Figure 6 - 89: SharePoint Calendar displayed in Outlook

Notice that the SharePoint calendar appears in the *My Calendars* navigation section on the left and that the calendar itself displays the same way an Outlook calendar displays and that you can overlay SharePoint calendars with Outlook calendars.

Using Team Discussions

Because the Project Site represents a centralized collaboration area for everyone involved in a project, you can use the *Team Discussion* feature to create and log threaded discussion topics between all parties. To use the *Team Discussion* feature, from the *Discussions* section of the *Quick Launch* menu, click the *Team Discussion* link and the system displays the *Team Discussion* page shown in Figure 6 - 90.

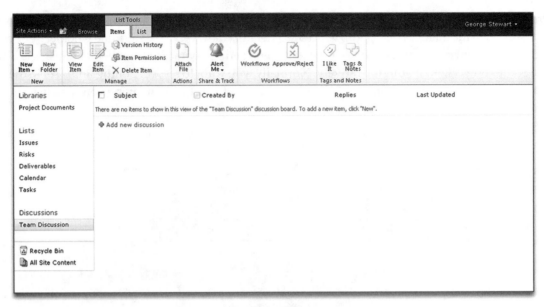

Figure 6 - 90: Team Discussion page

Creating a New Team Discussion

To create a new team discussion, click the *Items* tab to display the *Items* ribbon and from the *New* section, click the *New Item* pick list button and select the *Discussion* item. The system displays the *New Item* dialog for a team discussion as shown in Figure 6 - 91.

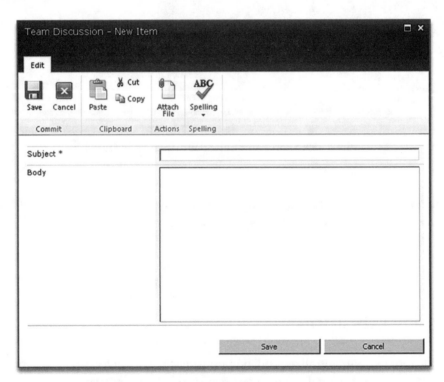

Figure 6 - 91: New Item dialog for a Team Discussion

Notice that the *Team Discussion* feature is simply another specialized SharePoint list. Use the *New Item* page to enter a subject for the discussion in the *Subject* field and enter your actual discussion post in the *Body* field. If you want to attach a file, in the *Actions* section of the *Edit* ribbon click the *Attach File* button. When you click into the *Body* field, the systems changes the ribbon display in the dialog to reveal the *Format Text* ribbon shown in Figure 6 - 92.

Figure 6 - 92: Format Text ribbon for discussions

You use familiar rich-text editing tools on the *Format Text* ribbon to style your post. Click on the *Insert* tab to display the *Insert* ribbon shown in Figure 6 - 93, which provides tools for you to add media, files and links to your discussion post.

Figure 6 - 93: Insert ribbon for discussions

When you finish composing your discussion list post, click the *Save* button at the bottom of the dialog or navigate to the *Edit* ribbon and click the *Save* button on the ribbon. The system returns to your *Team Discussions* homepage, which now displays your first post as shown in Figure 6 - 94.

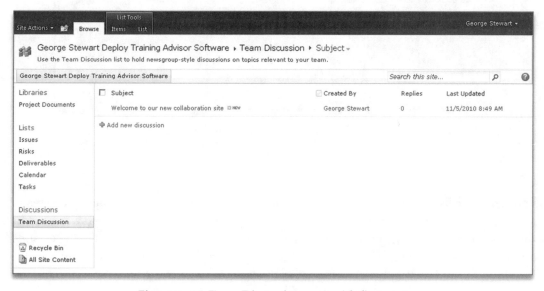

Figure 6 - 94: Team Discussion page with first post

Hands On Exercise

Exercise 6-16

Create a new Team Discussion in a Project Site.

1. In the *Discussions* section of the *Quick Launch* menu, click the *Team Discussion* link.

2. Click the *Items* tab to apply the *Items* ribbon and from the *New* section, click the *New Item* pick list button and select the *Discussion* item from the menu.

3. Enter a name for the discussion in the *Subject* field and enter a description of your post in the *Body* field.

4. Click the *Save* button to create the Team Discussion.

Working with a Team Discussion

To work with an existing discussion item, float your mouse pointer over the item in the *Subject* column and then click the pick list button. The system displays a pick list with available options, based on the permissions you have in the Project Site as shown in Figure 6 - 95.

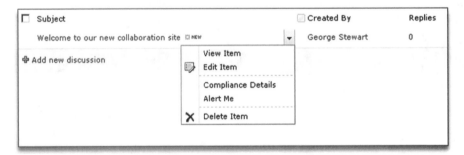

Figure 6 - 95: Pick list for working with discussions

The system presents pick list selections based on the permissions set by the project manager who created the discussion. If you want to view the original post, click the *View Item* option on the pick list. If you want to edit the original post, click the *Edit Item* option on the pick list and then edit the item. If you want to delete the existing discussion, click the *Delete Item* option on the pick list. If you want to subscribe to e-mail alerts about changes to the discussion, click the *Alert Me* option and set the alert options you want to use. To view the discussion, select the *View Item* selection from the list or simply click on the item's *Subject* link. The system displays the discussion as shown in Figure 6 - 96.

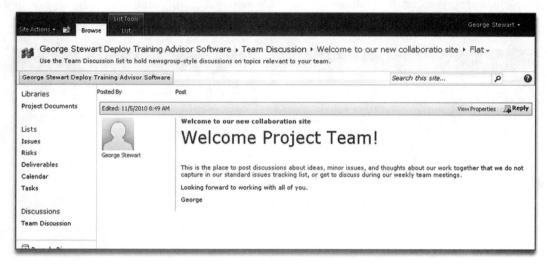

Figure 6 - 96: Discussion page displays discussion

Anyone with an interest in a project, and who has access to the Project Site, can add a reply or comments to an existing discussion. For example, a team member might add comments to the existing discussion shown in the figure by way of introduction to the team. To respond to a post, click the *Reply* button in the bar above the post at the far right. The system opens the *New Item* dialog to reply to a discussion as shown in Figure 6 - 97.

Figure 6 - 97: New Item dialog to reply to a post

Notice that the dialog for the reply reveals the author of the discussion (George Stewart) and shows the current text of the discussion. To add a reply, enter it in the *Body* section above the line that demarks the previous post. Click the *Save* button to complete the reply. Figure 6 - 98 shows the *Team Discussion* page displaying the original post and one reply using the *Threaded* option in the *Manage Views* section, *Current View* pick list.

Figure 6 - 98: Team Discussions page displays one post with one reply

When you view the page, such as the one shown previously in Figure 6 - 96, the system applies the default *Flat* view to the page. The *Flat* view shows all of the comments, listed in date order from the earliest response to the latest response. You can also apply the *Threaded* view of the page to see the comments listed as a threaded discussion.

Hands On Exercise

Exercise 6-17

Reply to a team discussion post.

1. From the *Team Discussions* homepage click the name of the team discussion you created in Exercise 6-15.

2. On the *Team Discussion* page, click the *Reply* button in the upper right corner of the page.

3. Add your reply or comments in the *Body* field and then click the *Save* button.

4. On the *Team Discussion* page, click the *List* tab to display the *List* ribbon. In the *Manage Views* section of the *List* ribbon, click the *Current View* pick list button and select the *Threaded* item.

5. Examine the *Threaded* view.

Working with Alerts in SharePoint

In previous sections of this module, you learned how to set alerts on individual list and document items. When your SharePoint site is email enabled, you can also set alerts for entire lists and libraries. Figure 6 - 99 shows the *List* ribbon for the *Team Discussions* list, which is similar across all SharePoint lists and document libraries.

Figure 6 - 99: List ribbon with Alert Me pick list expanded

Select the *Set Alert on this list* item on the pick list. The system displays the *New Alert* dialog shown in Figure 6 - 100.

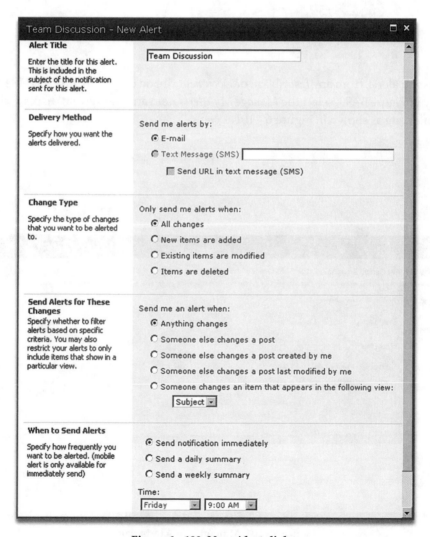

Figure 6 - 100: New Alert dialog

Notice that the *New Alert* dialog for an entire list or library looks very similar to the one for individual items. Here you can set alerts on a list-wide or library-wide basis rather than selectively for individual items or documents.

 SharePoint ribbon menu selections and picklist menu selections vary based on user, system configuration and other factors. In fact, as you increase the resolution on your system, many of the ribbons respond by expanding to display more detail and they contract intelligently when you reduce your resolution.

To manage your existing alerts, from any *List* ribbon or *Document* ribbon displaying the *Alert Me* pick list button, such as shown previously in Figure 6 - 99, select the *Manage My Alerts* item and the system displays the *Manage My Alerts* page for that particular site as shown in Figure 6 - 101.

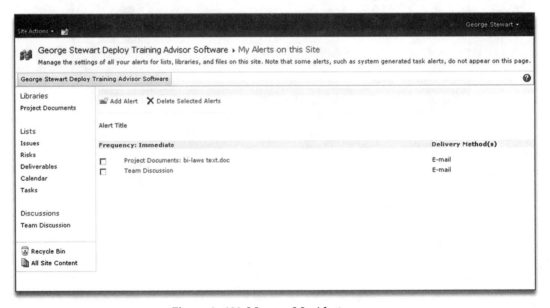

Figure 6 - 101: Manage My Alerts page

From this page, you can delete alerts that you previously created and add new list-wide or document-wide alerts. To remove an existing alert, select the checkbox to the left of the alert name, and click the *Delete Selected Alerts* button at the top of the page. To view an existing alert, click on the alert name. To set alerts across the entire site, click the *Add Alert* button at the top of the page. The system displays the *New Alert* page shown in Figure 6 - 102.

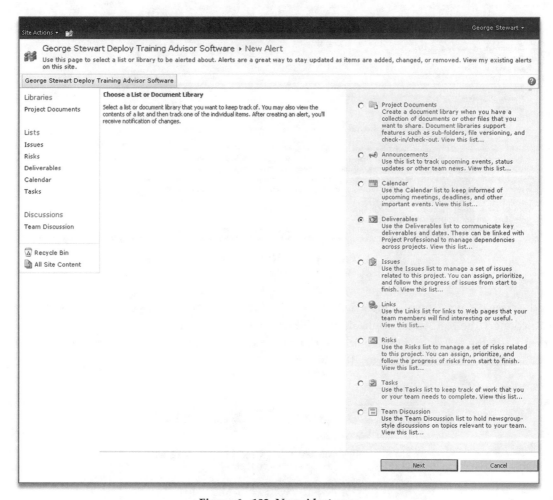

Figure 6 - 102: New Alert page

The *New Alert* page allows you to select any list or library contained in your site, and set a list-wide or library-wide alert.

Subscribing to an RSS Feed

Another option for sharing and tracking information about a SharePoint list or library is to use Really Simple Syndication (RSS) feeds. Each library and list automatically includes this capability. To setup an RSS subscription, from the *Share & Track* section of a *List* or *Document* ribbon, click the *RSS* button. The system displays the *RSS Feed* page for the selected document library or list as shown in Figure 6 - 103.

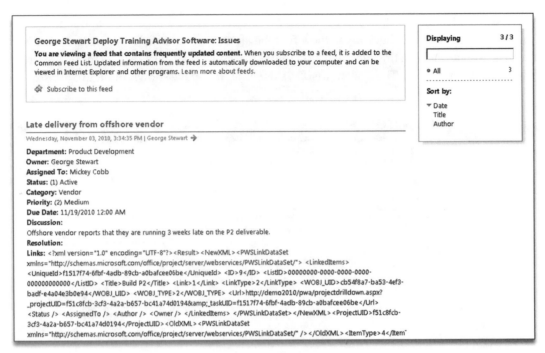

Figure 6 - 103: RSS Feed page

Notice that the page displays the feed in its native XML format. This is not a very good way to read the list! Instead, you want to connect the feed to an application like Microsoft Outlook that translates RSS raw feeds to human-readable form. Click the *Subscribe to the feed* link in the shaded area at the top of the page. The system displays the *Subscribe to this Feed* dialog shown in Figure 6 - 104.

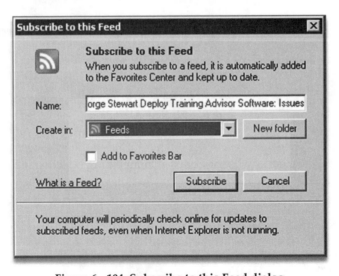

Figure 6 - 104: Subscribe to this Feed dialog

Notice that the system defaults to creating the feed link in your *Feeds* folder in Outlook. If you want to change the folder, you can create a new folder by clicking on the *New Folder* button. Click the *Subscribe* button to complete your subscription once you select or create the correct folder. Locate your new feed in your Outlook client.

Module 07

Working with Status Reports

Learning Objectives

After completing this module, you will be able to:

- Create and send a new status report request

- Edit and delete a status report

- Respond to a status report request

- Submit an unrequested status report

- View the status report archive

- View status report responses

- View unrequested status reports

Inside Module 07

Requesting a Status Report

Not only does Project Server 2010 provide time and task tracking, the system also allows managers to capture text-based information from resources using status reports. You can use the status reports feature to create periodic status reports due on a regular basis from specific resources or to request a one-time status report. To create a new *Status Report* request, click the *Status Reports* link in either the *Quick Launch* menu or the main content area of the *Home* page in Project Web App. The system displays the *Status Reports* page shown in Figure 7 - 1.

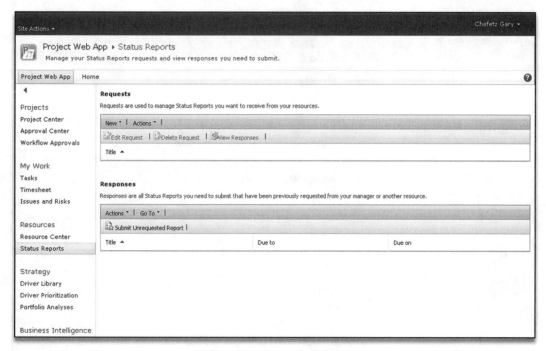

Figure 7 - 1: Status Reports page

 The *Request a Status Report* feature is dependent on permissions granted in groups in Project Web App. By default, this feature is available only to members of the following groups: Executives, Portfolio Managers, Project Managers, Resource Managers, Team Leads, and Administrators.

The *Status Reports* page includes two sections. Use the options in the *Requests* section to create and manage *Status Report* requests. Use the options in the *Responses* section to view and work with *Status Report* responses from your resources.

To create a new *Status Report* request, click the *New* pick list button in the *Requests* section and then click the *New Request* item on the pick list. Project Server 2010 displays the *Status Report Request* page shown in Figure 7 - 2.

Figure 7 - 2: Status Report Request page

On the *Status Report Request* page, enter a descriptive name for the *Status Report* request in the *Title* field. In the *Frequency* section, select the appropriate options to set the recurrence for the *Status Report* request. The system offers you a wide variety of options for setting a recurrence pattern, such as weekly, monthly, and yearly. Using the available options in the *Frequency* section, you can even create recurrences such as bi-weekly or quarterly. Click the *Start* pick list and select the starting date for the first reporting period.

Warning: Project Server 2010 does not allow you to select a Start date earlier than the current date. This means that you cannot create a monthly report in the middle of the month and set the Start date to the first day of the month!

In the *Available Resources* list, select the resources that must respond to your *Status Report* request and then click the *Add* button. Next, you set up the topical sections for the status report in the *Sections* part of the page. By default, the system offers three standard topical sections: *Major Accomplishments*, *Objectives for the Next Period*, and *Hot Issues*. You can delete, reorder, rename, add additional topical sections, add descriptions, or simply accept the default topical sections listed on the *Status Report Request* page.

When you complete your new *Status Report* request, click the *Send* button. Project Server 2010 sends an e-mail message to each resource, notifying them of the new *Status Report* request. The system displays your new *Status Report* request in the *Requests* section of the *Status Reports* page. Notice in Figure 7 - 3 that I created a monthly *Status Report* request for members of the Training team. Notice also that I included myself in the respondents list, so this new *Status Report* request displays in the *Responses* section as well.

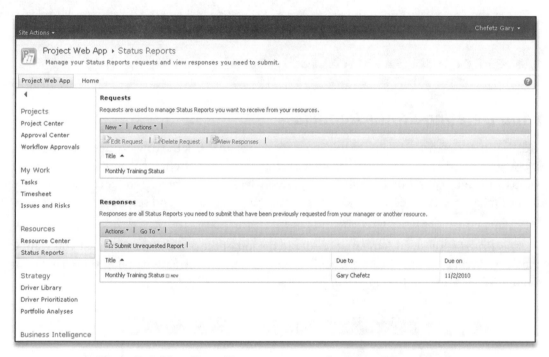

Figure 7 - 3: New Status Report request on the Status Reports page

Hands On Exercise

Exercise 7-1

Create a new status report request.

1. Navigate to the *Status Reports* page.

2. Click the *New* pick list button and select the *New Request* item from the pick list.

3. In the *Report Title* section of the *Status Report Request* page, enter a name for your new status report in the *Title* field followed by the phrase *Team Weekly Report*.

4. In the *Frequency* section of the *Status Report Request* page, set the *Recurrence* field to *weekly* due *every* week on *Thursday*.

5. In the *Start Date* section of the *Status Report Request* page, set the date to today's date.

6. In the *Resources* section of the *Status Report Request* page, add **yourself** and each member of your class as recipients of the *Status Report* request (include your instructor as well) by using the *Add* button.

7. In the *Sections* section of the *Status Report Request* page, keep the three default topical sections, but add a fourth section of your own choice by clicking on the *Insert Section* button.

8. Click the *Send* button when finished.

Editing and Deleting Status Reports

To edit an existing status report, navigate to the *Status Reports* page. Click the row header to the left of the *Status Report* request you want to edit and then click the *Edit Request* button. The system displays the *Status Report Request* page shown previously in Figure 7 - 2. Edit the information as you determine necessary and then click the *Send* button. You can also edit the *Status Report* request by clicking the *Actions* pick list button and selecting the *Edit Request* item on the list.

To delete a *Status Report* request, click the row header to the left of the *Status Report* request you want to delete and then click the *Delete Request* button. Project Server 2010 displays the confirmation dialog shown in Figure 7 - 4. In the confirmation dialog, click the *OK* button to complete the deletion.

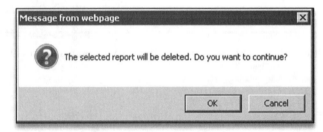

Figure 7 - 4: Delete a Status Report request confirmation

Responding to a Status Report Request

As I mentioned earlier in this module, when a manager sends a *Status Report* request, Project Server 2010 sends an e-mail message to each resource included in the *Status Report* request. Resources can see the *Status Report* request by clicking the *Status Reports* link in either the *Quick Launch* menu or the main content area of the *Home* page. The system displays the new *Status Report* request in the *Responses* area of the *Status Reports* page. For example, Figure 7 - 5 shows the Monthly Training status report on the *Status Reports* page for a resource named George Stewart.

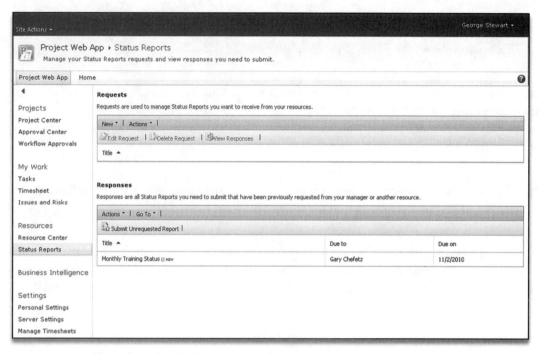

Figure 7 - 5: Status Reports page shows a new Status Report request

On the *Status Reports* page, resources may see multiple *Status Report* requests created by different managers. To respond to a *Status Report* request; click the link for the status report to which you want to respond. Project Server 2010 displays the *Status Report Response* page shown in Figure 7 - 6.

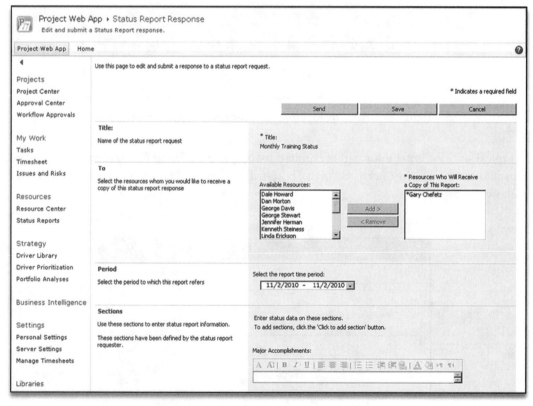

Figure 7 - 6: Status Report Response page

231

The *Status Report Response* page includes four information sections:

- The *Title* section shows the *Status Report* request name.

- The *To* section shows the *Available Resources* field where you will select the name(s) of the resource(s) who you want to respond to the *Status Report* request. You click the *Add* button to add these names to the *Resources Who Will Receive a Copy of This Report* field. This field also shows the name of the *Status Report* requestor, as indicated by an asterisk character (*) to the left of the manager's name.

- The *Period* section allows you to select the period to which the report refers. Click the *Select the report time period* pick list and choose the time period for which you want to respond.

- The *Sections* section contains the topical sections chosen by the manager who created the *Status Report* request. Notice in Figure 7 - 6 that the *Status Report* request image shows one topical sections: Major Accomplishments This Month. Not shown in the image are two additional default sections: Objectives for the Next Month and Hot Issues.

To enter information into any of the topical sections, click anywhere in the text field for the topic. Project Server 2010 activates the toolbar at the top of the text field giving you extensive formatting capabilities. For example, Figure 7 - 7 shows the activated toolbar for the *Major Accomplishments* field. Notice that the toolbar gives you text-formatting options such as font size, font style, alignment, and numbered or bulleted lists.

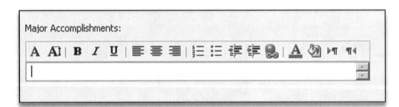

Figure 7 - 7: Activated toolbar for Major Accomplishments field

In each of the topical sections, enter information required to complete the *Status Report* response. If you need to add an additional topical section, click the *Click to add section* button at the bottom of the page. The system displays the *Section Name* dialog shown in Figure 7 - 8.

Figure 7 - 8: Section Name dialog

In the dialog, enter a unique name for the new section in the text field and then click the *OK* button. Enter additional information in the new topical section, as you require.

If you create a topical section that you no longer need, click the *Delete this section* button in the upper right corner of the section. You can delete any section that you add; however you cannot delete a section added by the requestor.

When you finish entering information in the topical sections, Project Server 2010 offers you two options:

- *Save the Status Report* response for additional editing and later submission.

- *Send the Status Report* response immediately.

If are working on an in-progress *Status Report* response and are not ready to send it to your manager, click the *Save* button. The system saves the *Status Report* response in your *Status Report Archive*, where you can edit it and send it at a later time. Project Server 2010 displays the *Status Report Archive* page with the saved *Status Report* response. For example, Figure 7 - 9 shows a *Status Report* response saved on October 19.

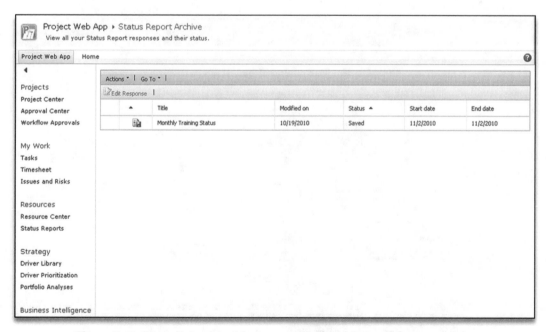

Figure 7 - 9: Status Report Archive page with saved Status Report response

To update an in-progress *Status Report* response, navigate to the *Status Reports* page, click the *Go To* pick list button, and select the *Status Reports: Archive* item on the pick list. Click the name of the *Status Report* response to update, then update it, save it, or send it.

If you are ready to submit the *Status Report* response to your manager, click the *Send* button. The system saves the *Status Report* response in your *Status Report Archive* and sends your manager an e-mail message notifying her of your *Status Report* response.

Submitting an Unrequested Status Report

You can create and send an ad hoc status report without a manager request. To submit an unrequested status report, navigate to the *Responses* section of the *Status Reports* page and click the *Submit Unrequested Report* button. Project Server 2010 displays the *Unrequested Status Report* page shown in Figure 7 - 10.

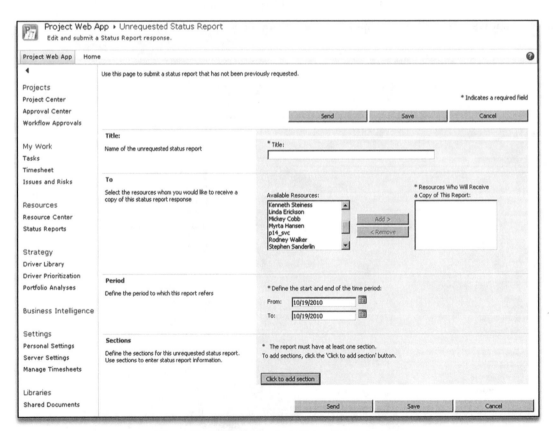

Figure 7 - 10: Unrequested Status Report page

To create the unrequested status report, enter the name of your status report in the *Title* field. In the *Available Resources* list, select the resources to which you want to send the unrequested status report and then click the *Add* button. In the *Period* section of the page, enter dates in the *From* and *To* fields to indicate the period for your report. Click the *Click to add section* button, enter a name for the topical section in the dialog, and then click the *OK* button. Enter data in the topical section and add additional topical sections until you complete your report and then click the *Send* button. The system adds your new unrequested status report to the status report Archive.

Viewing the Status Report Archive

The *Status Report Archive* page gives you access to your saved status reports and any previously submitted status reports. To access the *Status Report Archive* page, navigate to the *Status Reports* page, click the *Go To* pick list button in the *Responses* section, and then click the *Status Reports: Archive* item on the pick list. Project Server 2010 displays the *Status Report Archive* page shown in Figure 7 - 11.

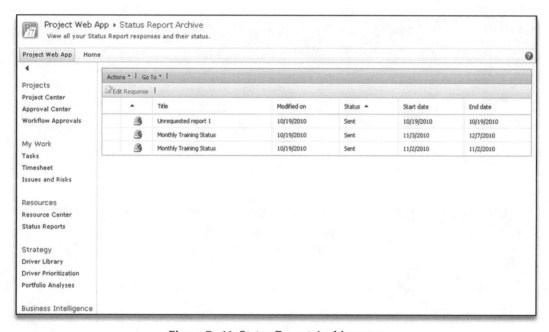

Figure 7 - 11: Status Report Archive page

Notice in Figure 7 - 11 that the user submitted two monthly status reports and one *Unrequested* status report. To edit an in-progress or previously submitted *Status Report* response, click the row header of the status report you want to edit and then click the *Edit Response* button. Project Server 2010 displays the *Status Report Response* page as shown in Figure 7 - 12.

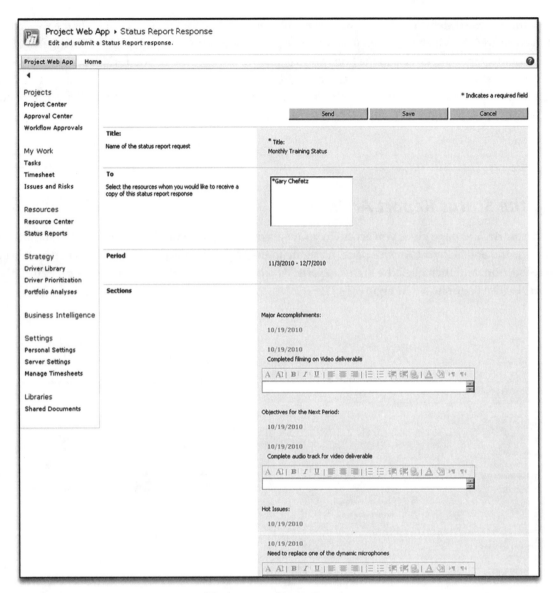

Figure 7 - 12: Status Report
Response page ready for editing

Because I previously submitted the status report response shown in Figure 7 - 12, notice how the system locks the information in the *To* and *Period* sections, as well as the text previously entered in each of the topical sections. Enter additional information in any of the topical sections and then click the *Send* button to send the status report response to your manager.

Hands On Exercise

Exercise 7-2

Respond to a status report request.

1. Click the *Status Reports* link in the *Quick Launch* menu to refresh your *Status Reports* page.

2. In the *Responses* section of the page, click the name of your own *Status Report* request.

3. In the *To* section of the page, select any two members of the class to receive copies of your response.

4. Make sure the setting in the *Period* section is for the current reporting period.

5. Enter report information in each of the topical sections and then click the *Send* button.

6. In the *Response* section of the *Status Reports* page, select the *Status Report* request from one of your fellow students and repeat steps #3-5.

7. From the *Responses* section of the *Status Reports* page, click the *Go To* pick list button, and then click the *Status Reports: Archive* item on the pick list.

8. Examine the two *Status Report* responses you sent during class.

Viewing Status Report Responses

When a resource sends you a *Status Report* response, Project Server 2010 automatically alerts you with an e-mail message. To view the *Status Report* responses from your resources, navigate to the *Status Reports* page and in the *Requests* section of the page click the name of the status report you want to view. The system displays the *View Responses* page for the selected status report. Figure 7 - 13 shows the *View Responses* page for my Monthly Training Status report.

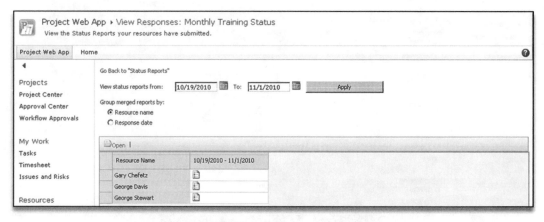

**Figure 7 - 13: View Responses page for the
Monthly Training Status Report**

The options at the top of the *View Responses* page allow you to view *Status Report* responses for specific reporting periods and to group the responses into a merged report. By default, the *View Responses* page shows the *Status Report* responses for each reporting period, with columns representing the current reporting period and all past periods. To display Status Responses for specific reporting periods, select the date range you want in the *From* and *To* fields and then click the *Apply* button.

If you select all of the cells, Project Server 2010 merges all selected *Status Report* responses into a merged team status report for each reporting period. The *Group merged reports by* option allows you to group by *Resource name* or *Response date*. Select the *Resource name* option to display the responses grouped by the name of each resource. Select the *Response date* option to display the responses grouped by the date each resource sent the response.

To view an individual *Status Report* response, click the cell to the left of the name of the person whose response you want to see and then click the *Open* button. To view the merged team *Status Report* response, select the names of all response cells and then click the *Open* button. The system displays the *Status Report Responses* page for the selected status report. Figure 7 - 14 shows the *Status Report Responses* page for the Monthly Training status report, grouped by resource name.

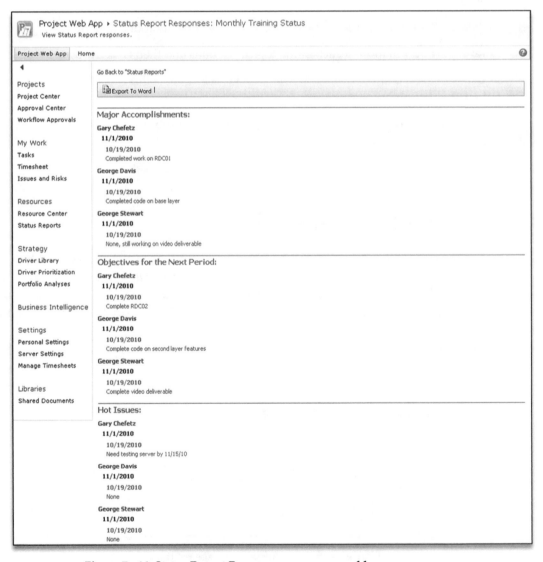

Figure 7 - 14: Status Report Responses page grouped by resource name

Beyond reading the responses on the *Status Report Responses* page, Project Server 2010 offers you one additional option; you can export the merged team status report to Microsoft Word. Click the *Export to Word* button and the system displays the *File Download* warning dialog shown in Figure 7 - 15.

If the merged team Status Report is associated with a particular project, MSProjectExperts recommends that you upload the saved copy of the merged team Status Report to the Document Library for that project. This allows you to share the Status Reports with the team and with other stakeholders.

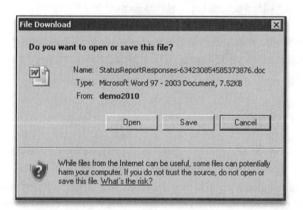

Figure 7 - 15: File Download warning

Click the *Save* button to save the Word document on your local computer or click the *Open* button in the dialog and the system opens Microsoft Word with the merged team status report in a new document. Figure 7 - 16 shows the Microsoft Word application with the top part of the merged team status report.

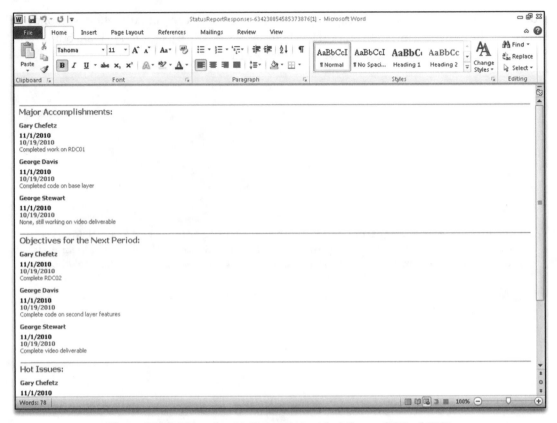

Figure 7 - 16: Merged team Status Report in Microsoft Word 2010

From the Microsoft Word application, you can edit the merged team status report document and then save it. After saving it, you can e-mail the document to your manager or upload the document to the Document Library of a related project for further sharing.

Viewing Unrequested Status Reports

Resources may occasionally send you an unrequested status report, or may include you as an additional recipient of a *Status Report* response to another manager. To view either of these types of status reports, navigate to the *Status Reports* page, click the *Go To* pick list button from the *Responses* section and click the *Status Reports: Miscellaneous* item on the pick list. Project Server 2010 displays the *Miscellaneous Status Reports* page as shown in Figure 7 - 17.

Figure 7 - 17: Miscellaneous Status Reports page

To view an *Unrequested* status report or the copy of a *Status Report* response, click the name of the status report you want to view. Project Server 2010 displays the *Status Report Responses* page for the selected status report. Figure 7 - 18 shows the *Status Report Responses* page for the Interim Training *Unrequested* status report from George Stewart.

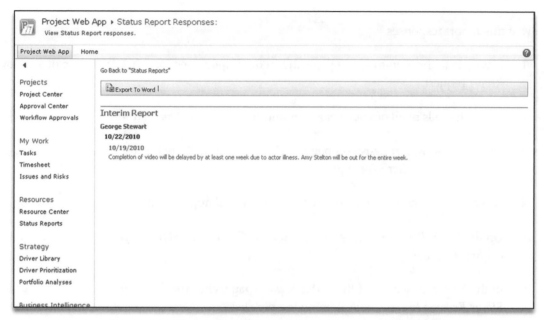

Figure 7 - 18: Unrequested Status Report from George Stewart

As with individual or merged team status reports, you can export the status report to Microsoft Word by clicking the *Export to Word* button. Click the *Go Back to "Status Reports"* link to return to the *Status Reports* page.

 Warning: When you click the *Go Back to "Status Reports"* link, the system returns you to the *Status Reports* page rather than the *Miscellaneous Status Reports* page. The only way to return directly to the *Miscellaneous Status Reports* page is to click the *Back* button in your Internet Explorer application.

Hands On Exercise

Exercise 7-3

View status report responses.

1. Navigate to the *Status Reports* page and in the *Requests* section, click the name of your own *Status Report* request.

2. Select the cells of all of your resources and then click the *Open* button.

3. On the *Status Report Responses* page, click the *Export to Word* button and export the merged team status report to Microsoft Word.

4. After viewing the report, close the Microsoft Word application and do not save the document.

5. On the *Status Report Responses* page, click the *Go Back to "Status Reports"* link to return to the *Status Reports* page.

6. In the *Responses* section of the *Status Reports* page, click the *Go To* pick list button and select the *Status Reports: Miscellaneous* item on the pick list.

7. On the *Miscellaneous Status Reports* page, review any miscellaneous status reports shown on the page.

8. Click the *Go To* button and select the *Status Reports: Home* item to return to the *Status Reports* page.

Module 08

Working with the Project Center and Project Views

Learning Objectives

After completing this module, you will be able to:

- Work with features in the Project Center

- Work with Project Center views

- Work with detailed Project views

- Access Project Workspace features from the Project Center

- Open projects from the Project Center page

- Check in a project

- Edit project details and open a project in the Project Center

Inside Module 08

Using the Project Center

In Project Server 2010, the Project Center is the central location for project and portfolio information, a launching point for new projects and the gateway to editing projects on the web, a new feature in Project Server 2010. To navigate to the *Project Center* page, click the *Project Center* link in the *Quick Launch* menu. Figure 8 - 1 shows the *Project Center* page with a custom view applied and the *Quick Launch* menu collapsed. The *Project Center* page displays a data grid with a project list on the left and a Gantt chart on the right. The project list displays a single line of information about each project and proposed project, with multiple columns of information about each item.

The Gantt chart displays one or two Gantt bars representing the life span of the project. When the system displays two Gantt bars, one represents the baseline schedule while the other represents the current schedule of the project.

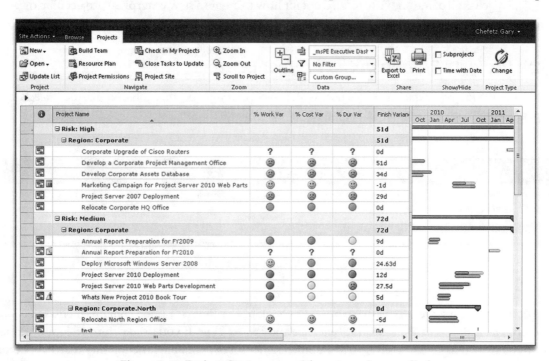

Figure 8 - 1: Project Center page with custom view applied

The *Project Center* page allows you to do each of the following:

- View the portfolio of active and proposed enterprise projects.

- View master projects and subprojects.

- Navigate to the Project Site for a project, or navigate directly to the *Risks, Issues, Documents,* or *Deliverables* page for the project.

- Create new enterprise projects and proposed projects.

- Edit the properties for an enterprise project or proposed project.

- Drill down to a detailed Project view to view or edit the project.

- Build a team or create a Resource Plan for any project.

- Open a single project or a group of projects in Project Professional 2010.

- Set individual permissions for a project.

- Close tasks to updates in a project.

- Check in a project stuck in a checked-out state.

In this module, I discuss all of the above topics except for how to create a new enterprise project plan or proposed enterprise project because I discussed these topics previously in Module 03.

Using the Projects Ribbon in the Project Center

Figure 8 - 2 shows the *Project Center* page for a user with project manager permissions. Notice the *Projects* ribbon at the top of the page, along with the *Projects* tab at the top of the *Projects* ribbon.

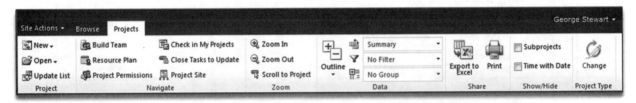

Figure 8 - 2: Project Center page Projects ribbon

The *Projects* ribbon has one context-sensitive tab, the *Projects* tab. The *Projects* ribbon contains menu selections in seven sections: *Project, Navigate, Zoom, Data, Share, Show/Hide* and *Project Type*. If you used prior versions of Project Server, you can see right away that Project Web App has a much richer set of available functionality than ever before. For example, Project Web App now supports project editing in the browser, a new feature in Project Server 2010. The *Project* section allows you to create new proposed enterprise projects and new enterprise projects. From here, you can drill down to projects for editing in the browser or open projects in Project Professional 2010, and you can synchronize data between projects and SharePoint lists.

The *Navigate* section provides familiar functions carried forward from previous versions including *Build Team, Resource Plan, Check in My Projects, Close Tasks to Update* and a button to navigate to the *Project Site* for a selected project, formerly known as the *Project Workspace* in Project Server 2007. You use tools in the *Zoom* section to zoom the timescale of the Gantt chart and scroll to projects in the Gantt chart. From the *Data* section you can collapse outline levels in views that contain multi-level grouping, select and apply views, and apply ad-hoc filters and grouping to your views. Use the *Share* section to export your view to Microsoft Excel or to send it to a printer. The *Show/Hide* section provides two toggle options, the first displays subprojects along with master projects and the second determines whether the system displays the time in date fields. Finally, the *Project Type* section contains one selection, *Change*. You use this to change the *Project Type* of a proposed or existing project.

Using Project Center Views

The *Project Center* page displays only the projects and proposed projects that you have permission to see, including projects and proposed projects that you own. Unless you have additional privileges in the system, these may be the only projects that you see. The first time you access the *Project Center* page, the system displays the default *Summary* view, unless your Project Server administrator removed that view. The system provides five standard views that you can select from the pick list in the *Data* section of the page:

- Summary

- Tracking

- Cost

- Earned Value

- Work

The *Summary* view, shown in Figure 8 - 3, displays the "vital statistics" for each project, with columns showing the project's *Start* date, *Finish* date, *% Complete*, *Work*, *Duration*, and *Owner*. The *Summary* view includes a Gantt chart with a single Gantt bar for each project and a black stripe indicating project progress. Notice in Figure 8 - 3 that several projects contain a black stripe within the blue Gantt bar, indicating the current progress for each project.

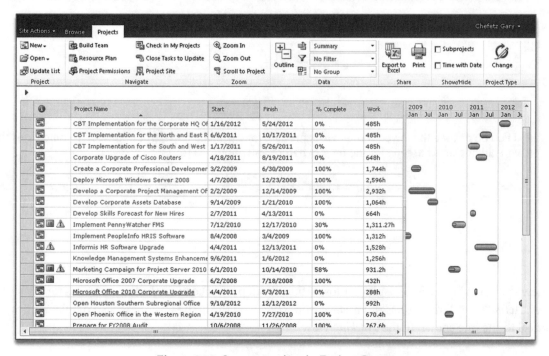

Figure 8 - 3: Summary view in Project Center

The *Tracking* view displays variance information about each project using the following fields: *% Complete, Actual Cost, Actual Duration, Actual Finish, Actual Start, Actual Work, Baseline Finish, Baseline Start, Duration, Remaining Duration, Finish,* and *Start.* The *Tracking* view, shown in Figure 8 - 4, displays a *Tracking* Gantt chart with two Gantt bars for each project. The top Gantt bar represents the current schedule for each project, while the bottom Gantt bar represents the baseline schedule for each project. The black stripe in the top Gantt bar indicates project progress.

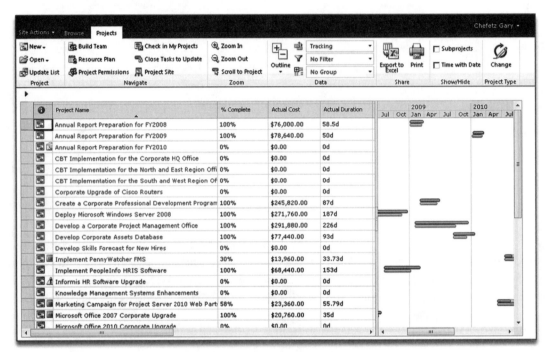

Figure 8 - 4: Project Center page with the Tracking view applied

 If you do not see the lower of the two Gantt bars for a project in the *Tracking* view, this indicates that you did not set a baseline for the project before you published it.

The *Cost* view shown in Figure 8 - 5 displays information about project costs, including columns for *Finish, Start, Cost, Baseline Cost, Actual Cost, Fixed Cost, Cost Variance,* and *Remaining Cost.* The *Cost* view also displays a *Tracking* Gantt chart identical to the one shown in the *Tracking* view.

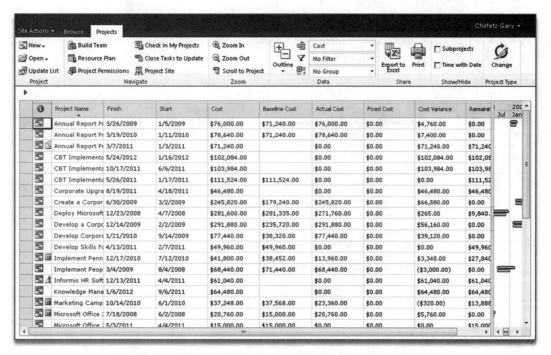

Figure 8 - 5: Project Center page with the Cost view applied

The *Earned Value* view displays the calculated earned value at the project level for each project. This view includes columns for *Finish, Start, Cost, Baseline Cost, BCWP, BCWS, SV, CV, ACWP,* and *VAC.* The *Earned Value* view shown in Figure 8 - 6 includes the same *Tracking* Gantt chart as the *Tracking* and *Cost* views.

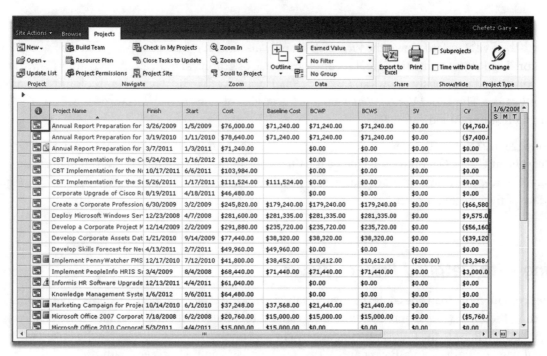

Figure 8 - 6: Project Center page with the Earned Value view applied

The *Work* view displays information about project work hours with columns for *% Work Complete, Finish, Remaining Work, Start, Work, Baseline Work, Actual Work,* and *Work Variance.* The *Work* view shown in Figure 8 - 7 displays the same *Tracking* Gantt chart found in all other *Project Center* views.

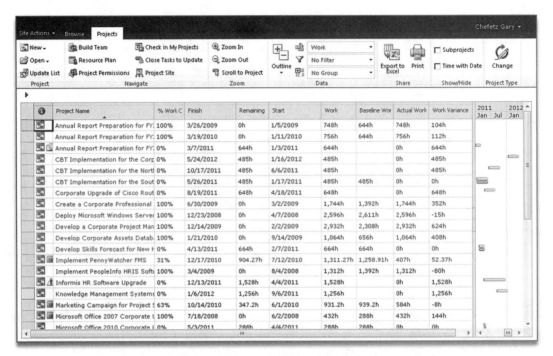

Figure 8 - 7: Project Center page with the Work view applied

In addition to the five standard views, the *View* pick list may also include custom views created by your Project Server administrator. The Project Center is a great forum for the use of graphical indicators in custom views. For example, Figure 8 - 1, displayed previously, shows an *Executive Summary* view that displays several columns containing custom graphical indicators. The *%Cost Var, % Work Var,* and *%Dur Var* columns reveal variance for each project using a red, yellow, or green stoplight indicator.

As with the *Resource Center* page, you can filter, group, or search the information presented in the *Project Center* page. Use the *Zoom In* and *Zoom Out* buttons to change the timescale of the Gantt chart. You can change the timescale to periods as small as 15-minute intervals or as large as half years. Use the *Scroll to Task* button to scroll the Gantt chart to the start date of the selected project.

Working with Detailed Project Views

Some pages contain more than one context-sensitive tab, such as the *Project Details* page. This page contains three such tabs, including the *Project, Task,* and *Options* tabs, grouped together under the *Schedule Tools* section, as shown in Figure 8 - 8. You navigate to the *Project Details* page by clicking on the name of a project in the *Project Center* page. The *Project Detail* page contains both a *Project* and a *Task* tab because you must access both project-level and task-level functions to use the features on this page. Notice the convenient *Status* bar notification just below the ribbon.

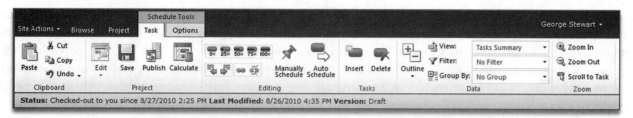

Figure 8 - 8: Project Details page with the Task ribbon selected

In the *Task* ribbon shown in Figure 8 - 8, notice the *Clipboard* section on the far left and the *Editing* and *Tasks* sections in the center. These three sections contain the new web-based project editing tools available in Project Server 2010 using familiar functionality similar to what you find in Project Professional 2010. This exciting new capability supports much stronger project management collaboration, allowing numerous users to participate in project schedule development, or even to manage simple projects from end to end, including project tracking, without using Project Professional 2010. Notice that the *Data* and *Zoom* sections provide you with tools to manipulate the data display and Gantt chart displays, respectively. Finally, the *Project* section makes the most common Project-level functions conveniently available without the need to switch to the *Project* tab.

In the preceding paragraph, I use the word "simple" to describe the project editing tools available using the Project Web App interface. These tools are a subset of the editing capabilities you find in Project Professional 2010, and are limited in their functionality. For example, you cannot specify a Units value when assigning one or more resources to tasks; the system uses the 100% units value automatically. When setting dependencies between tasks, the system limits you to only the Finish-To-Start (FS) dependency, and you cannot add *Lag* time or *Lead* time. Despite these limitations, this new capability represents a giant advance in Project Web App usability.

If you click the *Project* tab, the system displays the *Project* ribbon shown in Figure 8 - 9. This ribbon provides redundant *Edit* and *Save* buttons, and provides the only way to close and check in a project after editing on the web via the *Close* button in the *Project* section. The *Navigate* section provides navigation to the *Project Site* page using the *Project Site* button or to any of the four primary *Project Site* features using the *Documents, Issues, Risks* and *Deliverables* buttons. You also find *Build Team* and *Resource Plan* buttons to activate these two features and a new *Project Permissions* button that allows you to set project-level permissions specific to your selected project. Finally, the *Previous* and *Next* buttons allow you to switch between schedule pages and the *Project Fields* page where you can edit the *Project Name, Project Start Date* and *Project Owner* fields as well as any enterprise custom fields applicable to the specific project. Note in the figure that the system grays out the *Edit* button because the project is open for editing.

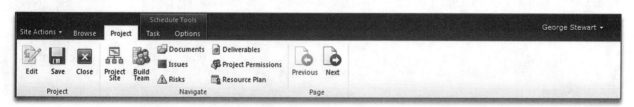

Figure 8 - 9: Project Details page with the Project ribbon selected

Click the *Options* tab and the system displays the *Options* contextual ribbon shown in Figure 8 - 10. In the *Share* section of the *Options* ribbon, notice that you can choose to print the project or export it to Excel. The *Link To* section contains buttons that allow you to create links from tasks to Documents, Issues and Risks contained in the Project's *Project Site*. You can even create any one of these objects and link them all in one operation. The *Show/Hide* option allows you to select to display the project summary task in the current view and allows you to change the date/time format. Finally, this ribbon also provides quick access to the *Close Tasks to Updates* feature also available in the Project Center.

Figure 8 - 10: Project Details page with the Options ribbon selected

In addition to viewing a single line of information about each project in the portfolio, the Project Center links you to detailed views of any project. Click the name of any project in the data grid of the *Project Center* page and the system displays the *Project Details* page, as shown for the Microsoft Office 2010 Corporate Upgrade project in Figure 8 - 11.

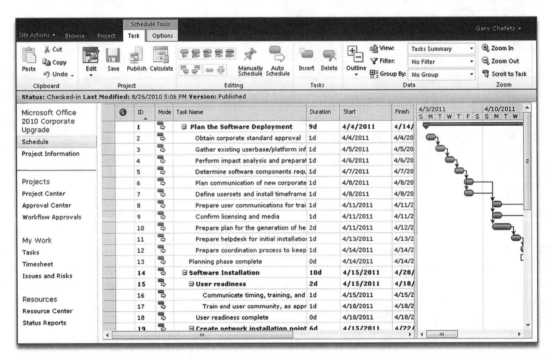

Figure 8 - 11: Project Details page of the selected project

The *View* pick list offers nineteen default views for the *Project Details* page along with any custom views created by your Project Server administrator. These nineteen views include three types of detailed project views: *Task* views, *Assignment* views, and *Resource* views. Table 8 - 1 lists the available views for each type.

 The system remembers which detailed project view you select each time you display the *Project Details* page, and returns to that view when you select another project from the *Project Center* page.

Task Views	Assignment Views	Resource Views
Tasks Cost	Assignments Cost	Resources Cost
Tasks Detail	Assignments Detail	
Tasks Earned Value	Assignments Earned Value	Resources Earned Value
Tasks Leveling		
Tasks Schedule		
Tasks Summary	Assignments Summary	Resources Summary
Tasks Top-Level		
Tasks Tracking	Assignments Tracking	
Tasks Work	Assignments Work	Resources Work

Table 8 - 1: Available Views on the Project Details page

Like *Project Center* views, you can apply grouping and filtering to any detailed project view. Use the *Zoom In* and *Zoom Out* buttons to change the Gantt chart timescale from periods as small as 15-minute intervals to as large as years. Use the *Scroll to Task* button to scroll the Gantt chart to the start date of the selected task.

Hands On Exercise

Exercise 8-1

Explore Project Center views.

1. Click the *Project Center* link in the *Quick Launch* menu.

2. In the *Data* section of the *Projects* ribbon, click the *View* pick list and apply each of the five default *Project Center* views individually.

3. Explore the information shown in each *Project Center* view.

4. Reapply the *Summary* view.

5. In the *Data* section of the *Projects* ribbon, click the *Group by* pick list and select the *Owner* field.

6. Note that the display changes to the grouped view.

7. In the *Data* section of the *Projects* ribbon, select the *Filter* pick list to create your own custom filter and note the results.

Exercise 8-2

Explore detailed Project views from the Project Center.

1. Click the name of a project in the *Project Center* data grid.

2. In the *Data* section of the *Task* ribbon, select any *Assignments* view from the *View* pick list.

3. In the *Data* section of the *Task* ribbon, select any *Resources* view from the *View* pick list.

4. In the *Data* section of the *Task* ribbon, select any *Tasks* view from the *View* pick list.

5. Click the *Project Center* link in the *Quick Launch* menu to return to the *Project Center* page.

Editing Projects in Project Web App

Not only can you view information in project detail views, you can also edit projects using these views. You can open a project for editing within Project Web App or open a project for editing in Project Professional from the *Project Center* page in Project Web App.

Editing Individual Projects in Project Web App

Select the header row for a single project in the *Project Center* data grid and then click the *Open* pick list from the *Project* section of the *Projects* ribbon. Select the *In Project Web App* item from the list and the system displays the *Schedule* page for the project as shown in Figure 8 - 12. Notice that the only items active on the *Task* ribbon are the *Edit* button in the *Project* section, the *Copy* button in the *Clipboard* section, and various options to control the view in both the *Data* and *Zoom* sections. Notice also the status bar below the ribbon telling you that the project is checked-in and the last modified date. You cannot use the scheduling tools until you check out the project for editing.

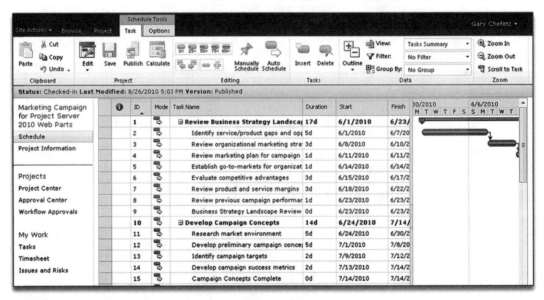

Figure 8 - 12: Project Schedule page

When you open a project that is in a stage of a workflow that occurs prior to allowing users to edit the schedule, you may not be able to access the *Schedule* page for the project. Instead, the system displays the set of *Project Detail Pages* that the creator of the workflow determined that you should see at the current stage.

To edit the project, click on the *Edit* pick list from the *Project* section of the *Task* ribbon and choose the *In Project Web App* item. The system opens the project for editing, refreshes the page, updates the *Status* bar below the ribbon to indicate the project is checked out, and makes all but the *Edit* button on the ribbon available for use as shown in Figure 8 - 13.

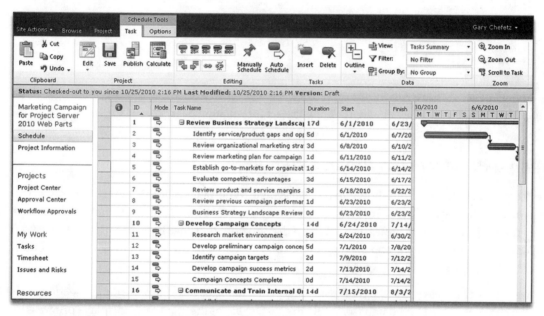

Figure 8 - 13: Project Open for Editing

When you open a project in Project Web App, you may see as few as one *Project Detail* page besides the *Schedule* page or you may see quite a few. If your project is not past a proposal stage, you might not see the *Schedule* page. Your Project Server implementer or administrator who manages your *Project Detail Pages* or workflow determines the pages that you encounter here as well as their contents. Because these can vary widely from system to system, I cannot predict everything that you might encounter. Some pages may contain data that you can edit while other pages may present data that you cannot edit. You should see the *Schedule* page once a project is beyond an approval stage that allows you to manage it, and you should see at least one *Project Detail* page that allows you to edit basic project information, such as the *Project Name*, and other general information as well as local and enterprise custom fields. In the example above, I select the *Project Information* page from the *Quick Launch* menu and the system displays the *Project Information* page shown in Figure 8 - 14. Note that similar pages in your system might not have the same name.

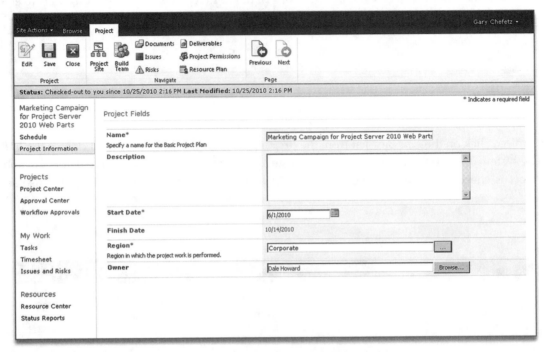

Figure 8 - 14: Project Information page

Renaming a Project using Project Web App

To rename the project, edit the name shown in the *Name* field. When you edit the name of the project, this action re-names the project in the Project Server 2010 database. Changing the name in the *Owner* field allows the new owner to see and open the project in Project Professional 2010, if they do not otherwise have permission to access the project. In addition to editing the *Project Name* and *Owner* fields, you can also edit the values in any custom enterprise Project fields.

After you make your changes on the *Project Details* page, click the *Save* button in the *Project* section of the *Project* rib-bon to save the changes in the *Draft* database. While the system saves the changes, it displays progress information in the upper right corner of the page.

Warning: To rename the project, you must both save and publish the project. When you save the project, the system changes the project name in the *Draft* database. When you publish the project, the system changes the project name in the *Published* database and in the Project Site associated with the project.

If you want to publish the changes to the *Published* database, click the *Schedule* link or the *Project Name* link from the *Quick Launch* menu. The system displays the *Schedule* page. On the *Tasks* ribbon, click the *Publish* button in the *Projects* section. While the system publishes the changes, it displays progress information in the upper right corner of the page. When finished, click on the *Project* tab to expose the *Project* ribbon and then click the *Close* button. The system displays the *Close* dialog shown in Figure 8 - 15.

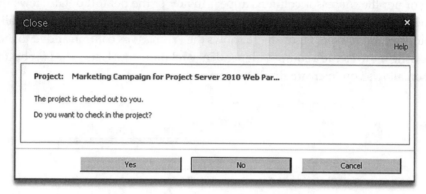

Figure 8 - 15: Close dialog

The *Close* dialog gives you the option to check in your project by clicking the *Yes* button or the option to check out your project by clicking the *No* button. Click the *Cancel* button if you want to cancel your action. Clicking the *Yes* button closes and checks in the project so that others can edit it.

Hands On Exercise

Exercise 8-3

Edit the Project details for an enterprise project.

1. Select the **Microsoft Office 2010 Corporate Upgrade** project by clicking on the row header in the *Project Center* data grid. In the *Project* section of the *Projects* ribbon, click the *Open* pick list and select the *In Project Web App for Editing* item.

2. Click the *Project Information* link in the *Quick Launch* menu to display the *Project Details* page.

3. Change the value in the *Region* custom enterprise project field.

4. In the *Project* section of the *Project* ribbon, click the *Save* button.

5. Click the *Schedule* link or the *Microsoft Office 2010 Corporate Upgrade* link from the *Quick Launch* menu.

6. Click on the *Project* tab to display the *Project* ribbon. In the *Project* section of the *Project* ribbon, click the *Save* button to save your project, then close and check in your project.

Editing the Project Schedule in Project Web App

With your project open for editing and the *Schedule* page displayed in Project Web App, you can edit your project schedule in a variety of ways. You can create, edit, and delete tasks and you can link tasks using Project Web App. You can add resources to tasks using Project Web App, but this feature is limited to assigning resources at 100% units only. For the most part, the system limits you to editing only what you can see. For instance, you can create complex dependency relationships such as finish-to-finish, start-to-start and add lead or lag time to dependencies; however, neither the predecessor nor the successor columns appear in any of the default detail views that ship with Project Server. Therefore, you should ask your Project Server administrator to create one or more detail views suited to perform the type of editing you want to do. Figure 8 - 16 shows the *Predecessors* column added to the *Tasks Detail* view in Project Web App allowing me to create a complex dependency relationship. Using the *Link* button on the *Editing* section of the *Tasks* ribbon allows you to create finish-to-start dependencies only.

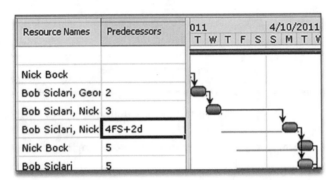

Figure 8 - 16: Predecessors added to Tasks Detail view

 MsProjectExperts recommends that your Project Server administrator or implementer create views specifically for editing projects as the product team designed all of the default views for viewing and not editing. By creating views specifically for this purpose, you can expose the information you need to edit and not information that you do not want edited in Project Web App.

When you float your mouse pointer over a cell in the *Resource Names* column, the system reveals a pick list menu with the resource names shown in Figure 8 - 17.

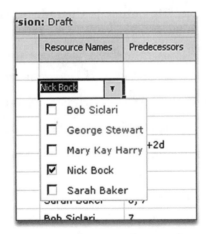

Figure 8 - 17: Resource Names column

Notice that the pick list allows you to select resources only, but it does not allow you to specify or edit the assignment units value. You also cannot specify the task type. Project Web App uses the default task type specified for the project. If you use *Fixed Work* as a task type in any of your projects, it renders them read-only in Project Web App.

Limitations when Editing Projects in Project Web App

There are a number of features not supported when you edit projects in Project Web App. The most important limitations are those that cause your project to be ineligible for editing as follows:

- Blank task lines or blank rows in a project schedule cause a project to open read-only and the system will not allow you to edit the schedule. Project in a stand-alone environment can handle blank lines, but realize that when you save your schedules to Project Server, you are saving to a database. Databases do not handle blank records very well. Besides making your schedule ineligible for editing in Project Web App, these can cause unexpected problems elsewhere in the system.

- The server-side scheduling engine cannot handle *Fixed Work* type tasks. If you include these in your schedule using Project Professional, you cannot edit your project in Project Web App.

- Other than using Project Web App to create master projects, you cannot edit master projects in Project Web App. These will always open read-only.

- Project Web App does not support editing projects with Task Calendars applied. If you include these in your project schedules, they will open read-only in Project Web App.

- Beyond those items that render your project read-only in Project Web App, you should be aware of functional limitations you face when editing a project on the web as follows:

- You cannot set a baseline from Project Web App. Before releasing your project to production, you must open it using Project Professional 2010 to save a baseline.

- You cannot edit assignment details in Project Web App. Actions like changing resource units or contouring work are beyond Project Web App's capabilities as is resource leveling. Just about everything you can think of doing to an assignment besides creating one at 100% units, is out of Project Web App's reach.

- You cannot make a task inactive using Project Web App.

- Cross-project links require that you use Project Professional 2010.

- You cannot make an assignment on summary tasks using Project Web App. Although there are some advanced scheduling techniques where assignments on summary tasks is useful, these are generally a bad idea and can cause unexpected results if you do not understand the ramifications.

- Cost and Material resource assignments are out of reach in Project Web App. You must use the Project Professional client to support these.

- Not surprisingly, you cannot set a *Task* type in Project Web App. Keep in mind the limitation of using *Fixed Work* tasks.

- You cannot edit a subproject, or create or edit master projects using Project Web App, except for the technique I showed you earlier in this module.

- You must set deadlines for tasks using Project Professional, as nothing in Project Web App that allows you to do this.

- You must edit WBS fields using Project Professional as Project Web App does not support setting or editing these.

- The web-scheduling engine does not support *effort-driven* scheduling; therefore, you must address effort-driven tasks using Project Professional. Notice that the system deselects the *effort-driven* option by default in Project 2010.

Tips for Editing Projects in Project Web App

Perhaps the most significant experience difference between editing in the client application versus editing in Project Web App is that Project Web App does not recalculate the schedule for you with every entry the way Project Professional does when you have the *Calculation* option set to *Automatic*. Opening and closing the file does invoke the scheduling engine similar to Project Professional. Because there is no automatic calculation setting for Project Web App, you must use the *Calculate* button from the *Project* section of the *Task* ribbon to see the effect your edits have on the schedule when you edit details that cause the schedule to change.

When you edit projects in Project Web App, it is very easy to forget to save and check in your projects. Unlike the Project client, which will continue to remain open on your desktop until you close it, it is very easy to wander off to other tasks without saving your changes or checking in your project. You must be constantly mindful of this or you are likely to cause frustration for yourself and others by forgetting these important steps. If you are trying to edit a project in Project Web App and you cannot, ask yourself whether you remembered to open it for editing. Remember that the status bar that appears just below the ribbon when you open a project for editing contains important information regarding the current state of your project.

Checking In a Project from Project Web App

Occasionally you will leave a project in a checked-out state caused by a network problem or a workstation crash. Fortunately, the system allows you to check in your own projects without seeking administrative help. To check in a project, navigate to the *Project Center* page and click the *Check in my projects* item in the *Navigate* section of the *Projects* ribbon. Project Server 2010 displays the *Force Check-in My Projects* page shown in Figure 8 - 18.

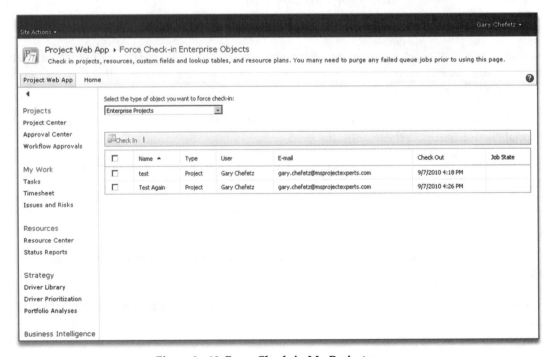

Figure 8 - 18: Force Check-in My Projects page

The *Force Check-in My Projects* page lists all projects currently checked out to you, including projects that are stuck in a checked-out state and projects that you currently have open in Project Professional 2010. Notice that Figure 8 - 18 displays only two projects.

To check in a project, select the option checkbox to the left of one or more projects to check in and click the *Check-In* button on the toolbar. The system displays the confirmation dialog shown in Figure 8 - 19. When you click the *OK* button, the system redisplays the *Force Check-in My Projects* page with the projects that you selected removed from the view.

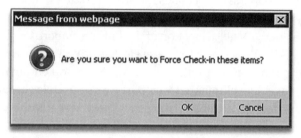

Figure 8 - 19: Confirmation dialog for Force Check-in

 If you have administrative rights to force check-in projects in the system, you see more than your own projects in the *Force Check-in My Projects* page.

Understanding Show/Hide Options

The *Show/Hide* section of the *Projects* ribbon contains two options: *Subprojects* and *Time with Date*. When you select the checkbox for *Time with Date* the system redisplays the page with a time in every date field as shown in Figure 8 - 20.

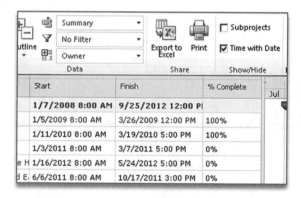

Figure 8 - 20: Showing Time with Date

Selecting the *Subprojects* checkbox produces a more subtle change to the page. When you deselect this in your view, and there are master projects in the system, you do not see the individual plans that are part of the master projects in the individual rows for projects. Instead, the system hides these from view and you must select the master project to drill down into the subprojects. When you select the *Subprojects* check box, the system displays the subprojects as in-

261

dividual project records and it displays the master project. Select the options that best fit your needs for any work session.

Navigating to the Project Site

You use the *Project Center* page to access the Project Sites for projects or to navigate directly to the *Risks, Issues, Documents,* or *Deliverables* page for a project. To navigate to the Project Site for any project, select the project row header and click the *Project Site* button from the *Navigate* section of the *Projects* ribbon. Project Server 2010 opens a new Internet Explorer window and displays the Project Site for your selected project as shown in Figure 8 - 21. The Project Center is your primary starting point for navigating to Project Sites as Microsoft eliminated a web part that displayed the sites in a list on the PWA home page. The eliminated web part was unpopular because it lacked display controls to make it useful for large project portfolios. Because I discussed Project Sites extensively in Module 06, I do not discuss this topic again in this module.

Figure 8 - 21: Project Site home page

From the Project Site home page, you can drilldown into any of the functional lists for the project such as Risks, Issues or Documents associated with the project. You can also access these directly from the *Project Center* page if any of these items exist for a project. Notice the *Indicators* column identified with the icon ⓘ in the *Project Center* page shown in Figure 8 - 22.

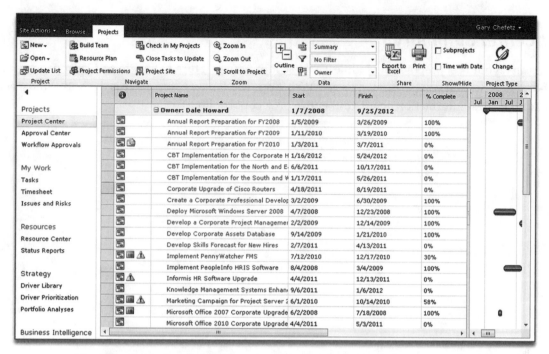

Figure 8 - 22: Project Center page shows indicators in the Indicators column

You can quickly see the meaning of the indicators by floating your mouse over any icon in the *Indicators* column for any project. The resulting tooltip displays the type of project and the number of Risks, Issues, and Documents associated with the project. Table 8 - 2 displays the indicators you may see in the *Indicators* column.

Indicator	Meaning
	Enterprise project
	Master Project
	Risks
	Issues
	Documents

Table 8 - 2: Indicators shown in the Project Center page

To access the *Risks, Issues, Documents,* or *Deliverables* page for any project, do one of the following:

- Click the *Risks, Issues,* or *Documents* indicator in the *Indicators* column to the left of the project.

- Select the row header for a project, click the *Project Site* button, and then select the *Risks, Issues, Documents,* or *Deliverables* in the Project Site home page.

Project Server 2010 opens a new Internet Explorer window and displays the Project Site for the selected project.

Project Center Summary

Since you created your first proposal in Module 03, you continuously return to the *Project Center* page to launch most of the day-to-day tasks that you perform in Project Web App. The *Project Center* page is the hub of most activity and the source for the latest information about your entire project portfolio.

Module 09

Working with Business Intelligence

Learning Objectives

After completing this module, you will be able to:

- Understand three common Business Intelligence uses for Project Managers

- Understand and be capable of using the Project Server 2010 Business Intelligence features

- Understand which data source is most applicable for a given need

- Create dashboard ready reports

- Create a basic dashboard

This module also assumes some basic knowledge of Excel operations, such as sorting and filtering.

Inside Module 09

Understanding Project Server 2010 Business Intelligence

What is Business Intelligence?

Business Intelligence (BI) is a set of processes, tools, and techniques for gathering, organizing, and analyzing large volumes of complex data in an effort to develop an accurate understanding of business dynamics, and you use it to improve strategic and tactical business decision-making. In other words, the purpose of BI is to capture large amounts of data, make some sense out of it, and use it to make sound business decisions. The ultimate goal is to develop the ability to spot problems and trends, and to make informed decisions to mitigate risks, improve efficiencies, and identify opportunities.

The data visualization aspects of the BI process are commonly referred to as reporting, a term with which you may be more familiar.

Project Server 2010 Business Intelligence differs from the Project Client Business Intelligence capabilities in that you are able to do analysis and reporting across multiple projects and resources across the organization. This enhanced scope enables you to see beyond your project plan and understand other impacts to your plan.

Levels of Business Intelligence

Business Intelligence needs are broken down into three major groups as shown in Figure 9 - 1. For Managers, the emphasis of this module will be on Personal and Collaborative BI.

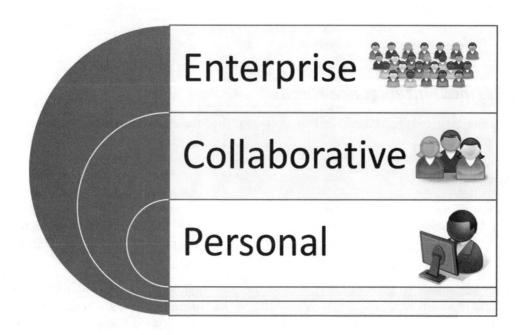

Figure 9 - 1: Levels of Business Intelligence

Personal Business Intelligence

Personal BI enables better decision-making for the person consuming the information in order to accomplish their work in a more effective manner. This type of BI can include personal ad hoc and single use reports, which you use to address short-term situations or specific questions, respectively. Personal BI also tends to be tactical in nature. An example of Personal BI is a Project Last Status Update report used by the Project Manager to ensure timely status updates from each Project Team member.

Collaborative Business Intelligence

Collaborative BI enables better information sharing and decision-making within an interested group of people where other methods of collaboration (email, face to face, etc.) can no longer meet the group's information needs effectively. Commonly, this BI addresses information needs of the Project Team, Project Stakeholders, Work Team or Department. This type of BI addresses both short term and long-term information needs of the group. An example of Collaborative BI is a Project Status Dashboard, which allows stakeholders to see current status, issues, risks and milestones.

Enterprise Business Intelligence

Enterprise BI enables better information sharing and decision-making where the system collects and uses requisite information across the Enterprise. Enterprise Business Intelligence typically focuses on long term needs. An example of Enterprise Business Intelligence is a Project Portfolio Cash Flow Projection report across all ongoing projects. Finance would use such a report as an input to their Enterprise Cash Flow Projection. Project Managers normally do not address Enterprise Business Intelligence needs.

Common Business Intelligence Needs

A project effort is similar to managing a car trip in many ways. The Project Manager's BI needs, as the driver, can be broken down as follows:

Analysis and Planning

The Project Manager's Analysis and Planning needs focus on what needs to occur to accomplish planned project goals and assumptions. Where there is deviation from the original plan, this need also encompasses the generation of alternatives to meet the plan. Lastly, there is an ongoing need to validate the plan against changing business conditions and project risks as to alert the Project Manager to potential issues.

Similarly, a driver determines where they are going and the best possible route to get there based on trip requirements. (We will take this route so we can see the World's largest ball of string!). The driver also plans out where they are going (outcome), where they will possibly stop (milestones), and makes adjustments to achieve progress as weather and road conditions affect the plan (risk management). Project BI systems make it easier to accomplish this need just as GPS-based navigation systems have made it much easier for drivers to meet similar needs through automatic route generation.

Status Reporting

The Project Manager's Status Reporting needs focus on communicating the current state of the effort and health of the plan to the Project Team and to other interested parties. The current state need ensures that all interested parties receive consistent information for decision-making and planning.

Similarly, the current position of a driver can be the most valuable information delivered by a navigation system. By knowing where you are, you can plan a path to a specific destination.

Progress Monitoring

Project Managers monitor progress so that they can clearly communicate short-term plans and ensure that the team is expending the effort required to meet the plan objectives. Variations of effort at this level can translate to larger progress issues over time. Similarly, a navigation system calculates the average speed of the driver and time to goal. If the driver decides to make a large number of stops, finds himself caught in traffic or decides to take a scenic detour, the navigation system shows the impact accordingly.

Understanding Business Intelligence Features

It is important for the Project Manager to understand what tools and data the system provides to meet their information needs. The Project Manager toolbox has three components: data, reporting tools and built-in content.

Understanding Available Data

Project Server 2010 generates a great deal of data about the current state of projects, resources, timesheets and the interactions between them. All Business Intelligence data for Project Server 2010 is contained within two data stores. The first is the relational data store, commonly referred to as either the *Reporting* database or RDB. This data store is always available, assuming your Project Server Administrator provided you with the appropriate security access. The other data store contains one or more optional OLAP analytical databases. The Project Server Administrator determines the number and content of these OLAP databases. I cover these two data stores in detail in subsequent sections. All OLAP analytical data derives from the Reporting Database.

Which Data Should I Use?

You should base your decision as to which data source to use on two primary factors, the timeliness of the data you need and the type of intelligence you require. Table 9 - 1 shows examples of needs and the appropriate data for such need. The data in the Reporting Database is most appropriate for factual intelligence needs that require near real time accuracy. The system places the data in the Reporting Database at nearly the same time that Project publishes and other save operations occur. Therefore, the RDB best serves any short term or near term information need. You can best use this data for situations where lists of information are necessary.

OLAP data, on the other hand, is best suited for analytical intelligence needs. The construction of the OLAP data structures the data in such a fashion as to optimize it for doing aggregation and summation of data. However, the freshness of the data is only as good as the last time you refreshed the OLAP data. In some cases, this data can be several days old. Therefore, OLAP data may be better suited to longer-term data analysis.

Example Question	OLAP Data	Relational Data
What are the differences in average Project Risk exposure between organizational regions?	X	
What projects will complete this month?		X
Have all timesheets been processed for the prior period?		X
How does the level of administrative time this quarter compare to that of past quarters?	X	

Table 9 - 1: Examples of Needs and Appropriate Data for Need

Relational Data

The primary data elements contained within the RDB are as follows:

- Project Decisions
- Projects
- Tasks
- Assignments
- Resources
- Issues
- Risks
- Deliverables
- Workflows
- Tasks by Day
- Assignments by Day
- Resources by Day
- Timesheet and Administrative Time
- Other Supporting entities such as Time reporting periods, etc.

You can visualize these elements as related elements using the diagram in Figure 9 - 2. You should use the diagram to decide what data entities are required to support a particular Business Intelligence need. For example, you create a report of timesheet entries which you group by Project Manager and Resource Type. You include Projects, Timesheet Lines, Resources and Resource Types in your query. You must also include the Resource entity because you make the relationship between Resource Type and Timesheet Lines through the Resource entity.

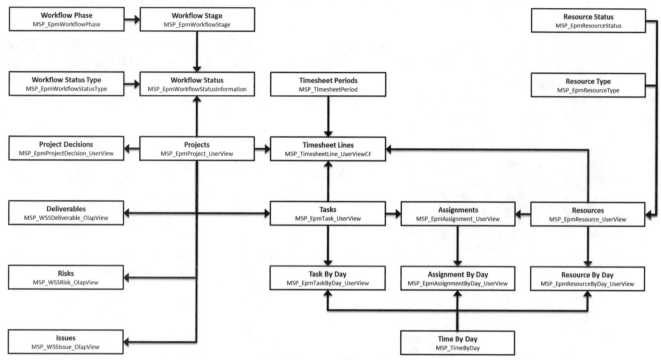

Figure 9 - 2: Reporting Database Item Relationships

Analytical Data

The OLAP data entities are similar to that present in the Relational data. You will see Projects, Tasks, Resources, Assignments, Timesheet, and Time itself. However, the system optimizes the organization of this data for analysis and exploration without the need for complex queries or knowledge of Structured Query Language (SQL).

Understanding how OLAP data is organized and the terms used helps you navigate your way to solving your information needs as well as making it easier for you to find additional information. A database contains each instance of OLAP data. Project Server supports multiple OLAP databases, your particular OLAP instance may contain all Project Server data or just data related to your Project and/or Resource department.

There are fourteen OLAP cubes within each Project Server OLAP database. Each cube organizes the data to support a particular information need. An Excel report template for each cube within a particular OLAP database provides easy access to the data. In order to get the most from OLAP, you should understand four terms and what they mean. These terms relate to Excel functionality, which you learn about when you author reports. You structure OLAP data by:

- Measures

- Dimensions

- Attributes

- Attribute properties

Measures are the aggregated factual data upon which you base your analysis. In Project Server, measures are *Cost*, *Duration,* or *Number* fields as the system can aggregate these values via summing, averaging, etc. Examples of measures are *Capacity* and *Work*.

Dimensions categorize and provide context to the underlying *Measure* data. For example, to breakdown *Capacity* and *Work* by Project, Resource, you use the Project List and Resource List Dimensions to provide requisite data breakdown.

Dimensions are collections of *Attribute* values where each attribute represents a unique value. You can also structure attributes as a hierarchy. The Resource Breakdown Structure dimension illustrates how each RBS value (Corporate, Corporate.Sales, Corporate.Sales and Corporate.IT) represents an attribute as shown in Figure 9 - 3. Because RBS is a hierarchical dimension, the *Corporate at Level 1* RBS value results in a rollup of data from Corporate.Sales and Corporate.IT at Level 2.

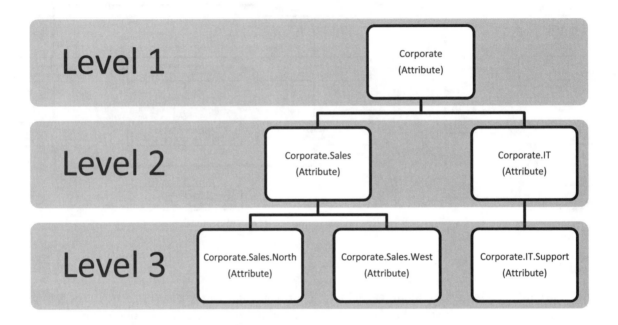

Figure 9 - 3: Example of the RBS Dimension with Hierarchy Levels and Attributes

Attributes can also have Properties, which extended information related to the attribute. For example, a project called *Implement PennyWatcher FMS*, which is an attribute in the Project List dimension, has properties such as a Project Start Date of 2/11/2011 and a Percent Complete of 0%.

Understanding the Toolset

Project Server 2010 has several Business Intelligence tools you can use to meet your needs. The primary tools covered here will be those that Project Managers most commonly use.

Excel

The cornerstone of Project Reporting depends on Excel 2007 or later versions and their PivotTable/Pivot Chart functionality shown in Figure 9 - 4. Pivot functionality is the only way to create Excel reports that can pull the latest data on demand from the Project Server. You use Excel to author new reports, change existing reports to meet current need and to view reports on the desktop. You use the Excel client exclusively to meet your Personal Business Intelligence needs.

Excel connects to the Project Server Data Stores via a file known as an Office Data Connection (ODC). The ODC file contains the details of how to connect to the data source. The Project Server Business Intelligence Center contains a library of ODCs that you can re-use to create new reports. I cover this topic in more detail in a later Hands On Exercise.

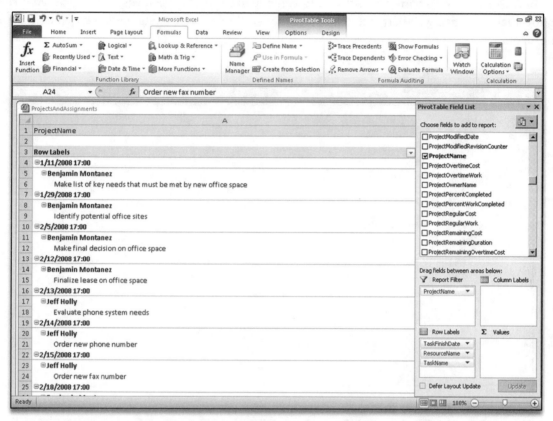

Figure 9 - 4: Example of Excel PivotTable

Excel Services

Excel Services is SharePoint functionality that enables you to publish and share Excel Reports via a SharePoint site as shown in Figure 9 - 5. When you create a report in Excel client, it publishes the report through Excel Services. Once published, anyone with the appropriate security rights can use the interactive report. Once enabled on a SharePoint farm, a report author can host and render reports on any site within the farm. This flexibility provides Project Managers with the ability to customize reporting specific to the needs of each project that they manage.

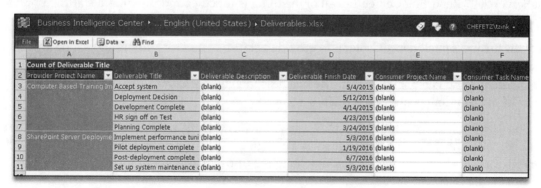

Figure 9 - 5: Example of an Excel Services Report

SharePoint Web Part Pages

SharePoint Web Part Pages, as shown in Figure 9 - 6, are pages that host web parts, and enable you to create customized BI dashboards as. Web parts are modular containers that enable you to create a customized experience without coding or IT involvement. Web parts can host specific content, like reports, RSS feeds, or text you type. You can also link them together so that all web parts act in unison to show different information related to the same project, resource and so on.

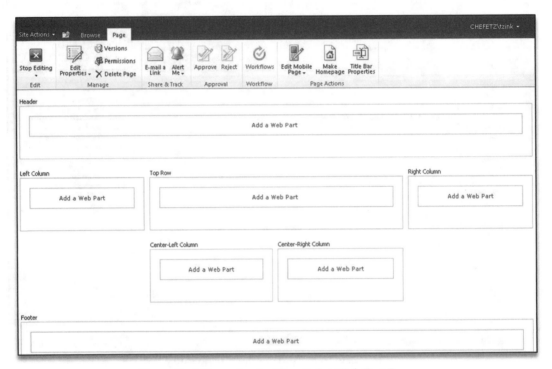

Figure 9 - 6: Example of a SharePoint Web Part Page

The Business Intelligence Center

The Business Intelligence Center, a sub-site of your PWA site in the SharePoint hierarchy, organizes and provides immediate access to all of these report delivery tools in a single location. This site, evolved from the Microsoft Office SharePoint Server 2007 Reporting Center, ties all of the BI tools together and provides a starting point for a Project Server BI portal.

The intent of the Business Intelligence Center is to provide a starting point for authors and to house BI content for Enterprise and Collaborative BI needs. In this module's Hands On Exercises, I show you how to use your Project Team Site as a Collaborative and Personal BI portal. The Business Intelligence Center also contains the central authorized library of all Office Data Connections used in the system.

To visit the Business Intelligence Center, click the *Business Intelligence* link in the *Quick Launch* menu. The system displays the *Business Intelligence Center* home page shown in Figure 9 - 7. To navigate back to the PWA site, click the *Project Web App* tab located above the *Quick Launch* menu in the upper left corner of the page.

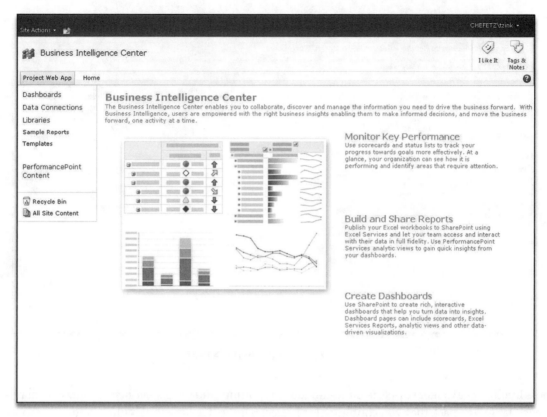

Figure 9 - 7: Business Intelligence Center home page

Understanding Sample Content

Project Server provides a number of content types that give your report development a significant boost. From Sample reports to report templates, and pre-provisioned Office Data Connections files for both the Reporting database and OLAP cubes, getting started with building reports in Project Server has never been easier. Using these basic parts as building blocks, you can quickly take advantage of the rich SharePoint and Office reporting tools at your disposal.

Built-In Sample Reports

Project Server 2010 provides sample Microsoft Excel reports that the system pre-connects to the Project Server Reporting Database through ODC files saved in the Project Server BI Data Store. Microsoft intended that these reports provide the report author with a starting point for creating new reports. The system targets some of these reports to PMO use and you can repurpose many of them for use on a specific project. To view these reports, visit the *Business Intelligence Center* site and click the *Sample Reports* link in the *Quick Launch* menu. The system displays the *Sample Reports* page shown in Figure 9 - 8.

Figure 9 - 8: Sample Reports page

The Business Intelligence Center supports multi-language reporting, and the *Sample Reports* library contains a separate folder for each language pack that you configure for Project Server. To view the English language reports, click the *English (United States)* folder in the *Sample Reports* library. The system displays the contents of the *English (United States)* folder as shown in Figure 9 - 9.

Figure 9 - 9: English language folder contents in the Sample Reports library

The *Sample Reports* library contains the following sample reports:

- Deliverables (Deliverables.xlsx)

- Issues and Risks (IssuesAndRisks.xlsx)

- Milestones Due This Month (MilestonesDueThisMonth.xlsx)

- Rejected Projects (RejectedProjectsLists.xlsx)

- Resource Capacity (ResourceCapacity.xlsx)

- Simple Projects List (SimpleProjectsList.xlsx)

- Timesheet Actuals (TimesheetActuals.xlsx)

- Top Projects (TopProjects.xlsx)

- Workflow Chart (WorkflowChart.xlsx)

- Workflow Drilldown (WorkflowDrillDown.xlsx)

Deliverables Report

The *Deliverables* report extracts a listing of all Project Server 2010 deliverables from the Project Server *Reporting* database and displays the data in Excel PivotTable format in your web browser, as shown in Figure 9 - 10.

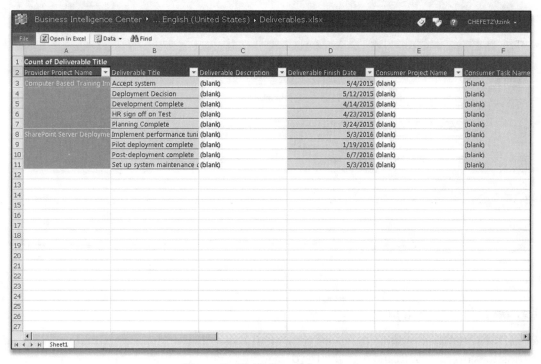

Figure 9 - 10: Deliverables report

Issues and Risks Report

The *Issues and Risks* report extracts a listing of all Project Server issues and risks from the Project Server RDB and displays the data in Excel PivotTable format in your web browser, as shown in Figure 9 - 11 and Figure 9 - 12.

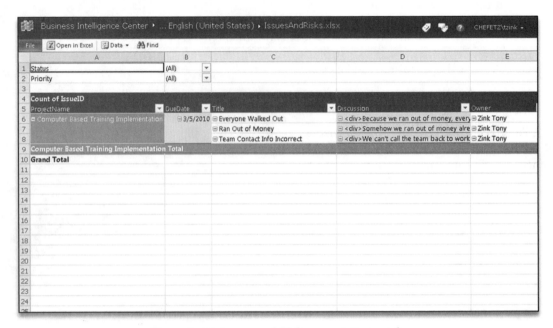

Figure 9 - 11: Issues and Risks report, Issues tab

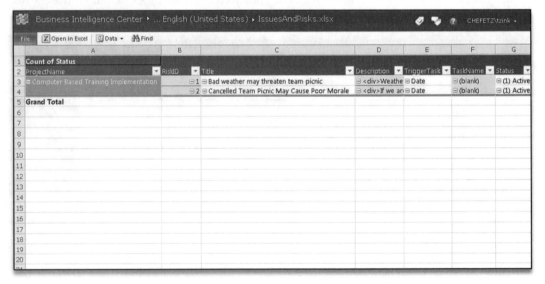

Figure 9 - 12: Issues and Risks report, Risks tab

Milestones Due This Month Report

The *Milestones Due This Month* report extracts a listing of all Project Server milestones that you have scheduled to complete during the current month and displays the data in Excel PivotTable format in your web browser, as shown in Figure 9 - 13.

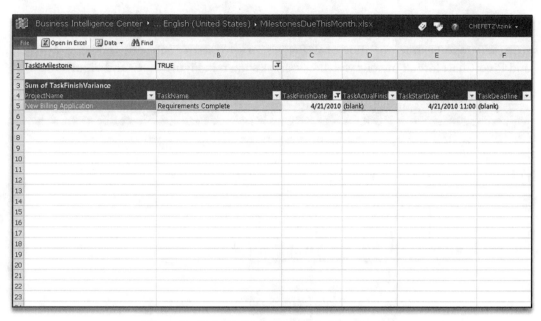

Figure 9 - 13: Milestones Due This Month report

Rejected Projects Report

The *Rejected Projects* report extracts a listing of all rejected Project Server projects and displays the data in Excel Pivot-Table format in your web browser, as shown in Figure 9 - 14.

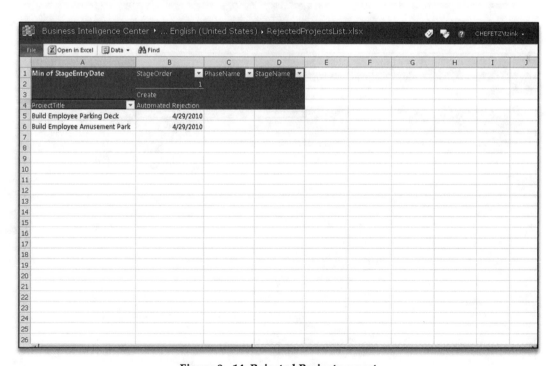

Figure 9 - 14: Rejected Projects report

Resource Capacity Report

The *Resource Capacity* report extracts a listing of all Project Server resource capacities and displays the data in Excel PivotTable and PivotChart format in your web browser, as shown in Figure 9 - 15 and Figure 9 - 16.

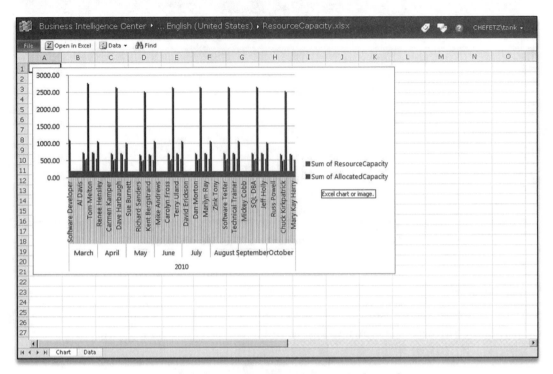

Figure 9 - 15: Resource Capacity report, chart tab

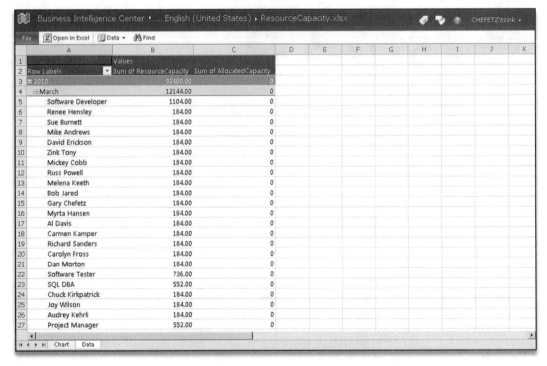

Figure 9 - 16: Resource Capacity report, data tab

Simple Projects List Report

The *Simple Projects List* report extracts a listing of all Project Server projects from the Project Server RDB and displays the data in Excel PivotTable format in your web browser, as shown in Figure 9 - 17.

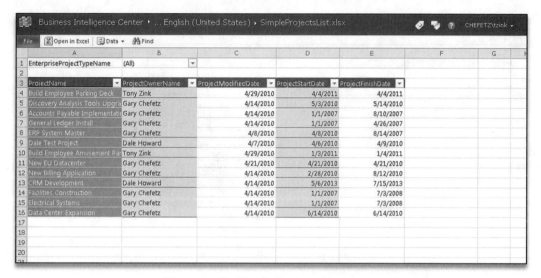

Figure 9 - 17: Simple Projects List report

Timesheet Actuals Report

The *Timesheet Actuals* report extracts a listing of all Project Server timesheet work hours from the Project Server RDB and displays the data in an approval process step grouping, in Excel PivotTable format in your web browser, as shown in Figure 9 - 18.

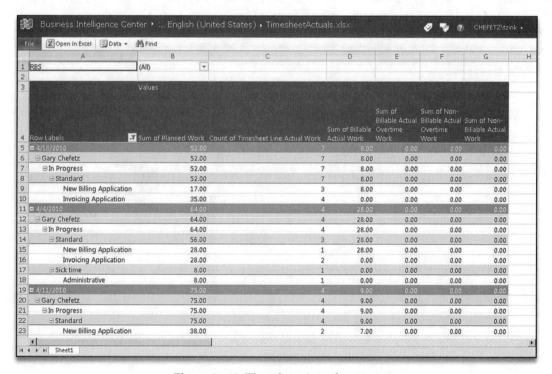

Figure 9 - 18: Timesheet Actuals report

Top Projects Report

The *Top Projects* report extracts a listing of top proposals and costs from the Project Server Reporting Database and displays the data in Excel PivotTable and PivotChart format in your web browser, as shown in Figure 9 - 19.

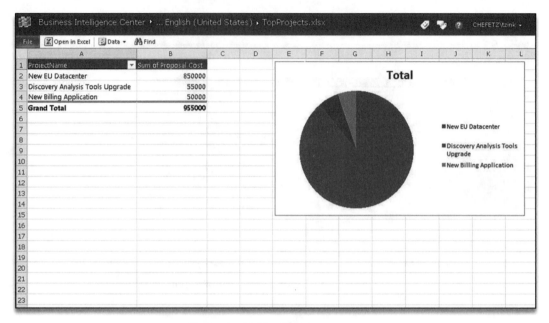

Figure 9 - 19: Top Projects report

Workflow Chart Report

The *Workflow Chart* report displays a count of all projects by system workflow stage from the Project Server RDB and displays the data in Excel PivotTable and PivotChart format in your web browser, as shown in Figure 9 - 20.

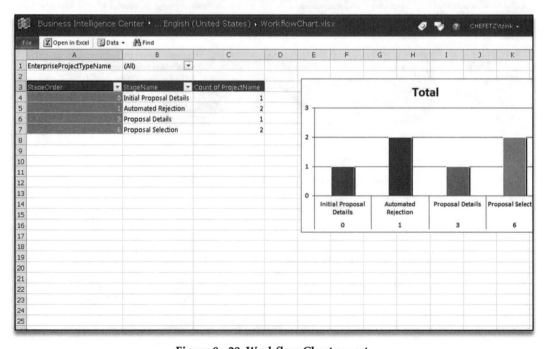

Figure 9 - 20: Workflow Chart report

Workflow Drilldown Report

The *Workflow Drilldown* report extracts a listing of detailed workflow stage status information from the Project Server RDB and displays the data in Excel PivotTable format in your web browser, as shown in Figure 9 - 21.

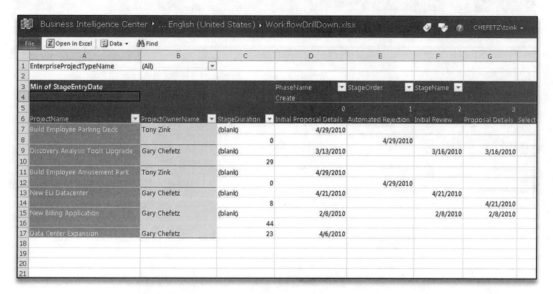

Figure 9 - 21: Workflow Drilldown report

Report Templates

Project Server provides you with Microsoft Excel report templates that use the pre-connected ODC files to get you quickly connected to your data. To view these report templates, from the Business Intelligence Center click the *Templates* link in the *Quick Launch* menu. The system displays the *Templates* page shown in Figure 9 - 22.

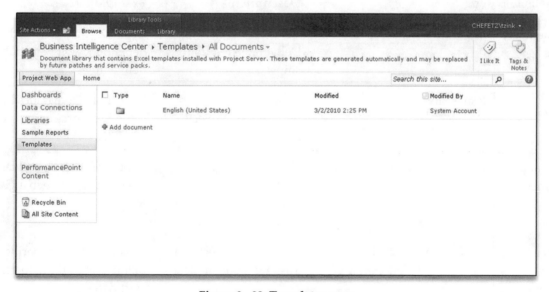

Figure 9 - 22: Templates page

The Business Intelligence Center supports multi-language reporting, and the *Templates* library contains a separate folder for each language pack that you provision for your Project Server. To view the English language reports, click the *English (United States)* folder in the *Templates* library. The system displays the contents of the *English (United States)* folder as shown in Figure 9 - 23.

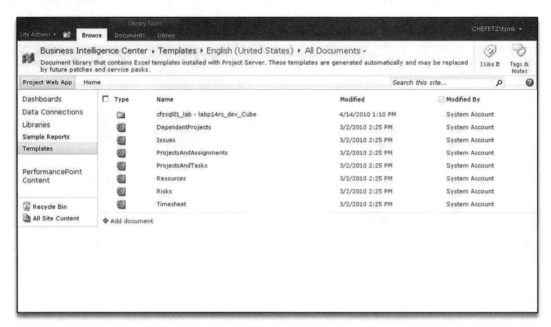

Figure 9 - 23: English language folder contents in the Templates library

The Excel report templates help you build new reports quickly. You can use these as starting points to develop your own custom reports. The system provides templates for each language available on the server.

The English language folder contains seven report templates that arrive pre-connected to the Project Server Reporting Database as shown in Table 9 - 2.

Report Name	File	Description	Example Use
Dependent Projects	DependentProjects.xltx	Visualizes Project to Deliverable relationships.	Report of projects which have a dependency on your published deliverables.
Issues	Issues.xltx	Visualizes Issues data with related Projects and Tasks data.	Report of active issues by assigned resource across your projects.
Projects and Assignments	ProjectsAndAssignments.xltx	Visualizes Project, Task, Assignment, Resource relationship data.	Report of projects and tasks by assigned resource in a given RBS node.
Projects and Tasks	ProjectsAndTasks.xltx	Visualizes Project and Task relationship data.	Task analysis comparing planned start dates to actual start dates.

Report Name	File	Description	Example Use
Resources	Resources.xltx	Visualizes Resource information.	Breakdown of Resource Standard Rates organized by Resource Breakdown Structure value.
Risks	Risks.xltx	Visualizes Risks data with related Project and Tasks data.	Average risk exposure by project.
Timesheet	Timesheet.xltx	Visualizes Timesheet data with related Project and Resource data.	Audit report comparing timesheet entered hours to planned hours.

Table 9 - 2: Built-In Report Descriptions

Every time you create a new OLAP database, the system automatically creates another folder in the *Templates* library containing an additional 14 report templates for that new OLAP database. Each folder contains 14 templates pre-connected to each of the 14 OLAP cubes in each OLAP database as shown in Table 9 - 3.

Report Name	File	Description	Example Use
OLAP Assignment Non-Timephased	OlapAssignmentNonTimephased.xltx	Visualizes point in time Assignment data with related Project, Task and Resource data.	Current Actual Cost total by Project.
OLAP Assignment Timephased	OlapAssignmentTimephased.xltx	Visualizes Assignment data over time with related Project, Task and Resource data.	Current Actual Cost total by Project by Month
OLAP Deliverables	OlapDeliverables.xltx	Visualize Deliverable data.	Count of projects consuming my project's deliverables.
OLAP EPM Timesheet	OlapEpmTimesheet.xltx	Visualize Timesheet data with related Task, Project and Resource data.	Timesheet entries by Project by Month.
OLAP Issues	OlapIssues.xltx	Visualize Issue data.	Active Issues for a particular Vendor across Projects.

Report Name	File	Description	Example Use
OLAP Portfolio Analyzer	OlapPortfolioAnalyzer.xltx	Visualize Assignment and Resource data over time with related Project, Task and Resource Plan data.	Resources by Project which have Resource Plan allocations.
OLAP Project Non-Timephased	OlapProjectNonTimephased.xltx	Visualize point in time Project data.	Projects and Remaining Work grouped by Region custom field.
OLAP Project SharePoint	OlapProjectSharePoint.xltx	Visualize point in time Project data with related Risk, Issue and Deliverable data.	Project Summary with Issue, Risk, Deliverable counts and Overall Risk Exposure
OLAP Project Timesheet	OlapProjectTimesheet.xltx	Visualize Project data over time with related Resource, Timesheet, and Task measures.	Analyze Capacity against Timesheet entries and Actual Work on Tasks against Capacity over time
OLAP Resource Non-Timephased	OlapResourceNonTimephased.xltx	Visualize point in time Resource cost data	Standard rate and Overtime rate of all resources grouped by RBS
OLAP Resource Timephased	OlapResourceTimephased.xltx	Visualize Resource capacity data over time.	Resource Capacity for Quarter 4 2011 by Skill resource custom field.
OLAP Risks	OlapRisks.xltx	Visualize Risk data.	List of risks across all projects which have an exposure of 5 days or more.
OLAP Task Non-Timephased	OlapTaskNonTimephased.xltx	Visualize point in time Task data.	Overallocated non-summary, active tasks across all Projects.
OLAP Timesheet	OlapTimesheet.xltx	Visualize Timesheet data.	Planned and actual administrative time by Month.

Table 9 - 3: Built-In OLAP Template Descriptions

Note that the file extension for the Excel report templates is *.xltx*, rather than *.xlsx*, indicating that they are Excel template files.

Warning: When saving a report created from an Excel report template, verify that you have changed the file extension to *.xlsx*. Otherwise, it will not render in Excel Services.

Office Data Connections

The system pre-connects the sample Excel reports and report templates in the Business Intelligence Center to their respective data sources in the Project Server BI Data Store via an Office Data Connection (ODC) file. The Business Intelligence Center manages these data connections centrally in the *Data Connections* library so that you can share these connections between report authors.

The key benefit for external ODC files is that different reports can use one connection. Therefore, if you are writing a new report, you can use an existing ODC to get to your data. This eliminates the need for you to know things like database server names and SQL queries.

The ODC library contains 13 shared Office Data Connection (ODC) files for connecting to the Project Server Reporting Database, and it contains 14 shared Office Data Connection (ODC) files for connecting reports to each OLAP Database that is available on the server. I show the relationship between Excel Reports, ODCs and your data in Figure 9 - 24.

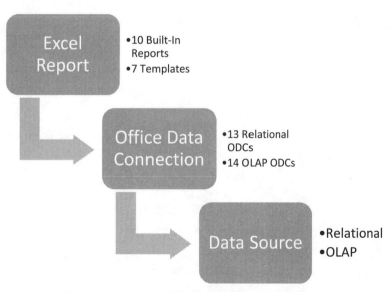

Figure 9 - 24: Excel - ODC - Data Source Relationship

To view these data connection files, navigate to the Business Intelligence Center and click the *Data Connections* link in the *Quick Launch* menu. The system displays the *Data Connections* page shown in Figure 9 - 25.

Figure 9 - 25: Data Connections page

To view the English language data connection files, click the *English (United States)* folder in the *Data Connections* library. The system displays the *English (United States)* folder partially shown in Figure 9 - 26.

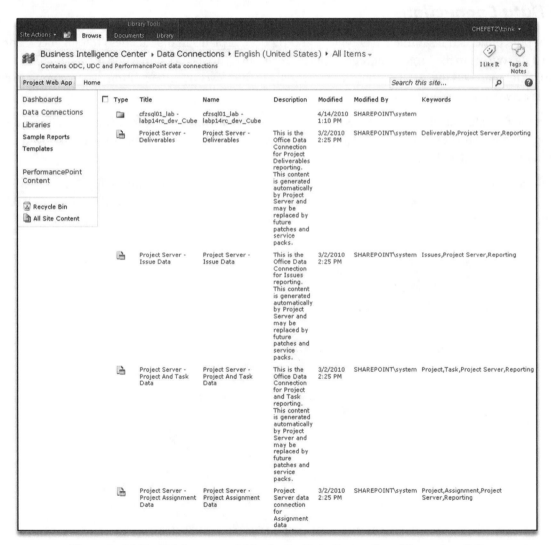

Figure 9 - 26: English language folder in the Data Connections library (partial)

The English language folder contains 13 data connection files for connecting reports to the Project Server Reporting database:

- Project Server - Deliverables (Project Server - Deliverables.odc)

- Project Server - Issue Data (Project Server - Issue Data.odc)

- Project Server - Project And Task Data (Project Server - Project And Task Data.odc)

- Project Server - Project Assignment Data (Project Server - Project Assignment Data.odc)

- Project Server - Rejected Projects List (Project Server - Rejected Projects List.odc)

- Project Server - Resource Capacity (Project Server - Resource Capacity.odc)

- Project Server - Resource Data (Project Server - Resource Data.odc)

- Project Server - Risk Data (Project Server - Risk Data.odc)

- Project Server - Simple Projects List (Project Server - Simple Projects List.odc)

- Project Server - Timesheet Data (Project Server - Timesheet Data.odc)

- Project Server - Top Projects Data (Project Server - Top Projects Data.odc)

- Project Server - Workflow Chart Data (Project Server - Workflow Chart Data.odc)

- Project Server - Workflow Drilldown Data (Project Server - Workflow Drilldown Data.odc)

I illustrate the ODC utilization in the Built-In Reports and Report Templates in Table 9 - 4 and Table 9 - 5.

ODC	Template Name	Description
Project Server - Deliverables.odc	Dependent Projects	Visualizes Project to Deliverable relationships.
Project Server - Issue Data.odc	Issues	Visualizes Issues data with related Projects and Tasks data.
Project Server - Project Assignment Data.odc	Projects and Assignments	Visualizes Project, Task, Assignment, Resource relationship data.
Project Server - Project And Task Data.odc	Projects and Tasks	Visualizes Project and Task relationship data.
Project Server - Resource Data.odc	Resources	Visualizes Resource information.
Project Server - Risk Data.odc	Risks	Visualizes Risks data with related Project and Tasks data.
Project Server - Timesheet Data.odc	Timesheet	Visualizes Timesheet data with related Project and Resource data.

Table 9 - 4: ODC to Template Cross-reference

ODC	Report Name	Description
Project Server - Deliverables.odc	Deliverables	Visualizes Deliverable data
Project Server - Issue Data.odc Project Server - Risk Data.odc	Issues and Risks	Visualizes Issues and Risks data
Project Server - Project And Task Data.odc	Milestones Due This Month	Visualizes all milestones across all projects due this month
Project Server - Rejected Projects List.odc	Rejected Projects	Visualizes projects that were rejected from Portfolio process
Project Server - Resource Capacity.odc	Resource Capacity	Visualizes timephased resource capacity for all resources
Project Server - Simple Projects List.odc	Simple Projects List	Visualizes a simple list of Projects
Project Server - Timesheet Data.odc	Timesheet Actuals	Visualizes all timesheet entries and their current process state by time reporting period
Project Server - Top Projects Data.odc	Top Projects	Visualize the top projects in terms of proposal cost
Project Server - Workflow Chart Data.odc	Workflow Chart	Visualize what projects are in which process stage
Project Server - Workflow Drilldown Data.odc	Workflow Drilldown	Visualize process status across processes.

Table 9 - 5: ODC to Report Cross-reference

The *English language* folder also contains a sub-folder for each OLAP database, each containing 14 data connection files for connecting reports to each of the 14 OLAP cubes in the OLAP database:

- OLAP Assignment Non Timephased (OlapAssignmentNonTimephased.odc)

- OLAP Assignment Timephased (OlapAssignmentTimephased.odc)

- OLAP Deliverables (OlapDeliverables.odc)

- OLAP EPM Timesheet (OlapEpmTimesheet.odc)

- OLAP Issues (OlapIssues.odc)

- OLAP Portfolio Analyzer (OlapPortfolioAnalyzer.odc)

- OLAP Project Non Timephased (OlapProjectNonTimephased.odc)

- OLAP Project SharePoint (OlapMSProjectSharePoint.odc)

- OLAP Project Timesheet (OlapProjectTimesheet.odc)

- OLAP Resource Non Timephased (OlapResourceNonTimephased.odc)

- OLAP Resource Timephased (OlapResourceTimephased.odc)

- OLAP Risks (OlapRisks.odc)

- OLAP Task Non Timephased (OlapTaskNonTimephased.odc)

- OLAP Timesheet (OlapTimesheet.odc)

Using the Project Server 2010 Business Intelligence Features

Viewing a report starts with accessing a report in SharePoint as shown in Figure 9 - 27. For discussion purposes, you will use the Sample Reports that you find in the Business Intelligence Center.

Figure 9 - 27: High Level View Report Process

Viewing Reports

To visit the Business Intelligence Center, click the *Business Intelligence* link in the PWA *Quick Launch* menu. The system displays the *Business Intelligence Center* home page shown in Figure 9 - 28. Notice in the figure that I am hovering my mouse pointer over the *Sample Reports* link. To navigate to the *Sample Reports* library, click on the link. To navigate back to the PWA site, click the *Project Web App* tab located above the *Quick Launch* menu in the upper left corner of the page.

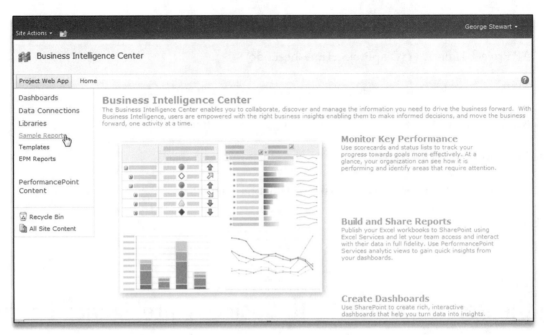

Figure 9 - 28: Business Intelligence Center - Navigate to Sample Reports

The Business Intelligence Center supports multi-language reporting, and the *Sample Reports* library contains a separate folder for each language pack that you configure for Project Server. To view the English language reports, click the *English (United States)* folder in the *Sample Reports* library as I am doing in Figure 9 - 29.

Figure 9 - 29: Select Sample Reports Folder by Language

The system displays the *Sample Reports* library shown in Figure 9 - 30. To view a report, you click on the link to select the name of the report.

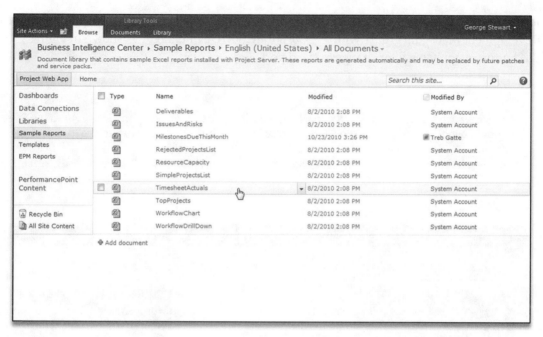

Figure 9 - 30: Select Sample Report to View

For example, George Stewart needs to see where timesheet entries are in the overall process. Aware that there is a *Built-In* report that shows this information, George navigates to the *Sample Reports* folder and selects the *TimesheetAc-tuals* report. After a few seconds, George sees the report shown in Figure 9 - 31. He sees that the system has not approved all time and that some entries show as *In Progress*.

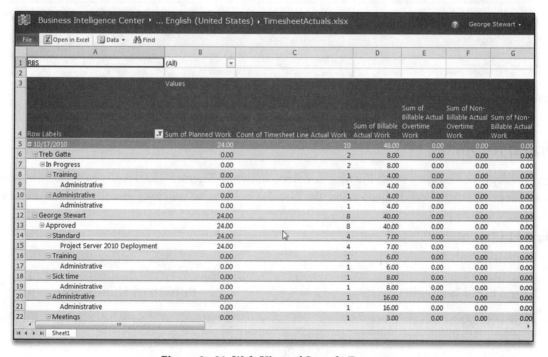

Figure 9 - 31: Web View of Sample Report

Because George is only interested in the data for his own group, he selects the *RBS* filter pick list to select only his Software Development Managers group, which is **Corporate.SoftDev.manager** as shown in Figure 9 - 32. He then clicks the *OK* button to apply his filter change to the report.

A quick way to select only one value in a long filter list is to first deselect the *Select All* value. This removes every selection from the filter. Then select just the values you wish to see in the report.

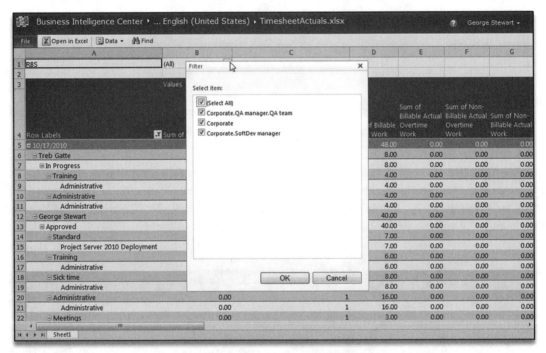

Figure 9 - 32: Example of Web Interactivity

Creating a Report

Creating a new report in Excel involves the four key steps shown in Figure 9 - 33. I cover each of these steps in detail in this topical section. At the end of this section, the Hands On Exercise will take you through the basic process.

Open the Excel Template

Figure 9 - 33: High Level Edit Process

Creating a new report starts with an Excel Template which can be found in the Business Intelligence Center. To visit the Business Intelligence Center, click the *Business Intelligence* link in the PWA *Quick Launch* menu. The system displays the *Business Intelligence Center* home page shown in Figure 9 - 34. To navigate back to the PWA site, click the *Project Web App* tab located above the *Quick Launch* menu in the upper left corner of the page.

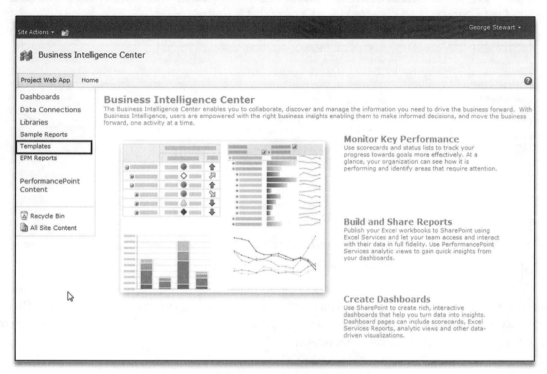

Figure 9 - 34: Business Intelligence Center - Navigate to Templates

The Business Intelligence Center supports multi-language reporting, and the *Templates* library contains a separate folder for each language pack that you configure for Project Server. To view the English language reports, click the *English (United States)* folder in the *Templates* library as shown in Figure 9 - 35.

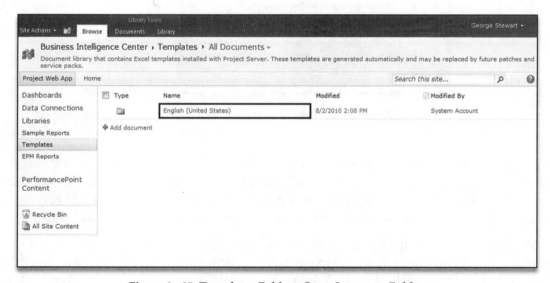

Figure 9 - 35: Templates Folder - Open Language Folder

Once you select the appropriate template for creating your report, hover over the template name to get the context menu as shown in Figure 9 - 36 and select the *Edit in Microsoft Excel* item.

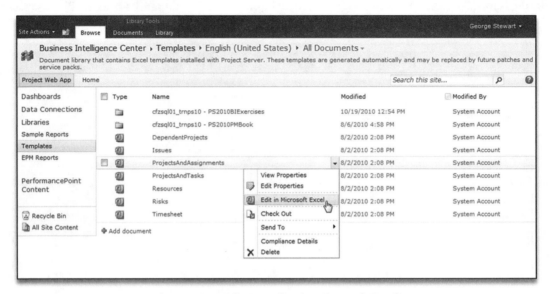

Figure 9 - 36: Edit Template in Microsoft Excel

The Business Intelligence Center will prompt you with a security warning as shown in Figure 9 - 37. This prompt allows you to cancel the template open process in case you opened this file accidentally. Click the *OK* button to continue the template open process and the Excel client opens.

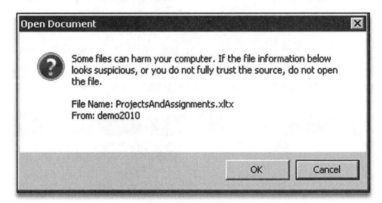

Figure 9 - 37: Open Document Confirmation

Depending on your system security configuration, Excel may disable data connections as a security precaution. This prevents you from accidentally opening a malicious file from the Internet. However, you will need to enable data connections for the template if you wish to create a report. If you are using Excel 2007, you will only see the prompt shown in Figure 9 - 38. You should click the *Enable Content* button to begin writing a report.

If you are using Excel 2010, you will see both prompts as shown in Figure 9 - 38 and Figure 9 - 39. You should click the *Enable Content* button. The system then presents you with the third security warning to make this a trusted document. As you are likely to use this template again, click the *Yes* button to make this template trusted and to begin writing your report.

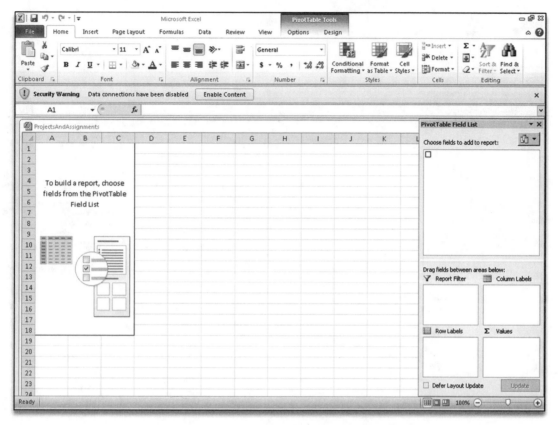

Figure 9 - 38: Data Connection Security Warning

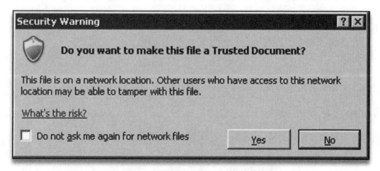

Figure 9 - 39: Make Template a Trusted Document

As the template continues to open, a series of messages will appear in the Excel status bar, indicating that Excel is connecting to the data source. After a few seconds, you see the empty PivotTable shown in Figure 9 - 40, where you will begin creating your report.

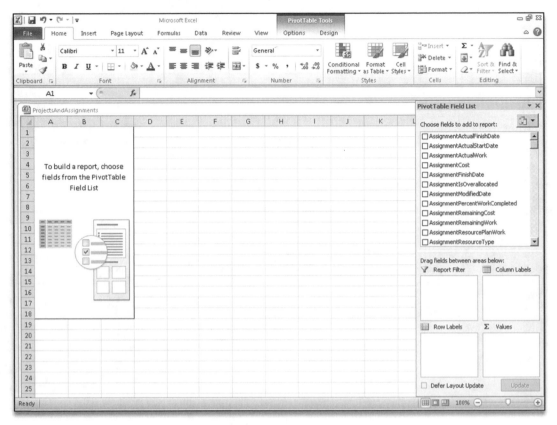

Figure 9 - 40: Template prior to making modifications

Edit the Report

I now move to the second step of the Edit Process as shown in Figure 9 - 41.

Open Excel Template   Publish to SharePoint

Edit the Report

Figure 9 - 41: High Level Edit Process

The PivotTable Field List is on the right side of the Excel template. This list is composed of 6 components which you should understand to write a report.

Figure 9 - 42 shows the list of available data fields for your report. The list is in alphabetical order to make it easier to find the data field you need. Product-generated data field names begin with the name of the data entity to which it belongs. For example, all project-related data fields have a name starting with Project. Therefore, Project Name is ProjectName in the list.

Figure 9 - 42: PivotTable Field List

Typically, you need to filter your data to what is relevant to your report user. Report Filters enable you to customize the data presented in the report. The *Report Filter* area, as shown in Figure 9 - 43, is where you designate fields as Report Filters. Any data field in this area will appear above the PivotTable and will act as a filter for the report. While there are other ways to filter a report, this method is a good way to make common Report Filters very visible to the report user. To specify a data field as a Report Filter, drag the data fields from the *Field* list into this area as shown in Figure 9 - 43.

Figure 9 - 43: PivotTable Report Filter Fields

It is likely you want to display rows of data in your report. To designate which data fields will appear in the row, you should drag them into the *Row Labels* area as shown in Figure 9 - 44. The order of the data fields in this area will determine where the field appears in the row. For example, if the topmost field is ProjectOwnerName, then ProjectOwnerName will be the left most field in the report row. If you need to reorder the fields, you can drag them around in the *Row Label* area.

Figure 9 - 44: PivotTable Report Rows

In some cases, you may need to create a *Cross-tabulation* or *Cross-tab* report. A *Cross-tab* report has both rows and columns where the intersection of the two values has meaning. A common column use is a time series where you need to show totals by month or by quarter. To designate a data field as a column, you drag it into the column label area shown in Figure 9 - 45.

Figure 9 - 45: PivotTable Report Columns

If your report requires totals or averages of a particular data field, you should place that data field in the $\sum$ *Values* area as shown in Figure 9 - 46. Fields in this area should be numeric or date type fields since you can only aggregate those field types.

Figure 9 - 46: PivotTable Calculated Values

Each time you make a change in these four areas, the report re-queries the database. If the report is over a large dataset, this behavior may not be desirable. At the very bottom of the PivotTable Field List is a checkbox and button, as shown in Figure 9 - 47. Selecting the *Defer Layout Update* item will defer the data refresh process until you tell Excel to do so. This is very handy if you are making many changes or are creating a new report. To update the data once you make your changes, click the *Update* button. Deselecting the *Defer Layout Update* item will return the report to its normal behavior.

Figure 9 - 47: PivotTable Defer Layout Setting

Warning: You must be a member of the Active Directory group that your organization uses for report authors in order to perform the exercises in this book.

Hands On Exercise

Exercise 9-1 for Excel 2007 and 2010 Users

Build a basic Tasks Due report from a report template.

1. In Project Web App, click on the *Business Intelligence* link on the *Quick Launch* menu to navigate to the Business Intelligence Center, click on the *Templates* link located in the *Libraries* section of the *Quick Launch* menu, then click on the *English* folder to display the available templates.

2. Open the *ProjectsAndAssignments* template by selecting it and in the *Open & Check out* section of the *Documents* ribbon, click the *Edit Document* button. If you see a Security Warning, click to allow the content. (Warning dialogs may vary).

3. Add the following fields into the *Row Labels* area:

    - TaskName

    - ResourceName

    - ProjectName

    - TaskFinishDate

    - Add the following fields to the *Report Filter* area:

    - ResourceIsTeam

    - ResourceType

    - TaskIsActive

    - TaskPercentCompleted

    - TaskIsManuallyScheduled

    - TaskIsMilestone

4. At the top of the report, change the values for the filter fields as follows:

    - Click the *ResourceIsTeam* pick list and set the value to *False* to exclude tasks assigned to team resources.

- Click the *ResourceType* pick list and set the value to 2 to show only tasks assigned to work resources.

- Click the *TaskIsActive* pick list and set the value to *True* to show only active tasks.

- Click the *TaskPercentCompleted* pick list and in the filter dialog, select the *Select Multiple Items* checkbox. Then deselect the *100* value in the filter value list so that completed tasks do not display and click the *OK* button.

- Click the *TaskIsManuallyScheduled* pick list and set the value to *False* to exclude manually scheduled tasks.

- Click the *TaskIsMilestone* pick list and set the value to *False* to display only non-milestone tasks.

- At the top of the report, change the labels for the *Filter* fields to make them more readable as follows:

- Select the *ResourceIsTeam* cell and type *Team Resource?* to rename it.

- Select the *ResourceType* cell and type *Resource Type.*

- Select the *TaskIsActive* cell and type *Active Task?*

- Select the *TaskPercentCompleted* cell and type *% Complete.*

- Select the *TaskIsManuallyScheduled* cell and type *Manually Scheduled?*

- Select the *TaskIsMilestone* cell and type *Milestone?*

5. Reorder the *Row Label* fields in this order:

    - TaskFinishDate

    - TaskName

    - ProjectName

    - ResourceName

6. Do not save this report yet as you use it for the next exercise.

Publish the Report

I now move to the last step of the edit process shown in Figure 9 - 48.

Figure 9 - 48: High Level Edit Process

In order to make a report accessible to others, you should publish the report to a SharePoint site as shown in Figure 9 - 49. *Publish* is different from *Save* or *Save As* since the *Publish* option makes it possible to designate the visibility of parts of the report to the report user. The *Save* command saves the report to SharePoint but does not give you any additional options.

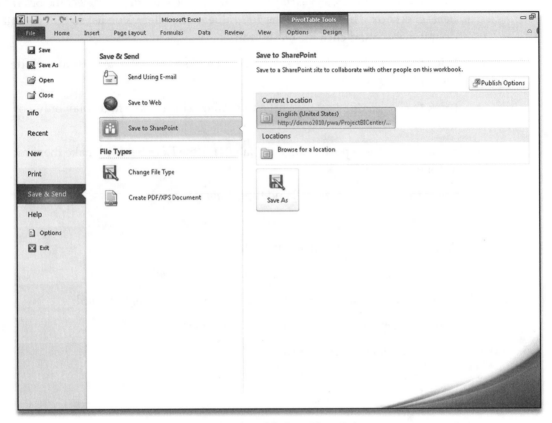

Figure 9 - 49: Publish to SharePoint

To publish a report, follow these steps:

1. Select the *File* menu

2. Select the *Save & Send* option

3. Select the *Save to SharePoint* item

4. Double click on the *Browse for a location* item

5. Because you opened a template from the *Templates* folder, Excel will attempt to publish your report there by default. You should not save reports in the *Templates* folder.

6. Select the *Save As* button and the *Save As* dialog appears as shown in Figure 9 - 50.

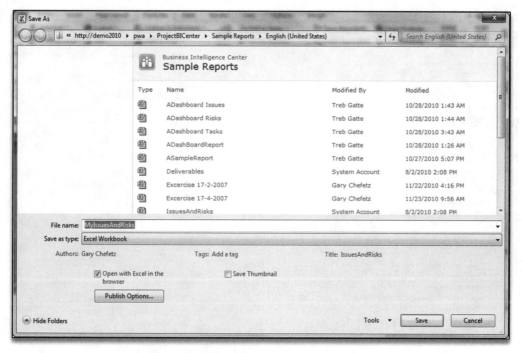

Figure 9 - 50: Browse to a Location dialog

- Before the final save, fill in the following values:

- Save your file to the following directory

- http://[*YourServerName*]/pwa/ProjectBICenter/Sample%20Reports/English%20(United%20States)/

- Rename your report with a unique name

- Select *Excel Workbook (*.xlsx)* in the *Save as type* field

- Select the *Open with Excel in the Browser* checkbox

- Click the *Save* button

- After a few seconds, you see a screen similar to Figure 9 - 51.

Warning: In the *Save As Type* pick list select the *Excel Workbook (*.xlsx)* item prior to saving! Otherwise, you will be saving a template to the BI Center, which will not render in the browser.

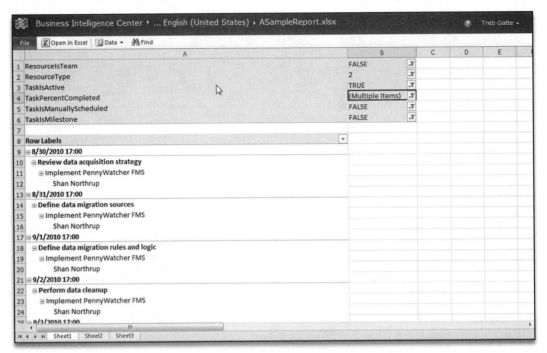

Figure 9 - 51: Web Rendered Report

Hands On Exercise

Exercise 9-2 for Excel 2010 Users

Publish the report from Exercise 9-1 to a SharePoint site.

1. Using the Excel client from the report in Exercise 9-1, select the *File* menu.

2. Select the *Save & Send* option in the Excel *Backstage*. Select the *Save to SharePoint* option.

3. Select the *Browse for a location* option.

4. Click the *Save As* button.

5. Update the directory location at the top of the dialog with your URL and press the **Enter** key on your computer keyboard to point the *Save As* dialog to that location.

6. http://[*YourServerName*]/pwa/ProjectBICenter/Sample%20Reports/English%20(United%20States)/

7. Give your report a unique name that you can recognize.

8. Change the *Save As type* field to *Excel Workbook (*.xlsx)*, if necessary.

9.   Select the *Open with Excel in the Browser* option.

10. Click the *Save* button.

You should see your report rendered in the browser.

Exercise 9-2 for Excel 2007 Users

Publish the report from Exercise 9-1 to a SharePoint site.

1.   Using the Excel client from the report in Exercise 9-1, click the *Office* button.

2.   Select the *Publish* item and select *Excel Services* in the fly-out menu.

3.   Select the *Browse for a location* option in the *Save As* dialog. Update the directory location by entering the URL for your sample reports library (sample shown below) in the *File name* field, add a forward slash at the end, and type a unique name for your report.

4.   http://[*YourServerName*]/pwa/ProjectBICenter/Sample%20Reports/English%20(United%20States)/

5.   Change the *Save As type* field to *Excel Workbook (*.xlsx)*, if necessary.

6.   Select the *Open in Excel Services* checkbox.

7.   Click the *Save* button.

You should see your report rendered in the browser.

Applying Basic Formatting

If you have used Excel before, I assume you know how to format a cell. Formatting in a PivotTable is similar but has some oddities of which you should be aware. The method to format *Date* or *Number* values differs based on whether they are in the *Rows Labels* area, *Columns Labels* area or the $\sum$ *Values* area of the PivotTable.

Row Labels

To format a *Row Label* data field, float your mouse pointer over the top of the first data field instance to format. When the cursor changes to a downward pointing arrow, as shown in Figure 9 - 52, select the cell. The system highlights all instances of the data field. Use the *Format* pick list on the Excel *Home* tab to format the cells accordingly.

Figure 9 - 52: Selection cursor for Row Labels

Column Labels

In a *Cross-Tab* report, dates and numbers can appear as columns. To format those values, select the row selector and use the *Format* pick list on the Excel *Home* tab to format accordingly.

∑ Values

To format a ∑ *Values* data field, double-click the column header in the report to open the *Field Settings* dialog. Select the *Number Format* button at the bottom to open the *Format Cells* dialog. Set the desired numeric or date format and click the *OK* button twice to return.

Adding Fit and Finish Formatting

The report you created in the Hands On Exercises is usable but not ready for production use. You use that report as the basis for going through the *Advanced Editing* options you need to make your reports effective.

When you select a PivotTable, you see two new contextual tabs that appear in the *Excel* ribbon. These are the *Design* tab and *Options* tab shown in Figure 9 - 53 and Figure 9 - 54, respectively. The *Design* tab functionality focuses on the look of your report while the *Options* tab contains a number of functions that enable you to control the report experience. I cover the functionality of both tabs in greater detail in the next topical section.

Figure 9 - 53: PivotTable Design tab

Figure 9 - 54: PivotTable Options tab

Using the Design Tab

The *PivotTable Tools Design* tab contains functionality that controls the visual look of your report. I cover the most common options for report writing in this topical section.

Subtotals Menu Button

The *Subtotals* pick list contains four options that control whether subtotals appear and where you would like them to appear in the report. This option is global for all fields in the report and requires a field in the ∑ *Values* area for you to see any impact. I list the options and what they do in Table 9 - 6.

In a later section, you learn how to control this setting on a data field basis, providing you with more control over totaling. Unless you have a need for totals on every field, I suggest that you select the *Do Not Show Subtotals* item and control this on a data field basis.

Option	Functionality
Do Not Show Subtotals	Removes all subtotals for all fields in the PivotTable.
Show all Subtotals at Bottom of Group	Inserts a totals row beneath each grouping data field in the report.
Show all Subtotals at Top of Group	Displays a total in line with the grouping data field without inserting lines into the report.
Include Filtered Items in Totals	This new for 2010 setting allows you to include items in the roll-up total, though you may have filtered them out of the report view.

Table 9 - 6: Subtotals Menu Button Options

Grand Totals Menu Button

The *Grand Totals* menu button contains four options that control what and where grand totals appear in your report. The options, which are self-explanatory, are as follows:

- *Off for Rows and Columns*
- On for Rows and Columns
- On for Rows Only
- On for Columns Only

Report Layout Menu Button

The *Report Layout* menu button contains five options, which control the presentation of the data fields in your report as shown in Table 9 - 7. This option controls one of the most important design decisions of your report. There is new functionality in Excel 2010, which enhances your ability to control the general layout of the report.

You can also control this setting at the field level, which I cover in a later section of this module, providing finer control over presentation.

Option	Functionality	Example	Uses
Show in **Compact** Form	Shows all data fields in a compact tree structure	XXX XXX XXX	Works best with when the number of data fields is greater than can be viewed horizontally and the report delivery is online. Enables the report user to open and close groups.

Option	Functionality	Example	Uses

Show in Outline Form	Shows all data fields in a wide outline form, sometimes resembling a staircase	XXXXX
		
		   XXXXX
		
		      XXXXX
			Works best with a small number of data fields and the report delivery is online.
			
			Enables the report user to open and close groups

Show in Tabular Form	Shows all data fields as a table but does not show repeating values by default	XXXX XXXX XXXXX
		
		    XXXX XXXXX
		
		        XXXXX
			Works best for printed report delivery and a number of data fields that will fit across the medium.
			
			Can be used online with the open/close functionality

Repeat All Item Labels	Note: This function has no impact on the Compact Form. Repeats all item labels for each group of repeating values	Outline Form looks like: XXXX XXXX XXXXX XXXX XXXXX XXXXX Tabular Form looks like: XXXX XXXX XXXXX XXXX XXXX XXXXX XXXX XXXX XXXXX	Can be very useful for printed reports for place keeping or where there are a lot of lined under a particular group and group will span a page or screen. Use cautiously in online reports as repeating data can make reports hard to read.
Do Not Repeat All Item Labels	Default value that does not show all values for repeating values.	See defaults for Outline Form and Tabular Form above.	Useful for online report presentation where repeated same values can create visual clutter.

Table 9 - 7: Report Layout options

Blank Rows Menu Button

The *Blank Rows* menu button contains two options that control whether a blank line appears between data groups in your report. Blank lines provide additional visual breaks between data groups and are effective for printed reports. The options, which are self-explanatory, are as follows:

- *Insert Blank Line after Each Item*
- Remove Blank Line after Each Item

PivotTable Styles Gallery

The *PivotTable Styles* gallery is the quickest way to format the look and feel of your report as shown in Figure 9 - 55. Your report layout strongly influences how these gallery options appear to you. As you hover your mouse over each option, you can see the *Active Preview* of the selection's impact if chosen. You should choose a style that makes the data presented as easy to view and understand as possible.

Also note, that the system links colors for these gallery items to the *Page Layout* tab, *Colors* pick list. Any changes made there will have an immediate impact on your report colors. Unless you truly desire a pink report, I advise you use caution.

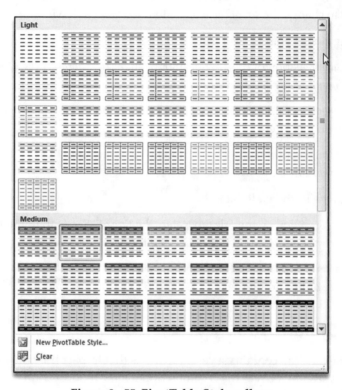

Figure 9 - 55: PivotTable Style gallery

Hands On Exercise

Exercise 9-3 for Excel 2007 and Excel 2010 Users

Modify a report to be a Tabular report with column totals.

1. Open the report you created in Exercise 9-1 in the Excel client, if necessary.

2. Add the *TaskRemainingWork* data field to the ∑ *Values* area.

3. Hover your mouse pointer over the first occurrence of the *TaskFinishDate* field, to expose the down arrow. When the down arrow appears, click to select all occurrences.

4. Click the *Home* tab and from the *Number* section use the pick list in the upper area to apply the *Short Date* format.

5. Click on the *Sum of TaskRemainingWork* header and change it to *Remaining Work*. In the *Number* section of the *Home* ribbon, use the *Number* pick list to format using the *Accounting with 2 decimal places* option and change the *Symbol* value to *None*.

6. Click the *Design* tab in the *PivotTable Tools* ribbon group and from the *PivotTable Styles* section use the gallery to change the *PivotTable Style* item to *Pivot Style Medium 9*.

7. Hover your mouse pointer over a style to display its name.

8. From the *Layout* section of the *Design* ribbon, click the *Subtotals* pick list button and select the *Show all subtotals at top of group* item.

9. From the *Layout* section of the *Design* ribbon, click the *Grand Totals* pick list button and select the *On for Columns Only* item.

10. From the *Layout* section of the *Design* ribbon, click the *Report Layout* pick list and select the *Show in Tabular form* item.

11. Resize columns to show all data.

12. Excel 2010 users, click on the *File* tab, select the *Save & Send* tab in the *Backstage* and the double-click the *Current Location* item to publish the report to the server.

13. Excel 2007 users, click on the *Office* button, select the *Publish* item then the *Excel Services* selection. Click the *Save* button to save the updated report.

Working with the Options Tab

The PivotTable *Options* contextual tab contains several functions that impact how the PivotTable behaves and what core elements appear. In this section, I cover the common options for report writing.

PivotTable Options

The PivotTable *Options* pick list shown in Figure 9 - 56 is very important when creating a new report that you intend to use on a regular basis. You should review these settings during report creation as they control the basic visual properties and refresh data settings for the report. You typically set these only once during report creation.

Figure 9 - 56: PivotTable Options - Options pick list

Click the *Options* item and the system displays the *Pivot Table Options* dialog shown in Figure 9 - 57 and Figure 9 - 58. The first figures displays the *Layout & Format* tab while the second figure shows the *Data* tab.

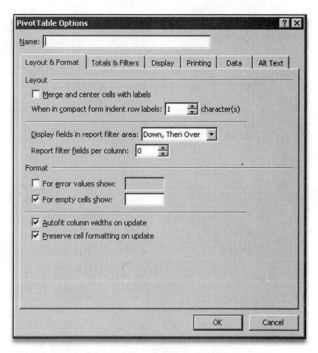

Figure 9 - 57: PivotTable options - Layout & Format tab

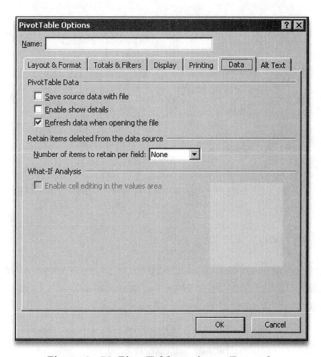

Figure 9 - 58: PivotTable options - Data tab

I list the most common four settings found in the aforementioned tabs in Table 9 - 8 along with explanations of their functionality and recommended settings.

Tab	Figure	Option	Function	Recommended Setting
Layout & Format	Figure 9 - 57	PivotTable Name	Enables you to designate a name for the PivotTable	**Recommend: Name your PivotTable** Give the PivotTable a name that you can easily identify. You will use this name later when conditional publishing is covered.
Layout & Format	Figure 9 - 57	Autofit column widths on Update	When selected, Excel autofits your columns automatically on data refresh.	**Recommend: Deselect** This functionality makes it hard to control the format of the report, which can lead to the report being wider than your screen resolution.
Layout & Format	Figure 9 - 57	Preserve cell formatting on update	When selected, prevents Excel from resetting the PivotTable formatting to the default settings on data refresh	**Recommend: Select** Otherwise, you lose any conditional formatting and other modifications on a data refresh
Data	Figure 9 - 58	Refresh data when opening the file	When selected, the Excel report automatically retrieves the latest data and gets rid of any cached data.	**Recommend: Select** Otherwise, user confusion occurs when the system uses out-of-date data to make a decision.

Table 9 - 8: List of Pertinent PivotTable Option Settings

Working with Field Settings

Use the *Active Field* field to change the name of the selected data field. For example, you decide that the *TaskWorkPercentComplete* value is too long; select the field and change the value to *% Work Comp*. When you press the **Enter** key, the system reflects your change in the PivotTable.

Clicking on the *Field Setting* button, shown in Figure 9 - 59, provides options that enable you to control the display of data at the individual data field level rather than at the report level.

Figure 9 - 59: Field Settings Button on the PivotTable Options tab

You can find the key settings on the *Layout & Print* tab of the dialog shown in Figure 9 - 60.

Figure 9 - 60: PivotTable Data Field Settings dialog - Layout & Print tab

I list examples of how each setting impacts the PivotTable in Table 9 - 9.

Setting	Effect	Example

Show item labels in outline form	When selected, the data field appears in a wide outline form, sometimes resembling a staircase	XXXXX
		
		    XXXXX
		
		        XXXXX

Show item labels in tabular form	When selected, the data field appears as a table but does not show repeating values by default	XXXX XXXX XXXXX
		
		      XXXX XXXXX
		
		            XXXXX

Repeat item labels	When selected, the data field is repeated for each group of repeating values	Outline Form looks like: XXXX XXXX XXXXX XXXX XXXXX XXXXX Tabular Form looks like: XXXX XXXX XXXXX XXXX XXXX XXXXX XXXX XXXX XXXXX

Setting	Effect	Example

Insert blank line after each item label	When selected, inserts a blank line between each group of like values for the data field.	XXXXX
		    XXXXX
		        XXXXX

Insert page break after each item	Whenever the value of the data field changes, the system inserts a page break. This is very useful in reports that are to be printed	XXXX XXXX --------------------------------------- YYYYY

Table 9 - 9: Data Field Setting Examples

Applying Grouping

The *Group* group of the Excel PivotTable *Options* tab contains three buttons:

- The *Group Selection/Ungroup* buttons enable you to dynamically group contiguous rows or columns into a collapsible group. If you are analyzing large amounts of data, you use these buttons to create dynamic groups that fit your analytical needs.

- The *Group Field* button enables you to meet a common Project Management reporting need of reporting data by week, month, and quarter. The *Group Field* button enables dynamic grouping of date data fields or number data fields into groups you specify.

You select the date or number field to group in the PivotTable by clicking the *Group Field* button. If you selected a date field, you see Figure 9 - 61. Note that the date groupings are *Days, Months, Quarters,* and *Years*. What happens if you want to group by week? Figure 9 - 61 illustrates the configuration for week grouping where you select *Days* and designate the number of days as *seven*. This approach enables other possibilities for date grouping such as bi-weekly reporting needs.

For grouping data by week, msProjectExperts recommends you use *Group by Days* and *number of days* set to 7.

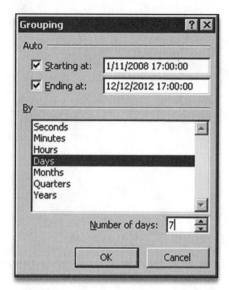

Figure 9 - 61: Grouping dialog, Date by Week Grouping

If you selected a numeric field, you see Figure 9 - 62. You define the groups by starting and ending values and define how wide to make each group.

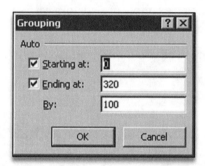

Figure 9 - 62: Grouping Dialog Example for Numeric Data

Summarizing Values

The *Summarize Values* menu button shown in Figure 9 - 63 enables the type of value aggregation performed on the selected field in the ∑ *Values* area of the PivotTable. You can also use this button to change the default calculation assigned by Excel to the numeric data field you placed in the ∑ *Values* area of the PivotTable in cases where it assigned an incorrect operation. Select the field in question in the PivotTable and use this button to correct the operation.

Figure 9 - 63: Calculations pick list of PivotTable Options Tab

The most used choices in the *Summarize Values* menu are:

- Sum

- Count

- Average

- Min

- Max

- Product

There is also a *More* options selection to provide five more aggregation alternatives.

Fields, Items and Sets Menu Button and Calculated Fields Menu Item

Use the *Fields, Items and Sets* button from the *Calculations* pick list to create your own calculated fields in the ∑ *Values* area of the PivotTable. Figure 9 - 64 shows an example of a custom calculation where the user is comparing Baseline Work to Work. This value is calculated automatically when the system refreshes the PivotTable data.

Most of the formula operators in Excel are available for use and Excel provides you with a list of data fields that you can use in a formula in the *Fields* list.

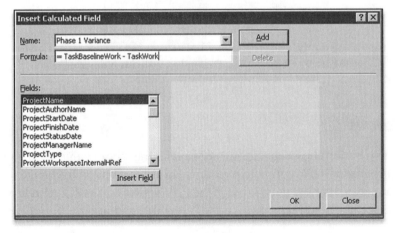

Figure 9 - 64: Insert Calculated Field dialog

+/- Buttons

Use the *+/- Buttons* button at the right side of the *Options* tab to hide or show the collapse/expand buttons next to each field in the PivotTable. If you intend to print a report, this option will help reduce visual clutter in the report.

Hands On Exercise

Exercise 9-4 for Excel 2007 and Excel 2010 Users

Update the report developed in Exercise 9-1 to make it printer friendly.

1. Open the report you created in Exercise 9-1 in the Excel client, if necessary.

2. From the *PivotTable* section of the *Options* ribbon, click the *Options* pick list and select the *Options* item. Give your pivot table a name in the *Name* field. In the *Layout & Format* tab of the *PivotTable Options* dialog, deselect the checkbox for the *Autofit column widths on update* option. Click the *OK* button.

3. Click on the *TaskFinishDate* item in the *Row Labels* section and select the *Field Settings* item from the popup menu. Click on the *Layout & Print* tab, select the *Show item labels in outline form* option, and then click the *OK* button to close the *Field Settings* dialog.

4. Hover your mouse pointer over the *TaskFinishDate* field header in the spreadsheet and click to select all when the downward arrow appears. In the *Group* section of the *Options* ribbon, click the *Group Selection* button and use the *Grouping* dialog to group the item by week, by selecting the *Days* option and entering a value of 7 in the *Number of days* field. Click the *OK* button in the dialog.

5. Add the *AssignmentWork* item to the ∑ *Values* area of the PivotTable.

6. In the ∑ *Values* area of the PivotTable, click on the *AssignmentWork* item and select the *Value Field Settings* item from the popup menu. Change the *Summarize Values By* setting from *AssignmentWork* to *Sum*. Click the *OK* button to close the *Value Field Settings* dialog.

7. Add the *Task Work* item to the ∑ *Values* area of the PivotTable and use the same technique you used in the previous step to verify that it is set to *Sum*.

For Excel 2010 Users

8. Click the *Calculations* button and click on the *Fields, Items, & Sets* pick list, then select the *Calculated Field* item to add a calculated field named *% of Task*. In the *Calculated Field* dialog, enter the name in the *Name* field. Enter "AssignmentWork/TaskWork" without the quotes in the *Formula* field. Click the *OK* button.

For Excel 2007 Users

8. In the *Tools* section of the *Options* ribbon, click the *Formulas* button and select the *Calculated Field* item to add a calculated field named *% of Task*. In the *Calculate Field* dialog, enter the name in the *Name* field. Enter "AssignmentWork/TaskWork" without the quotes in the *Formula* field. Click the *OK* button.

For Excel 2007 and Excel 2010 Users

9. Float your mouse pointer over the header for your new field until you see the downward pointing arrow and click to select all instances. Right-click on the header and select the *Format Cells* item. In the *Format Cells* dialog, format the *Sum of % of Task* item as a percentage with no decimals and click the *OK* button.

10. Resize columns in your spreadsheet to best display the data to your liking.

11. Update the field names as follows:

    *   *TaskFinishDate* to *Finish Week*

    *   *TaskName* to *Task*

    *   *ProjectName* to *Project*

    *   *Resource Name* to *Resource*

    *   *RemainingWork* to *Remaining Work*

    *   *Sum of TaskRemainingWork* to *Remaining*

    *   *Sum of AssignmentWork* to *Assigned*

    *   *Sum of TaskWork* to *Task Work*

    *   *Sum of % of Task* to *% Task*

12. Right Justify the column headers that display numeric data.

13. Publish your report to SharePoint.

Advanced Formatting

In this section, I cover advanced aspects of Excel where there is relevance to Project Server Business Intelligence.

Data Field Level Filtering for Date Fields

PivotTables offer support for special *Date* field filtering for *Date* data fields as shown in Figure 9 - 65. This feature enables you restrict report data to the current month or quarter without user intervention. To specify a date filter:

*   Select a *Date* data field in the PivotTable

*   Select the *Filter* dropdown button in the data field heading

*   Select the *Date Filters...* item

*   Select the date filter to apply

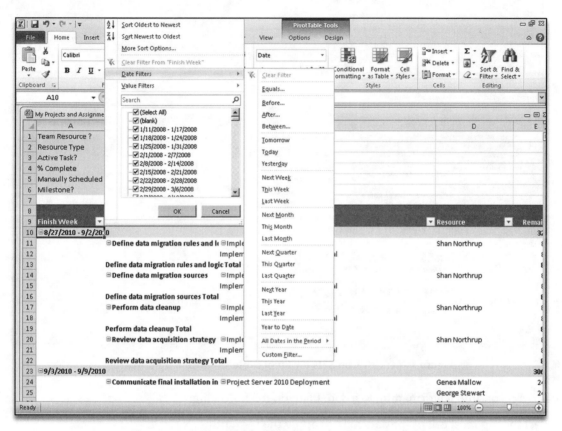

Figure 9 - 65: PivotTable Date filters for Date Data fields

Key Performance Indicators using Conditional Formatting

Your Business Intelligence need likely includes Key Performance Indicator (KPI) reporting. You can accomplish this type of reporting, in addition to other data visualizations, using an *Icon Set* conditional formatting as shown in Figure 9 - 66. KPIs, when used properly, provide visual indicators that draw the user's attention to significant data.

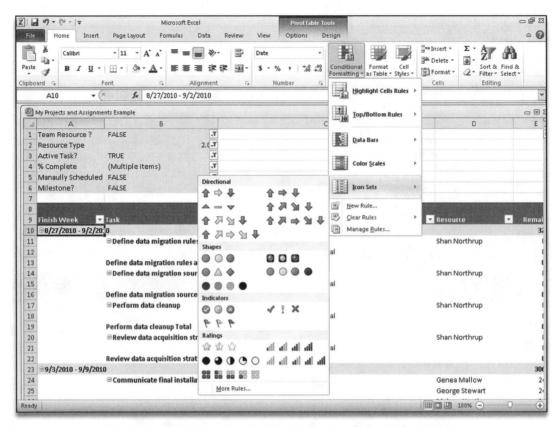

Figure 9 - 66: KPI Icon Sets for PivotTable Conditional Formatting

To apply *Icon Set* conditional formatting to a data field, do the following:

1. Select the top most cell of the data field to apply the formatting.

 Warning: Due to an Excel quirk, do not select the entire column, just the first value cell in the column.

2. On the *Home* tab, select the *Conditional Formatting* menu button.

3. Select the *Icon Sets…* item.

4. Select an Icon Set. The system will apply the Icon Set to that cell. A new menu appears next to that cell as shown in Figure 9 - 67. Select the *All cells showing 'Remaining' values for 'Resource'* option.

Figure 9 - 67: Icon Set Formatting menu

This procedure is to avoid the Excel quirk that applies conditional formatting to Totals rows. If you have based your KPI on % of Total, including the Column Total in this calculation will give you incorrect results. If you follow this procedure, the system only applies conditional formatting to the detail rows.

5.   The system will apply conditional formatting to all detail rows.

The default *Conditional Formatting* rules applied are probably not using the criteria you desire. To change this, you need to edit the *Conditional Formatting* rule by doing the following:

- In the *Home* tab, select the *Conditional Formatting* menu button.

- Select the *Manage Rules…* item. The system displays the *Conditional Formatting Rules Manager* dialog shown in Figure 9 - 68.

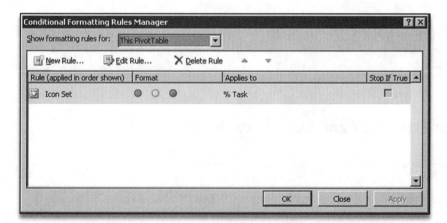

Figure 9 - 68: Conditional Formatting Rules Manger

- Select the rule to edit and click the *Edit Rule* button and the system displays the dialog shown in Figure 9 - 69. This dialog enables you to change the basis for displaying each icon, reversing the order of icons, and showing icons only.

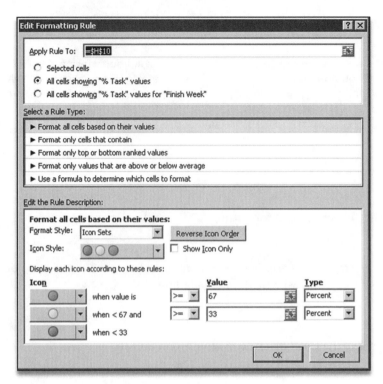

Figure 9 - 69: Edit Formatting Rule Dialog

Hands On Exercise

Exercise 9-5 for Excel 2007 and Excel 2010 Users

Apply date filtering and conditional formatting to a report.

1. Open the report you created in Exercise 9-1 in the Excel client, if necessary.

2. Select the TaskFinishDate item (now called Finish Week), apply the Next Month date filter to the field by clicking on the pick list button in the field header, and then select the Date Filters item from the popup menu. Next, select the Next Month filter from the fly-out menu.

3. Click on the first value in the Remaining data field and from the Styles section of the Home ribbon, click the Conditional Formatting button and select the Icon Sets item from the menu. Select the Green Yellow Red icon set.

4. Click the Formatting button next to the first value and select the All cells showing "Remaining" values item.

5. From the Styles section of the Home ribbon, click on the Conditional Formatting button and select the Manage Rules button. The system displays the Conditional Formatting Rules Manager dialog. Select the Icon Set item in the dialog and click the Edit Rule button. The system displays the Edit Formatting Rule dialog.

6. Apply KPI formatting to the Remaining data field as follows:

    •   Numbers greater than or equal to 200 display red icons.

    •   Numbers less than 200 or greater than or equal to 100 display yellow icons.

    •   Numbers less than 100 display green icons.

7. Click the OK button in the Edit Formatting Rule dialog, then click the Apply button in the Conditional Formatting Rules Manager dialog, and then click the OK button to close the dialog.

8. Close your report.

Understanding Dashboards

Dashboards are a highly desired Business Intelligence capability but often people implement them badly. Dashboards are a way of bringing a small number of distinct data visualizations together to answer a specific need or tell a story. A dashboard **is not** a random set of 25 charts thrown together on a screen because they look good together. A dashboard also does not need to have fancy charts or other graphics. It simply needs to address the information need effectively.

The most effective dashboards have the minimum number of data visualizations needed to tell the story and no more. It is important that when you develop dashboards, you resist the temptation of "one more report". As a rule of thumb, keep the number to 3-6 components to prevent scrolling. You should endeavor to minimize scrolling and prioritize key data to appear on the initial screen.

The dashboard functionality covered here is SharePoint-based dashboards. You can emulate a dashboard within Excel, using slicers to link PivotTables. However, SharePoint dashboards allow you to aggregate content from other sources beyond Excel. Excel-based dashboards are very useful for meeting Collaborative Business Intelligence needs and you can easily modify them to meet changing business needs.

Dashboards are relatively easy to build once you understand the basics of how they work. In order to build a dashboard, I introduce you to a few more concepts before I delve into the construction process.

Dashboard Components

The dashboard you learn how to build next is a *SharePoint Web Part* page hosting Excel *Web Access* web parts and a *Page Filter* web part, which the system links together via *Parameter* connections. You can add other types of web parts but these are the core to Project Business Intelligence. I depict these relationships in Figure 9 - 70.

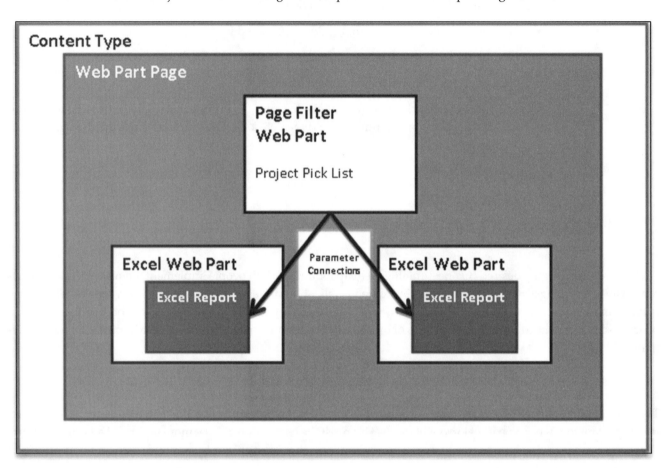

Figure 9 - 70: SharePoint Dashboard Component Relationships

Content Types

A content type is a SharePoint template for a specific type of reusable data. A content type can contain information items such as specific column information, attached workflows, document templates, and other settings. *Web Part* pages are a content type and thus, will have a different behavior from a regular document even though you can store both types of items in a Document Library.

Web Part page

The *Web Part* page is a SharePoint document that hosts the dashboard components. The primary decisions you make when you create a *Web Part* page is to determine the name of the page and the layout to use.

Web Parts

These are the individual containers for your reports on the *Web Part* page. The primary functions of the web parts are:

- To control what actions users can take with your report

- To manage the visual layout of the report on the page

- To enable filter connectivity with other web parts so that they act in concert

Page Filter Web Part

A *Page Filter* web part is a special SharePoint web part that uses parameters to connect multiple web parts together. These connections enable the web parts to function in unison. There are several types of *Page Filters* and these perform different actions. Some require the person configuring the web part to enter a list of allowable values. Other *Page Filter* web parts retrieve information based on the current logged-in user.

Excel Parameter

A parameter is a special Excel range, usually defined for a PivotTable filter field that enables the Excel report to receive filter values from a *Page Filter* web part.

Conditional Publishing

The Excel *Conditional Publishing* function enables control of which specific parts of your Excel report are visible within Excel Services and can determine which items the system are designated as parameters.

Dashboard Implementation Process

The process of building a dashboard is broken up into four steps. The first three steps are planning steps as it is important to define what you are building and why before delving into the mechanics. Following this process, shown in Figure 9 - 71, ensures that you create your dashboard in an efficient manner.

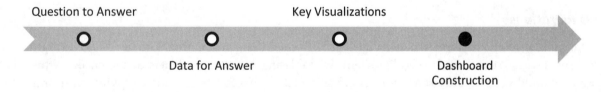

Figure 9 - 71: Dashboard Development Process

Question to Answer

Before building a dashboard, you should be clear on the question you want your dashboard to address. This information helps you determine what elements to present and how best to structure these elements. Questions do not need to be complex but should be straightforward and easy to describe.

You should also understand what type of action you want to result from this information. If your intent is to spur action, then you should structure the data presentation to support that goal. For example, if you want individual accountability, then the responsible individual's name should be prominent in the presentation.

For example, you your team to have easy access to the data answering the question "What activities are due on the project next week?" You also need your team to act upon these items in a timely manner, especially those due next week. You want to build this for a 3-month project so you do not want to invest a lot of building it.

Data for Answer

To answer the question "What activities are due on the project next week?" you want data for project tasks, issues, and risks. For this dashboard, you decide that the complete data set you need is as follows:

- Tasks
- Task Name
- Task Finish Date
- The name of the person assigned to the task
- Project Name
- Issues
- Title
- Assigned to
- Due Date
- Project Name
- Risks
- Title
- Assigned to
- Due date
- Project Name

Key Visualizations

To keep it simple, you create three separate data lists with conditional formatting. You use *Yellow* to highlight dates occurring next week. You use *Red* to highlight items with missing data. It is prudent to document everything that you need to do to build your reports. The report specification tables that follow provide you with one example of such documentation. First, select the appropriate template for each list as shown in Table 9 - 10.

Report	Template	Rationale
Upcoming Tasks	ProjectAndAssignments	Need resource name, which requires assignment data
Upcoming Issues	Issues	Has the data needed
Upcoming Risks	Risks	Has the data needed

Table 9 - 10: Match Reports to Templates

I outline the requirements for the Upcoming Tasks report display in Table 9 - 11.

Item	Details
Row Labels	TaskFinishDate ResourceName TaskName
Setup PivotTable filter	Use ProjectName
Set up field filter as a Report parameter	Assign range name ProjectName to field
PivotTable formatting	Show in Tabular Form No Subtotals No Grand Totals PivotTable Name: PVTasks Use default theme +/- buttons on Dates formatted as Short Date
Conditional formatting	Use date filters to show only this week.

Table 9 - 11: Upcoming Tasks Specifications

I outline the Upcoming Issues report specification in Table 9 - 12.

Item	Details
Row Fields	Status Due Date Assigned To Title
Setup PivotTable filter	Use ProjectName
Set up field filter as a Report parameter	Assign range name ProjectName to field

Item	Details
PivotTable formatting	Show in Tabular Form
	No Subtotals
	No Grand Totals
	PivotTable Name: PVIssues
	Use default theme
	+/- buttons on
	Dates formatted as Short Date
Conditional formatting	Highlight dates due next week

Table 9 - 12: Upcoming Issues Specification

I outline the Upcoming Risks report specification in Table 9 - 13.

Item	Details
Row Fields	Status
	Due Date
	AssignedToResource
	Title
Setup PivotTable filter	Use ProjectName
Set up field filter as a Report parameter	Assign range name ProjectName to field
PivotTable formatting	Show in Tabular Form
	No Subtotals
	No Grand Totals
	PivotTable Name: PVRisks
	Use default theme
	+/- buttons on
	Dates formatted as Short Date
Conditional formatting	Highlight dates due next week

Table 9 - 13: Upcoming Risks Specification

Dashboard Construction

For discussion purposes, you have already built the reports as specified above. Now, it is time to bring the pieces together to begin creating your dashboard.

Creating a Parameter

In each of the reports above, you use *ProjectName* as a *Report* filter. In order for this filter to be usable in the Dashboard, you define the filter as a parameter so that the filter can receive its setting from the *Page Filter* web part on the *Dashboard* page.

There are three steps to create and use a parameter:

- Define the *Filter* field as a one cell Named Range

- Add it as a *Published* parameter

- Connect it to the *Page Filter* web part

Define the Filter Field as a One Cell Named Range

In order for a field to be visible external to the Excel Report, it has to be defined as a *Named Range* as shown in Figure 9 - 72.

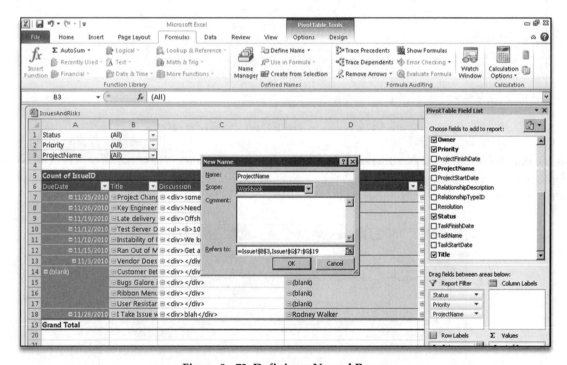

Figure 9 - 72: Defining a Named Range

To define the *Filter* field as such, do the following:

1. Select the *Filter* field value.

2. Click the *Formulas* tab.

3. Select the *Define Names* pick list.

331

4. Enter the Range Name in the *Name* field.

5. Click the *OK* button.

Conditional Publishing

In the *Backstage,* there is a *Publish Options* button that I did not include as part of the regular publishing steps. To publish a parameter, select the *Publish Options* button **before publishing** your Excel Report. The *Publish Options* dialog displays as shown in Figure 9 - 73.

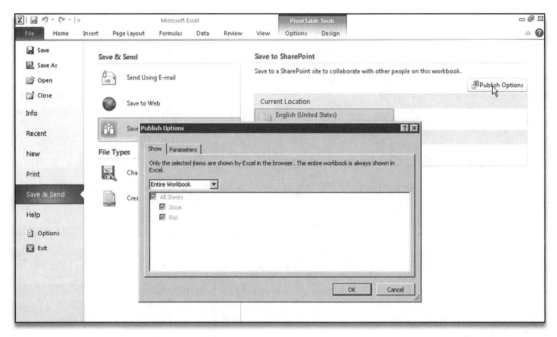

Figure 9 - 73: Backstage with Publish Options dialog

The *Show* tab enables you to control which aspects of the report are visible in Excel Services. This can be especially handy if you have a report that you would like to share but you do not want to share all of the information. To define a parameter, go to the *Parameters* tab shown in Figure 9 - 74.

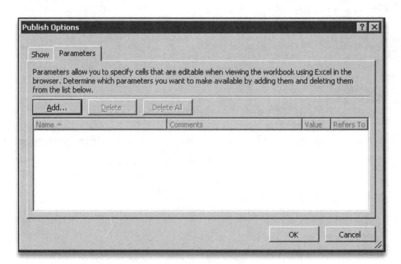

Figure 9 - 74: Publish Options - Add Parameter

Click the *Add* button and the system opens the *Add Parameters* dialog shown in Figure 9 - 75.

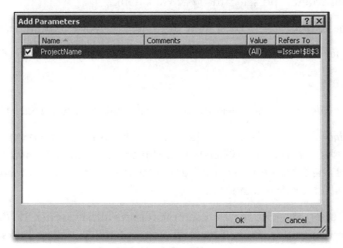

Figure 9 - 75: Add Parameters dialog

Select the checkbox next to the name of your new parameter and click the *OK* button.

Hands On Exercise

Exercise 9-6 for Excel 2007 and Excel 2010 Users

Build the Upcoming Tasks report.

1. Navigate to the Business Intelligence Center and click the *Templates* link in the *Quick Launch* menu. Click on the *English (United States)* link to open the English language folder. Click on the *ProjectsAndTasks* template name to launch the template. In the *Open* dialog, select the *Read Only* option and click the *OK* button. The system launches the template in Excel.

2. Click the *Enable Content* button if prompted by a security warning. Make the file trusted if prompted.

3. Add *TaskFinishDate, ResourceName,* and the *TaskName* fields to the *Row Labels* area.

4. Add the *ProjectName* field to the *Report Filter* area.

5. In the *Layout* section of the *Design* ribbon, click the *Subtotals* button and select the *Do Not Show Subtotals* item. Click the *Grand Totals* button and select the *Off for Rows and Columns* item. Click the *Report Layout* button and select the *Show in Tabular Form* item.

6. Select the *ProjectName* field and from the *Defined Names* section of the *Formulas* ribbon, click the *Define Name* button. Enter the name "ProjectNM" without the quotes in the *Name* field and click the *OK* button.

7. Format the *TaskFinishDate* column as a short date.

8. Click the filter pick list on the *TaskFinishDate* column header and float your mouse pointer over the *Date Filters* item, and select the *Next Week* item.

9. Arrange the column sizes to best view the data, give your column headers friendly names.

10. On the *Options* ribbon, enter the name "PVTasks" without the quotes in the *PivotTable Name* field.

For Excel 2010 Users

11. Click on the *File* menu and select the *Save & Send* tab. Select the *Save to SharePoint* option.

12. Click the *Publish Options* button in the upper right corner of the page and select the *Parameters* tab in the *Publish Options* dialog. Click the *Add* button and select the named item you created in step 6. Click the *OK* button to close the *Add Parameters* dialog and then click the *OK* button to close the *Publish Options* dialog.

13. Locate and select the URL for your sample reports library under the *Recent Locations* section and click the *Save As* button. In the *Save As* dialog, enter "Upcoming Tasks" without the quotes in the *File Name* field and select the *Excel Workbook* item in the *Save as Type* pick list. Click the *Save* button to save your new report.

14. Close your report

For Excel 2007 Users

11. Select the *Publish* item and select the *Excel Services* item in the fly-out menu.

12. Select the *Browse for a location* option in the *Save As* dialog. Update the directory location by entering the URL for your sample reports library (sample shown below) in the *File name* field and add a forward slash at the end and type "Upcoming Tasks" without the quotes as the name for your report.

    - http://[*YourServerName*]/pwa/ProjectBICenter/Sample%20Reports/English%20(United%20States)/

13. Change the *Save As type* field to Excel Workbook (*.xlsx), if necessary. Select the *Open in Excel Services* checkbox. Click the *Save* button

14. Close your report.

Exercise 9-7 for Excel 2007 and Excel 2010 Users

Build the Upcoming Risks report.

1. Navigate to the Business Intelligence Center and click the *Templates* link in the *Quick Launch* menu. Click on the *English (United States)* link to open the English language folder. Click on the *Risks* template name to launch the template. In the *Open* dialog, select *Read Only* and click the *OK* button. The system launches the template in Excel.

2. Click the *Enable Content* button if prompted by a security warning. Make the file trusted, if prompted.

3. Add *Status, DueDate, AssignedToResource,* and the *Title* fields to the *Row Labels* area.

4. Add the *ProjectName* field to the *Report Filter* area.

5. In the *Layout* section of the *Design* ribbon, click the *Subtotals* button and select the *Do Not Show Subtotals* item. Click the *Grand Totals* button and select the *Off for Rows and Columns* item. Click the *Report Layout* button and select the *Show in Tabular Form* item.

6. Select the *ProjectName* field and from the *Defined Names* section of the *Formulas* ribbon, click the *Define Name* button. Enter the name "ProjectNM" without the quotes in the *Name* field and click the *OK* button.

7. Format the *TaskFinishDate* column as a short date.

8. Click the filter pick list on the *DueDate* column header and float your mouse pointer over the *Date Filters* item, and select the *Next Week* item.

9. Arrange the column sizes to best view the data, give your column headers friendly names.

10. On the *Options* ribbon, enter the name "PVIssues" without the quotes in the *PivotTable Name* field.

For Excel 2010 Users

11. Click on the *File* menu and select the *Save & Send* tab. Select the *Save to SharePoint* option.

12. Click the *Publish Options* button in the upper right corner of the page and select the *Parameters* tab in the *Publish Options* dialog. Click the *Add* button and select the named item you created in step 6. Click the *OK* button to close the *Add Parameters* dialog and then click the *OK* button to close the *Publish Options* dialog.

13. Locate and select the URL for your sample reports library under the *Recent Locations* section and click the *Save As* button. In the *Save As* dialog, enter "Upcoming Risks" without the quotes in the *File Name* field and select the *Excel Workbook* item in the *Save as Type* pick list. Click the *Save* button to save your new report.

14. Close your report.

For Excel 2007 Users

11. Select the *Publish* item and select the *Excel Services* item in the fly-out menu.

12. Select the *Browse for a location* option in the *Save As* dialog. Update the directory location by entering the URL for your sample reports library (sample shown below) in the *File name* field and add a forward slash at the end and type "Upcoming Risks" without the quotes as the name for your report.

13. http://[*YourServerName*]/pwa/ProjectBICenter/Sample%20Reports/English%20(United%20States)/

14. Change the *Save As type* field to Excel Workbook (*.xlsx), if necessary. Select the *Open in Excel Services* checkbox. Click the *Save* button.

15. Close your report.

Exercise 9-8 for Excel 2007 and Excel 2010 Users

Build the Upcoming Issues report.

1. Navigate to the Business Intelligence Center and click the *Templates* link in the *Quick Launch* menu. Click on the *English (United States)* link to open the English language folder. Click on the

Issues template name to launch the template. In the *Open* dialog, select the *Read Only* item and click the *OK* button. The system launches the template in Excel.

2. Click the *Enable Content* button if prompted by a security warning. Make the file trusted, if prompted.

3. Add *Status, DueDate, AssignedToResource,* and the *Title* fields to the *Row Labels* area.

4. Add the *ProjectName* field to the *Report Filter* area.

5. In the *Layout* section of the *Design* ribbon, click the *Subtotals* button and select the *Do Not Show Subtotals* item. Click the *Grand Totals* button and select the *Off for Rows and Columns* item. Click the *Report Layout* button and select the *Show in Tabular Form* item.

6. Select the *ProjectName* field and from the *Defined Names* section of the *Formulas* ribbon, click the *Define Name* button. Enter the name "ProjectNM" without the quotes in the *Name* field and click the *OK* button.

7. Format the *TaskFinishDate* column as a short date.

8. Click the filter pick list on the *DueDate* column header and float your mouse pointer over the *Date Filters* item, and select the *Next Week* item.

9. Arrange the column sizes to best view the data and give your column headers friendly names.

10. On the *Options* ribbon, enter the name "PVIssues" without the quotes in the *PivotTable Name* field.

For Excel 2010 Users

11. Click on the *File* menu and select the *Save & Send* tab. Select the *Save to SharePoint* option.

12. Click the *Publish Options* button in the upper right corner of the page and click the *Parameters* tab in the *Publish Options* dialog. Click the *Add* button and select the named item you created in step 6. Click the *OK* button to close the *Add Parameters* dialog and then click the *OK* button to close the *Publish Options* dialog.

13. Locate and select the URL for your sample reports library under the *Recent Locations* section and click the *Save As* button. In the *Save As* dialog, enter "Upcoming Issues" without the quotes in the *File Name* field and select the *Excel Workbook* item in the *Save as Type* pick list. Click the *Save* button to save your new report.

14. Close your report.

For Excel 2007 Users

11. Select the *Publish* item and select the *Excel Services* item in the fly-out menu.

12. Select the *Browse for a location* option in the *Save As* dialog. Update the directory location by entering the URL for your sample reports library (sample shown below) in the *File name* field and add a forward slash at the end and type "Upcoming Issues" without the quotes as the name for your report.

13. http://[*YourServerName*]/pwa/ProjectBICenter/Sample%20Reports/English%20(United%20States)/

14. Change the *Save As type* field to Excel Workbook (*.xlsx), if necessary. Select the *Open in Excel Services* checkbox. Click the *Save* button.

15. Close your report.

Adding the Content Type to the Document Library

The *Dashboard* page can live in any SharePoint site to which you have the rights to add content. For this example, I am building a dashboard intended for the Project Team site, which allows me to take advantage of the site's security access so that the dashboard is only available to Project Team members.

Web Part pages are documents and must be stored in a document library. You can choose to use the *Project Documents* folder in your Project Team site or you can create another folder for this purpose. I use the *Project Documents* folder for this example. *Web Part* pages are not normally a default content type for document libraries. Therefore, you must execute a **one-time** procedure on this document library to add this content type so that you can create *Web Part* pages.

Hands On Exercise

Exercise 9-9

Add the Web Part page content type to your Deploy Training Advisor Software project site.

1. Navigate to your Deploy Training Advisor Software project site.

2. Click the *Project Documents* link from the *Quick Launch* menu.

3. Click the *Settings* button on the *Library* tab.

4. In the *General Settings* section, select the *Advanced Setting* item.

5. In the *Content* section, set the *Allow management of content types* value to *Yes* and click the *OK* button.

6. Scroll to the *Content Types* section of the *Document Library Setting* page and click the *Add from existing site content types* link.

7. In the *Available Site Content Types* list, scroll to, and select the *Web Part Page* item and click the *Add* button.

8. Click the *OK* button. Verify that you now see the *Web Part* page content type listed as shown in Figure 9 - 76. You can now create *Web Part* pages in this document library.

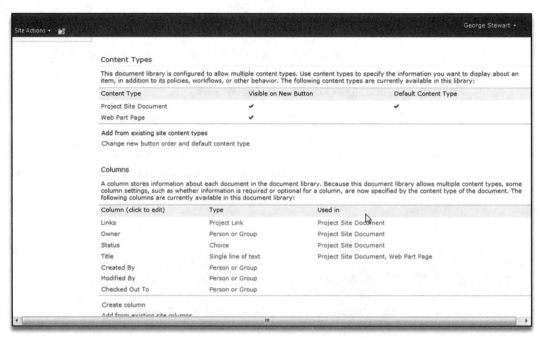

Figure 9 - 76: Document Library Content Types

Create a Web Part Page

Return to your document library and click the *Documents* tab to display the *Documents* ribbon. Select the *New Document* menu button and select the *Web Part Page* item as shown in Figure 9 - 77.

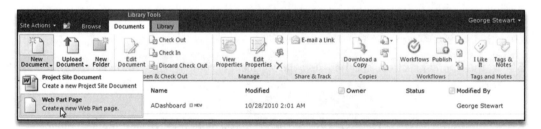

Figure 9 - 77: Create Web Part page button

On the *New Web Part Page* page shown in Figure 9 - 78, specify the name of your *Web Part* page and the layout of the page.

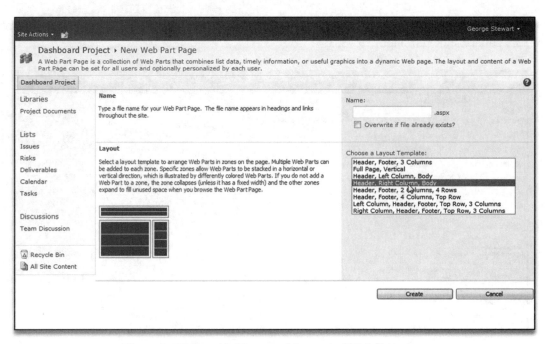

Figure 9 - 78: Specify Name and Layout of Web Part page

Adding Reports to the Dashboard

You now see the *Edit Web Part* page shown in Figure 9 - 79. *Zones* are the boxes on the page, where the name of the zone is in the upper left corner of the box.

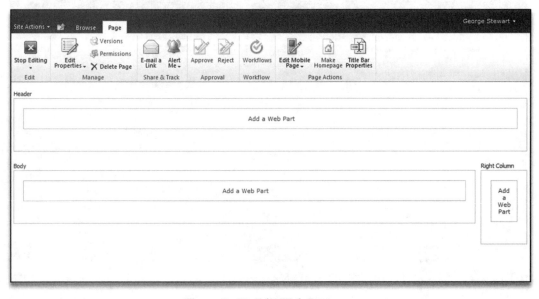

Figure 9 - 79: Edit Web Part page

Click the *Add a Web Part* link in the *Body* zone to add an *Excel Web Access* web part. When you click this link, you will see the *Web Part* gallery shown in Figure 9 - 80.

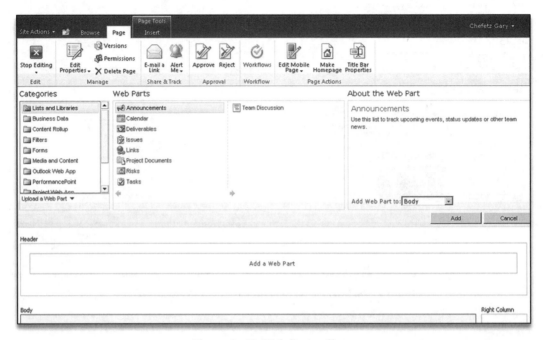

Figure 9 - 80: Web Part gallery

In the *Categories* section, select the *Business Data* item; in the *Web Parts* section, select the *Excel Web Access* item and click the *Add* button. The system redisplays the Dashboard page as shown in Figure 9 - 81.

Figure 9 - 81: Web Part Page with Excel Web Access Web Part

Select the *Click here to open the tool pane* link. The *Web Part* tool pane allows you to set the properties for the web part as shown in Figure 9 - 82. These properties can include the title, toolbar options, and which Excel report to display. You can also access the tool pane via the *Web Part* menu by selecting the down arrow in the upper right corner of the web part and selecting the *Edit Web Part* item.

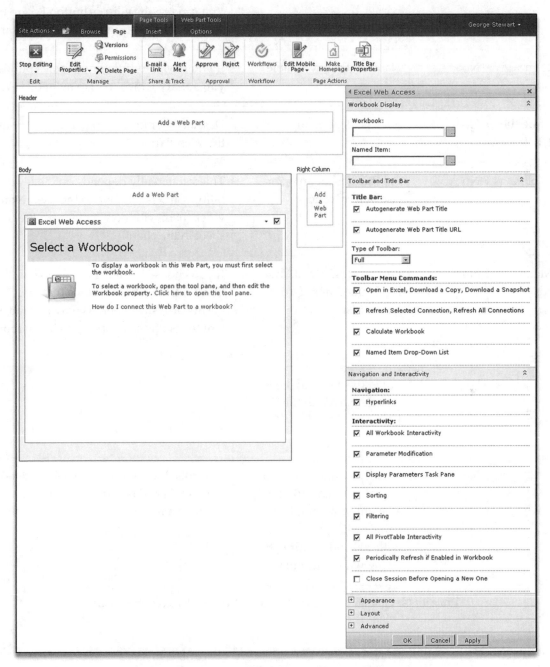

Figure 9 - 82: Excel Web Part Tool Pane Settings

Table 9 - 14 presents a list of commonly used settings for the tool pane.

Setting	Required?	Value	Rationale
Workbook	Yes	Full URL to your Excel report	The Excel Report to display in this Web Part. You can use the ellipsis button […] to browse to your Excel Report in the SharePoint farm.
Named Item	No	Name of the PivotTable	If you have multiple PivotTables published, you specify which to display in this Web Part.
Autogenerate the Web Part Title	No	Suggest deselecting	Deselecting means you get to specify the title of the Web Part.
Type of Toolbar	No	For this dashboard exercise, select None	This value really depends on the level of capability you wish to give to the user. None provides them with no way to open the Spreadsheet in the client.
Toolbar Menu Commands	No	For this dashboard, deselect Named Item Drop-Down List	If you choose to give users a toolbar, this section controls which options they see. For this dashboard, since there is only one tab, the system turns off the drop-down list to reduce clutter.
Title (Expand Appearance Section)	No	Put in the name of the Report displayed in the Web Part	
Height	No	*Note:* This function has a bug so you have to specify a height or it defaults the value to 400 pixels. Start with 200 and modify after trying with your data.	Controls the amount of visual space taken by the Web Part. The proper setting can keep space usage to a minimum.

Table 9 - 14: Commonly Used Settings for Excel Web Access Web Parts

You repeat this process for each Excel Report web part you add to the page. Note: You can rearrange web parts by dragging them around on the page.

Hands On Exercise

Exercise 9-10

Create a web part page and add your Excel reports.

1. Navigate to the home page of your Deploy Training Advisor Software project site and click the *Project Documents* link in the *Quick Launch* menu.

2. From the *New* section of the *Documents* ribbon, click the *New Document* pick list and select the *Web Part Page* item from the list.

3. In the *New Web Part Page* page, enter "Next Week" without the quotes in the *Name* field, and select the *Header, Right Column, Body* item in the *Choose a Layout* selector and click the *Create* button.

4. In the *Body* section of the new web part page, click the *Add a Web Part* link. After the system opens the *Web Part Gallery* at the top of the page, in the *Category* section select the *Business Data* item. In the web part list, select the *Excel Web Access* web part and click the *Add* button.

5. In the *Select a Workbook* area, click on the *Click here to open the tool pane* link. In the tool pane, click the *Ellipsis* button for the *Workbook* field to open the *Select an Asset* dialog. Use the navigation tool on the left of the dialog to expand the Business Intelligence Center, and locate and expand the English folder of the *Sample Reports* folder.

6. Select the *Upcoming Tasks* workbook and click the *OK* button. In the *Named Item* field, type "PVTasks" without the quotes, which is the name you gave your pivot table. In the *Type of Toolbar* pick list select the *None* option. Deselect all of the options in the *Toolbar Menu Commands* section. Expand the *Appearance* section, in the Title field remove the "Excel Web Access" text, and in the *Height* section set the *Height* value to *200*. Click the *OK* button at the bottom of the tool pane.

7. In the *Body* section of the page, click the *Add a Web Part* link, select the *Excel Web Access* web part from the gallery, and click the *Add* button.

8. In the *Select a Workbook* area, click on the *Click here to open the tool pane* link. In the tool pane, click the *Ellipsis* button for the *Workbook* field to open the *Select an Asset* dialog. Use the navigation tool on the left of the dialog to expand the Business Intelligence Center, and locate and expand the English folder of the *Sample Reports* folder.

9. Select the *Upcoming Issues* workbook and click the *OK* button. In the *Named Item* field, type "PVIssues" without the quotes, which is the name you gave your pivot table. In the *Type of Toolbar* pick list, select the *None* option. Deselect all of the options in the *Toolbar Menu Commands* section. Expand the *Appearance* section, in the *Title* field remove the "Excel Web Access" text, and in the *Height* section set the *Height* value to *200*. Click the *OK* button at the bottom of the tool pane.

10. Repeat steps 7 – 9 to add the *Upcoming Risks* report to your new dashboard. For the *Name* item, type "PVRisks" without the quotes.

Add the Choice Filter Web Part

For this discussion, I limit the reporting range to one project. Therefore, the built-in *Choice Filter* web part easily meets the requirement.

> If you use this technique in a production environment, any changes to the project name will require a change to this filter.

Click the *Add a Web Part* link in the *Right Column* zone to add a *Choice Page Filter* web part. When you click this link, you will see the *Web Part* gallery as shown previously in Figure 9 - 80. Select the *Filters* category on the left, and then select the *Choice Filters* item under the *Web Parts* section.

Select the *Open the tool pane* link to open the *Web Part* tool pane. Change the *Web Part* settings as set forth in Table 9 - 15.

Setting	Required?	Value	Rationale
Filter Name	Yes	For this discussion, change this to Project	This is the name used in the Connections.
List of Choices	Yes	Enter or copy/paste the name of the project for this dashboard	
Title	No	For this discussion, change this to Project	This name displays next to the filter.
Default Value (Expand the Advanced Filter Options)	No	For this discussion, enter or copy/paste the name of the project for this dashboard	This setting eliminates the need for the user to select any value to see the reports.

Table 9 - 15: Choice Filter Settings

Connect the Page Filter to the Excel Web Access Web Parts

The final step of constructing the dashboard is to connect the *Choice Page Filter* item to each Excel Web Access web part.

1. Select the *Web Part menu arrow* item in the upper right corner of the *Choice Page Filter* web part.

2. Select the *Connections, Send Filter Values To* item to the name of the Excel Report as shown in Figure 9 - 83.

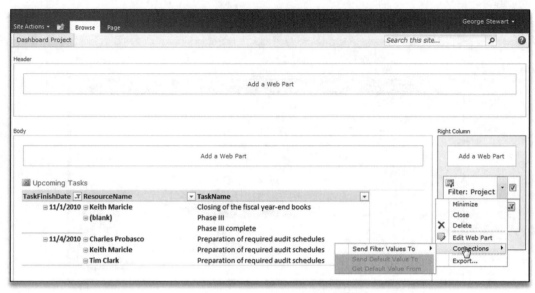

Figure 9 - 83: Edit Connections between Web Parts

3. Select the *Send Filter Values To…* item from the pick list and chose a web part from the fly out menu as shown in Figure 9 - 84.

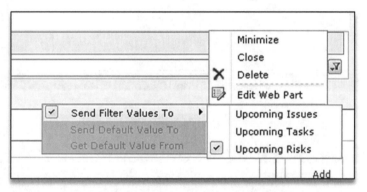

Figure 9 - 84: Select Web Part Connection Type

4. The system displays the *Choose Connection* dialog shown in Figure 9 - 85.

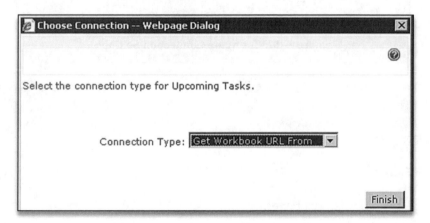

Figure 9 - 85: Choose Connection dialog

5. In the *Connection Type* pick list, select the *Get Filter Values From* item. The dialog display changes as shown in Figure 9 - 86.

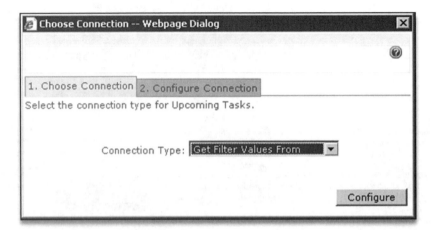

Figure 9 - 86: Choose Connections dialog - Configure Connections

6. Click on the *Configure* button or the *Configure Connection* tab and the display changes as shown in Figure 9 - 87.

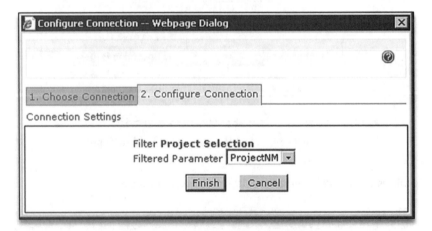

Figure 9 - 87: Configure Connection Settings

7. Verify that you selected ProjectNM for the *Filtered Parameter*. Repeat for each Excel Web Access web part on the page.

8. When complete, select the *Page* tab in the Ribbon.

9. Click the *Stop Editing* button.

You now have a complete functional dashboard.

Hands On Exercise

Exercise 9-11

Add the Choice Filter web part to your dashboard page and configure the connections to your reports.

1. Return to your new dashboard page and click the *Add a Web Part* link in the *Right Column* zone to open the Web Part gallery. Select the *Filters* category on the left, and then select the *Choice Filter* item in the gallery and click the *Add* button.

2. Select the Web Part menu arrow item in the upper right corner of the *Choice Filter* web part and select the *Connections, Send Filter Values To* item and select the name of one of your Excel Reports.

3. In the *Connection Type* pick list in the dialog, select the *Get Filter Values From* item. In the dialog, click on the *Configure* button or the *Configure Connection* tab. Select ProjectNM in the *Filtered Parameter* pick list and click the *Finish* button.

4. Repeat steps 2 - 4 for the other two Excel reports.

5. Select the Web Part menu arrow item in the upper right corner of the *Choice Filter* web part and select the *Edit Web Part* item.

6. In the web part tool pane, rename the filter to "Project" without the quotes in the *Filter Name* field.

7. In the *Type each choice on a separate line…* section, enter the exact name for your Deploy Training Advisor Software project. Expand the *Advanced Filter Options* section and enter the same value into the *Default Value* field.

8. Expand the *Appearance* section and set the *Title* field to "Project" without the quotes, and select the *None* option in the *Chrome Type* pick list. Scroll to the bottom and click the *OK* button.

9. In the *Edit* section of the *Page* ribbon, click the *Stop Editing* button. Your new dashboard page should look something like the one shown in Figure 9 - 88.

Figure 9 - 88: Completed dashboard page

Business Intelligence Summary

In this module, you learned the basic skills you need to start building useful reports and dashboards. This is only the beginning. To take this to the next level, you might add the dashboard page you just created to the *Project Site* template for your system making this a permanent fixture for all project sites. You can add styling to the page to make it more interesting and you might use conditional formatting techniques you learned about earlier in the module to render the data more visibly pleasing.

Index